American Infidel:
ROBERT G. INGERSOLL

ALLOW ME TO SAY

THAT THE CAUSE NEAREST MY HEART,

AND TO WHICH I AM WILLING

TO DEVOTE THE REMAINDER OF MY LIFE,

IS THE ABSOLUTE, THE *ABSOLUTE*

ENFRANCHISEMENT

OF THE HUMAN MIND

R. G. Ingersoll

American Infidel:
ROBERT G. INGERSOLL

A BIOGRAPHY

by ORVIN LARSON

New York: **THE CITADEL PRESS**

To DR. A. CRAIG BAIRD,
Professor Emeritus, the State University of Iowa,
who started it all

920
I 47L
95047

American Infidel: Robert G. Ingersoll

FIRST EDITION

Copyright © 1962 by Orvin Larson
Published by The Citadel Press
222 Park Avenue South
New York 3, N. Y.

Library of Congress Catalog Card No. 62-01223
Manufactured in the United States of America

Contents

Part One:
WANDERINGS

THE DEVIL MOVES IN MYSTERIOUS WAYS

THE Reverend John Ingersoll in the early morning of August 11, 1833, looked down at the son just born to him and saw, no doubt, another soul for the Lord. It was not possible that the son would one day stand on the platforms of the land crying out against church and cleric, dogma and Holy Writ, and that the name of the son would be a household word for an agent of the devil.

For the boy would be brought up amid circumstances favorable to piety. The father was an impassioned man of God, a revivalist whose converts were legion. Every Sunday the boy would go to Sunday school and to church; he would sit up front to hear his father and others preach. At home there would be prayers and reading from the Bible and the father's devout talks with visiting clergy. God and Christ and the Holy Ghost were compelling everyday concerns. The Devil had little chance at the Ingersoll fireside.

The son was named Robert Green. The Green was after Beriah Green, the Reverend Ingersoll's close friend and a colleague in the winning of souls. Beriah, like his friend, was also an ardent abolitionist. Slavery, to John and Beriah, was a national sin, an abomination to God. Boldly they preached against it, at a time when many of their hearers were for it.

Mary, John's wife, also favored the name Green. She too was an abolitionist, as ardent as John and Beriah. In spite of household cares and the impropriety of being a woman she actively worked for the cause. In a political speech which her son Robert was to make on September 7, 1870, in Peoria,

Illinois, it would come to light that she was the first to sign a petition, which she also circulated, for the abolition of slavery in the District of Columbia.

Was this the flaw through which the Devil wormed himself —discontent in the blood with the established order? Here was the father who espoused the "niggers" and here was his help-meet—a woman! a mother! a wife of a clergyman!—who should know better than to flaunt herself in a dubious cause. Moreover, this woman, even as she was carrying the child to be named Robert Green, was reading pernicious literature! A Lady Somerset in an article on pre-natal influences in the *Arena,* March, 1895, reported that Robert Ingersoll had once told her that sometime prior to his birth his mother recoiling from his father's Calvinism regularly went to a friend's house and read Voltaire. So, said Lady Somerset, Robert was "from the first a pronounced unbeliever in the divine revelation!"

Robert Green Ingersoll was not impressed with lineage, so he was never tempted to genealogy. He once wrote, "I know little about my ancestors,—not much more than they do about me." He never said more about his grandfather than in what he said about how his father and mother first met: "One Robert Livingston, of the town of Lisbon, as was his duty visited the school for the purpose of finding out whether the young teacher [John Ingersoll] was in all respects qualified to discharge the duties of his position. By some accident, Mr. Livingston took with him on that day, probably for company, his daughter, Mary." The fact is that Mr. Livingston was a judge of the county court, St. Lawrence County, New York. He was the son of John Livingston (not of the illustrious Livingston line), who had come from Scotland or Ireland in the period 1767-1777, in the Scotch-Irish Presbyterian emigration.

If there was little that Robert said about the Livingstons, there was less that he could say about the Ingersolls, who were without renown. But Grandfather Ebenezer Ingersoll did serve in the American forces in the Revolution from May, 1775, to August, 1776. And he had another merit, of which his grandson was aware: he "had sense enough and courage enough," said Robert, "to be a Universalist . . . if any were spared, all would be." Ebenezer's wife, however, was a true believer. She believed in eternal damnation.

It was in the late spring of 1821 that Mary Livingston, age twenty-one, met John Ingersoll, age twenty-nine. John graduated that year, bachelor of arts, from Middlebury College, in Vermont, where "he received," said Robert, "the rudiments of ignorance," namely Hebrew, Greek, and Latin. He then commenced studies in theology with the Reverend Joseph Hopkins of New Haven, Vermont. Finding it hard to make a living in New Haven, he made his way by foot to Lisbon, New York. Here he had just started to teach school when Mary came into his life. They were married in September, 1821. They lived in Lisbon until the spring of 1823. Having kept up his studies with the Reverend Hopkins, John was ordained a Congregational minister, in 1823, and accepted a call to a church at Pittsford, Vermont, the town of his birth. He held this charge until 1826.

The three years at Pittsford was the longest period that John Ingersoll, as a minister, was to spend in one place. A revivalist by temperament, as well as by vocation, he was highly susceptible to "calls." And he was called often. When he had revived a locality, he would move on. The quiet rounds of the pastor were not for him. He would rescue and win souls; let someone else tend them.

It was well that the Reverend was ready to move on when the Lord called. For there were those in the various communities that he came to who did not like his talk against slavery. He mixed abolitionism with sin and salvation, particularly after 1830, and the mixture got pretty strong at times. And so some wanted him gone and said so, and hinted that if he tarried too long he might depart on a rail.

The Reverend stayed three years in Pittsford because of the multiplication of his domestic burdens. By 1826 three children had arrived: Ruth, born July 5, 1822; John Livingston, October 24, 1823; and Mary Jane, June 14, 1826.

By the fall of 1826 the urge to be up and doing in benighted regions was too much for the Reverend. Pittsford was pretty well in the fold, but to the west, in the state of New York, there was much to be done. John knew the great Charles Finney, who in 1824 forsook the practice of law to be a Presbyterian missionary to two little frontier towns, Evans Mills and Antwerp, in Jefferson County, New York, where with his powerful preaching he started a wave of revivalism that spread over the East. John had heard Finney several times and had talked with him. Finney pointed to regions of darkness in New York, and John went there.

The itinerary of the Ingersolls in New York was one of rapid flux—a month here, a month there, maybe two or three months —the tempo not slowing until 1831 when the Reverend accepted a call to the Congregational Church in Marshall, Oneida County. In Marshall, December 12, 1831, his second son, Ebenezer Clark, was born. In the spring of 1833 he moved to a church in Pompey, Onondaga County, where, again, he stayed about a month. Then on to Dresden, where Robert Green was born.

The Ingersolls were in Dresden less than a year. In March, 1834, they came to New York City, where on April 2 John became associate pastor of the Second Free Presbyterian Church. He had received the call through Charles Finney, the pastor and tutelary genius of the church.

The second Free Presbyterian Church was two years old. Just prior to its organization in February, 1832, Finney had held revival meetings in New York City. Among his hearers was Mr. Lewis Tappan, of the well-known business firm of Arthur Tappan and Company, who was so moved by the preaching that he proposed the formation of a church which Finney should head. Tappan also provided for a suitable habitation, financing the conversion of the Chatham Street Theater to the Chatham Street Chapel.

The Reverend Ingersoll preached in Chatham Street Chapel, where he baptized Robert Green, and then in a new structure planned by Finney, the Broadway Tabernacle. But he was not long at the Tabernacle, resigning in February, 1835. Yet this would have seemed an ideal situation for him. He admired Finney, whose doctrines and methods were akin to his. Moreover, unredeemed sinners swarmed into the Tabernacle, a heady sight for any revivalist.

The trouble was that John Ingersoll could not temper his abolitionism. When the Broadway Tabernacle was under construction, a mob set fire to the walls and roof. They had heard that miscegenation was to be championed. In July, 1834, Finney returned from a six months' sojourn in Europe and found that many in his congregation were wrought up over slavery. He cautioned Ingersoll to be more discreet. But it was not in the man's nature to be discreet. To be so was to palaver with Satan.

The Ingersolls were on the move again. It was a great trial for Mary Ingersoll, this frequent packing and unpacking of her family. Life was bouncing wagons and snail-paced river boats. The next stop was Cazenovia, in Madison County, upstate New York. It was the last stop for Mary. Here, the day after Christmas, in 1835, worn out and an easy prey to disease, she died.

Now there was less stability in the family than ever. Fortunately, for Robert, there was his sister, Mary. Only nine years old, she made him her special charge and tried to be everything that she thought a mother should be. She also took care of Ebenezer, "Ebon," but he was four and less helpless than Robert, who was one and a half. The eldest child, John, who was twelve, and Ruth, who was ten, assumed other responsibilities of the household.

In Cazenovia the Reverend Ingersoll had a congregation composed of members who two years before had broken away from the Presbyterian Church to form a church with a free pew and a free pulpit. The free pulpit meant that a preacher could disavow the doctrine of the elect and the damned and could offer salvation through Christ to all; it also meant that he could advocate temperance and the abolition of slavery. It was a congenial situation to the Reverend and he made the most of it. As usual, he did not stay long. In February, 1836,

he went to Hampton (now Westmoreland) in Oneida County
to conduct a special series of evangelistic services in the Congregational Church. He was immediately successful and, on
February 26, thirty new members came into the church. The
regular pastor resigned and Ingersoll was left in complete
charge. One convert said, "When I went to hear Priest Ingersoll, I could scarcely take time to eat my dinner. I knew my
soul was in jeopardy, and fearing lest I lose one moment, I ran
all the way back. He made salvation seem so plain, so easy, I
wanted to take it to my heart without delay."[1] Ingersoll stayed
at Westmoreland two years.

The next and last pastorate that the Reverend held in New
York State was a Presbyterian Church at Belleville, in Jefferson County. And now for a time Robert, age six, was in touch
with a personality that may have slightly bent the twig. On a
farm near Belleville lived a sister of John Ingersoll, a Mrs.
Sykes, known to Robert as Aunt Candace. She was a peppery
woman with a heterodox streak and a tendency to ridicule the
messengers of fire and brimstone. During one of Robert's stays
on the Sykes' farm he went with them to a schoolhouse nearby
to attend a revival meeting. The revivalist treated his hearers to
a horrendous discourse on eternal damnation. On their way
home the Sykeses, particularly Aunt Candace, made fun of
the revivalist and as soon as they got home Robert jumped on
a stool and mimicked him. One day Robert was to say to Aunt
Candace that she was "the first relation I ever saw that had
sense enough to deny the infamous doctrine of eternal punishment. I thank you from the bottom of my heart for your good
and brave words."

The Reverend, if he had heard of it, would not have taken
lightly his son's burlesque of a revivalist. He had little sense
of humor where religion was concerned. Innate depravity and
eternal punishment were too much on his mind. It was a long,
hard struggle to overcome one's sinful nature, with little chance
of victory without the proper discipline. This meant to the
Reverend, in the later words of Robert, that "Every real or

supposed infraction of a divine law must, to accord with his views, be visited with severe and immediate punishment."

"My father," said Robert, "whipped his children to keep them out of hell." And yet this father "was a man of great tenderness and loved his children almost to insanity. . . . When I think of the kind of God my father adored and the awful consequences which he supposed would follow each infraction of the *divine law,* I am amazed that he was as kind, loving and lenient as he really was."[2]

THE BOY LEARNS OF GOD

THE Sabbath to Robert was an ordeal. Sunday began at sundown on Saturday night. "We commenced at that time," said Ingersoll, "for the purpose of getting a good ready and when the sun fell below the horizon . . . there was a darkness fell upon the house ten thousand times deeper than that of night. Nobody said a pleasant word; nobody laughed; nobody smiled; the child that looked the sickest was regarded as the most pious. That night you could not even crack hickory nuts."[1] On Sunday morning the gloom deepened and the Sabbath was on in earnest.

The church was a plain wood structure. If a stove were at the rear, it warmed only the early comers close to it. Usually there was no stove. "It was thought to be a kind of sin to be comfortable while you were thanking God." The pews, hard and straight-backed, did not seduce the flesh; too often they left slivers in Robert's rump and legs. The pulpit, to Robert, was twenty feet high.

He had to attend two Sunday services, one in the morning, one in the afternoon, the intermission affording time for Sunday school. The essentials of each service were an opening prayer; a hymn sung by a volunteer mixed choir; the sermon;

another hymn by the choir; and a concluding prayer. The opening prayer was a local newspaper. It contained the vital statistics of the community and data on business, social, and cultural matters. Names were not mentioned. Guesswork heightened interest.

The congregation seldom participated in the singing because of the absence of hymnbooks with tunes. The choir, however, had tune-books like *The Dulcimer, The Shawm,* or the *Carmina Sacra.* Getting a key with a tuning-fork, the choir sang without accompaniment. Sometimes the music could revive a nodding Robert, particularly such hymns as "How Lovely Is Zion," "By the Rivers of Babylon," and "When the Worn Spirit Wants Repose."

Then came the sermon. "The minister," Ingersoll said, "commenced at 'first' and went on and on and on to about 'twenty-thirdly.' Then he made a few remarks by way of application; and then took a general view of the subject, and in about two hours reached the last chapter in Revelation."

The morning service over, Sunday school set in. "Then came the catechism with the chief end of man . . . . We sat in a row with our feet coming in about six inches of the floor. The minister asked us if we knew that we all deserved to go to hell, and we all answered 'Yes.' Then we were asked if we would be willing to go to hell if it was God's will, and every little liar shouted 'Yes.' "[2]

Next, everybody had a quick lunch to allow a little time before the afternoon service so that they could visit the graveyard and study epitaphs. The epitaphs, said Ingersoll, were a "great comfort. The reflection came to my mind that the observance of the Sabbath could not last always." But he was afraid that the comfort was illusory because every so often the congregation would sing a hymn with the lines:

> "Where congregations ne'er break up,
> And Sabbaths never end."

"These lines prejudiced me a little against even heaven," he remarked.

The sermons though long were yet powerful in arousing in

Robert the fear of hell. He was wracked with terrifying images of devils and prodigious fires. He saw himself ceaselessly tormented. He never forgot an illustration, used often by a preacher, of the length of time a child would have to stay in hell if he misbehaved: " 'Suppose that once in a billion years a bird should come from some far-distant planet, and carry off in its little bill a grain of sand, a time would finally come when the last atom composing this earth would be carried away; and when this last atom was taken, it would not even be sun-up in hell.' " No wonder it was difficult to love God. "I have a dim recollection," said Ingersoll, "of hating Jehovah when I was extremely small."[3]

THE BOY LEARNS OTHER THINGS TOO

Robert learned to read when he was five. His father assigned selections in the Bible and in the Shorter Catechism of the Westminster divines and, later, portions of these works to memorize. Then Robert memorized passages in Hebrew, Greek, and Latin. Years later he denounced "the acquisition of the useless, or of the almost useless . . . . the acquisition of dead languages."

Although Robert's formal schooling was frequently interrupted by his father's changes of locale, the schools that he attended differed little. The schoolhouse was much like the church in its structure, plainness, and lack of comfort. There were no individual seats, just primitive benches.

Robert was one of twenty-five to fifty students, ages five to twenty, grades one to ten or twelve, all in one room. The attendance went down during planting time and harvest time but during the winter the little schoolhouse buzzed with activity. There was instruction in the three "R's," sometimes in algebra, physics, and astronomy. About the fifth year in school Robert began to have weekly exercises in declamation.

In Ashtabula, Ohio, where the Ingersolls moved in 1841, Robert attended an academy in the Baptist Church, the only school in town. An Ashtabula resident recalled that the boy showed promise as a declaimer and that he was particularly effective with Thomas Hood's poem that begins "I remember, I remember, the cot where I was born." With this poem, however, Robert came to grief. His rendition having attracted public notice, he was invited to perform at an entertainment in the Baptist Church. When his part in the program came, he walked to the platform, bowed appropriately, but could not remember a word. Bewildered and tearful he started toward his seat but before he reached it he remembered. Well-wishers urged him to try again. He returned to the platform, bowed again, and—forgot again.[1] As he left the platform he could only say, "Clark [his brother] knows it."[2] For a long time after, Robert avoided speaking in public.

For textbooks Robert used, by common necessity, whatever books he could find at home. It might be Cruishank's *Primary Geography* or Goodrich's *Universal History upon the Basis of Geography*. It might be Hutchison's *Class Book on Rhetoric* or Ebenezer Porter's *The Rhetorical Reader*. And he had Mc-Guffey's *Readers*.

Regardless of the type of book, moral and religious instruction was the keynote. McGuffey's *Readers* abounded with Christian precept and example. Cruishank's *Primary Geography* taught that "God made the world for man to live in and has fitted it for man's convenience and comfort." In the preface to *The Rhetorical Reader,* Ebenezer Porter wrote: "If this little book be found useful in advancing the interests of Christian Education, the best wishes of its author will be answered."

The teacher too was a source of religious instruction. If he had gone to college, his professors were often clergymen. He himself might be one. A hundred colleges sprang up in the fifty years following the Revolution and almost all of them had as their primary purpose the training of students for the ministry.

All this emphasis on God and goodness did not, however,

make Robert a model of virtue. A John P. Roberts of Ashtabula said that "Ingersoll, as a boy, seemed to be always on the negative side of things;"[3] and a Dr. Samuel Wetmore, a schoolmate of Ingersoll in Ashtabula, said, "Life seemed to burst out on the face of that boy. . . ."[4] Mix such ingredients and you have mischief. Roberts said that the Reverend Ingersoll frequently took his children to the woodshed and birched them; he suggests that Robert went to the woodshed more than the other children.

There were many attractive secular interests for a boy in Ashtabula. There were skating, fishing, swimming, and hunting. There were the stagecoaches, the Conestoga wagons, and the steamboats. Robert often went down to the shore of Lake Erie and saw not too far off the *Illinois* or the *Pennsylvania* or the *Commodore Perry* or the *James Madison* or the *Great Western,* romance-laden steam packets going all the way from Buffalo to Chicago with stops at Cleveland and Detroit. Passengers on the upper deck waved to him and he waved back. The very captain himself, a gigantic man with a foghorn voice, might boom out a greeting. It was a great time to be alive. The dust on the main street of Ashtabula never settled. See the horses drawing the gaily colored stage coaches put on their greatest burst of speed just before pulling up in front of the Stoll House. See the ever-increasing number of Conestoga freighters drawn by six brawny horses and burdened with merchandise from the East and farm products from the West. See the still greater number of smaller wagons, wagons from New England, New York, and Pennsylvania, wagons of the pioneers, bound for Indiana, Illinois, Missouri, Wisconsin, and other points West. Dust and noise and confusion swirled around the herds of cattle, hogs, and sheep on the way to Cleveland whence they would go down the Ohio and Erie Canal to the Ohio River and the abattoirs of the Queen City of the West, Cincinnati. It would be an odd boy whose imagination was not fired by the bustle and pageantry of a nation on the move.

But Robert was more than a spectator of this uprooting

westward process, he was part of it. The Ingersolls had come from Buffalo to Cleveland by steamboat and after a short stay in Oberlin, Ohio, they came to Ashtabula. Next they were in North Madison; then they lived in several other Ohio towns. Finally, in 1849, they reached Milwaukee, Wisconsin.

In Milwaukee the Reverend Ingersoll found it necessary to supplement his earnings with a grocery business. Robert, now sixteen, was his father's assistant. "We are doing a pretty good business," wrote Robert to his brother John, "our sales being from eight to twenty dollars a day." John, the only one of the five Ingersoll children to get a college education, had attended Oberlin College for three years and Rush Medical College for two years. In 1849 he was practicing medicine in Waukesha, Wisconsin. Robert's other brother, Clark, obtained a position with Putnam and Company, of Milwaukee, and was soon making twenty-five dollars a month buying wheat.

Somewhere on his travels the Reverend Ingersoll had taken unto himself a wife, who was a widow with two children. This was an unhappy match and they were not in Milwaukee long before the Reverend Ingersoll did an unheard of thing for a minister, he sued for and won a divorce. The main cause of the breakup is suggested in what the Reverend wrote John when the latter was about to get married, "You cannot but be aware of the importance of such an event so vitally connected with future weal or woe. . . . God grant you wisdom in this matter. Is the woman you have in view the daughter of a wise and judicious mother? Has she first rate good natural sense? Is her wit good? Is she industrious? Is she neat? You *cannot* live *happily* with a slack woman. I know."[5]

After the divorce, the Reverend decided to leave Milwaukee. His congregation was now not too pleased with him. And the grocery business deteriorated, partly because the community sense of propriety had been outraged. The Reverend was broke. He could not pay the court fees for the divorce and he could not pay his lawyer, General Pain. He also owed money to one Foot Tailor, a Milwaukee merchant. General Pain pressed for settlement, threatening legal action. So Robert, who had become a schoolteacher, resorted to the drastic expedient of letting Pain have an order for payment on the trustees of his school district.[6] This did not enhance Robert's standing with the trustees. Leaving Milwaukee, the Ingersolls went eastward.

Robert took a long jump eastward. In April, 1851, he was in Conneautville, Pennsylvania, where he had gone in the expectation of finding work in the lumber business of his father's nephew, Ebenezer Wright. But the work did not materialize and he was stranded in Conneautville under the most trying circumstances. "I am hard up for money I tell you," he wrote his brother John April 12. "I have not a cent in the world and I owe for board and I can't get away and can get nothing to do." His father who was preaching in the vicinity of Toledo, Ohio, had asked him to come to Toledo. But how could he go, not having a cent? He wrote his father, who replied that he would send the money soon. It had not arrived, as of April 12. But Robert was in good health, and summoning out of his woe a little levity he said to John, "Look out for the women."

Aid soon came from his father but Robert chose to visit John for a while, who had moved to New Berlin, Wisconsin. On June 2, the father wrote John telling him that if Robert had not already arrived he was on the way—"let him not remain *long* there." The father, who was now preaching in Palestine, Illinois, wanted Robert to join him: "Robert might get a ride as I did to Beloit [Wisconsin], and from Beloit to Rockford [Illinois] and from there he could take the stage to Grand Detour or to Dixon if he could find no better chance and from Dixon he could get a ride here any day." But Robert remained with his brother. On July 5, the father who was now in Greenville, in southern Illinois, wrote John: "I am utterly dissatisfied with the present situation of Robert. In case I am likely to stay here some months, I may send for him to come here . . . ." The father was becoming very much concerned over his son's lack of education. Both Robert and Clark, he wrote, are *"quite capable . . .* of being men among men with suitable advantages." He suggested that Robert might study law with a Judge

Dale of the county court, in Greenville, but he wondered, "Will it do to let him go into the study of Law without a better education than he *now* has?"

Greenville offered the Reverend Ingersoll fair prospects of a relatively long stay and in the fall of 1851 both Robert and Clark came to live with him. Clark secured employment in G. W. Hill's General Store. Robert entered the Greenville Academy which, according to the Reverend, had "a very good Teacher the Rev. M. S. S. Smith, a New School Man"—one of the S's stood for Socrates.

The Academy was in the basement of the Congregational Church, of which the Reverend Ingersoll was the pastor. A *History of Greenville* states that " 'Bob,' who was then seventeen years old, was extraordinarily bright for one of his age."[7] And that he was "very devout in those days." But Mr. and Mrs. J. T. Russell, two of Robert's schoolmates in the Academy, recalled that the Reverend Ingersoll kept his son "in the 'amen corner' every Sunday."[8] No one would be kept in the "amen corner" who did not have much to repent of.

It would take a lot of sitting in that corner to make amends for what Robert supposedly did to Socrates Smith. Socrates opened every school day with scripture reading and prayer and in reading scripture he read for days at a time the same chapter. He had a desk with a top that could be raised. One morning as he was about to commence devotionals he raised the top to find his Bible and he found a large dead goose propped up, with its bill resting on the current chapter. Socrates quizzed the students to find the culprit and as he was doing so Robert cried out, "Are there any Judases in this school?"[9] Robert was now suspected but he protested his innocence even after a girl named Theresa Fuller testified that she had seen him the night before chasing a flock of geese. This evidence was deemed too circumstantial. The culprit was never caught.

The goose incident may have figured in Socrates Smith's suggestion to the Reverend Ingersoll that Robert had nothing more to gain by remaining in the Academy. Or it may have been Smith's appreciation of a student of uncommon parts.

While in the Academy Robert was distinguished for having at the tip of his tongue much of Burns, Byron, and Thomas Moore.[10] His grounding in religious literature was also conspicuous. Again, Smith had read some of Robert's poetry which was published in the Greenville *Journal*. At any rate, Robert's attendance at the Academy ended, after one year, in June, 1852.

The poetry that Robert was writing was high-blown. Here are some stanzas from his poem "The Wavy West," published in the Greenville *Journal,* in June, 1852:

> Thou glorious world of bloom,
> Where bending flowers gently blow
> And o'er the breast their leaflets throw
> In beauty's soft perfume;
>
> Where dark-haired Indian girls,
> Reclining on thy dewy breast,
> In morning dew and sunlight dressed,
> Adorned with dewy pearls,
>
> First felt the tender flame,
> Saw Lover's lips in rapture move
> And felt the trembling beat of love
> Thrill wildly o'er their frame.

A critique of this fledgling verse would find many defects. Yet oratory notable for its vivid imagery and poetic rhythms was in the making. Robert was under no illusion as to the merit of his efforts. In a letter to John in which he enclosed a copy of his poem "A Dream," he doubted "if it can be called poetry" and he went on to say, "I dasn't hardly send it to you for you can find simple expressions in almost anything but here it is." This is part of the poem, à la Shelley:

> Last night as I lay on the bosom of sleep—
> T'was the mantle of dreams that enveloped my soul.
> Entranced and enraptured while visions did sweep
> Through the chambers of thought too sweet to control.

. . . .

> T'was the form of my mother I clasped to my breast
> When I thought t'was a dream and tears filled my eyes
> She whispered t'is not, while the body doth rest,
> The spirit unchained doth in ecstacy rise
>
> When the curtain of night is flung o'er the sky
> And creation lies hushed on the breast of repose
> The spirit then gleams like the crescent on high
> O'er the universe sweeps exults and adores.

Robert's poetic period lasted several years and coincided with his discovery of Burns, Moore, Goldsmith, Shelley, Keats, Byron, Coleridge, Poe, and Shakespeare. Robert found Shelley's "Queen Mab" to be "one of the finest compositions in the world."

Of Poe's "Raven" he wrote, "I tell you what, John, Edgar Poe's Raven takes my eye." He was deeply affected by Goldsmith's "Deserted Village," particularly the lines descriptive of Goldsmith's father, a minister, which reminded him of his father:

> As some proud cliff that lifts its awful form
> Swells from the vale and midway leaves the storm
> Though round its base the rolling clouds are spread
> Eternal sunshine settles on its head.

But Robert's literary passions became Burns and Shakespeare. "Shakespeare is my Bible, Burns my hymn-book," he often said.

He came upon Burns and Shakespeare accidentally. "I went to get my shoes mended, and I had to go with them. And I had to wait until they were done. . . . When I went into the shop of the old Scotch shoemaker he was reading a book, and when he took my shoes in hand I took his book, which was 'Robert Burns.' In a few days I had a copy; and, indeed, gentlemen, from that time if 'Burns' had been destroyed I could have restored more than half of it. It was in my mind day and night."[11]

Ingersoll first met Shakespeare "at a little hotel in Illinois, many years ago, when we were not quite civilized, when the footsteps of the red man were still in the prairies. While I was waiting for supper an old man was reading from a book, and among others who were listening was myself. I was filled with wonder. I had never heard anything like it. I was ashamed to ask him what he was reading; I supposed that an intelligent boy ought to know. So I waited, and when the little bell rang for supper I hung back and they went out. I picked up the book; it was Sam Johnson's edition of Shakespeare. The next day I bought a copy for four dollars. My God! more than the national debt! You talk about the present straits of the Treasury! For days, for nights, for months, for years I read those books. . . ."[12] In September, 1852, Robert wrote to John about *Richard III* and *The Taming of the Shrew,* "I have read them so often that I have learned them by heart." In later years he delivered two popular lectures on his idols, *Robert Burns* given first in 1878; *Shakespeare,* in 1891.

Robert also became familiar with his father's library, which was large with sacred works. He read the commentators Adam Clark, Scott, Henry and MacKnight, and Cruden.[13] He found in Adam Clark "that the serpent seduced our mother Eve, and was in fact the father of Cain," and that "the animals, while in the Ark, had their natures changed to that degree that they devoured straw together and enjoyed each other's society— thus pre-figuring the blessed millennium." He discovered in Scott "such a natural theologian that he really thought that the story of Phaeton—of the wild steeds dashing across the sky— corroborated the story of Joshua having stopped the sun and moon." Henry and MacKnight taught him that "Go so loved the world that he made up his mind to damn a large majority of the human race." Cruden tried to take the miraculous from the miracles: "I remember that he explained the miracle of feeding the wandering Jews with quails, by saying that even at this day immense numbers of quails crossed the Red Sea, and that sometimes when tired, they settled on ships that sank beneath their weight. The fact that the explanation was as hard to believe as the miracle made no difference to the devout Cruden."

Calvin's *Institutes* succeeded only in arousing a "considerable respect for the Devil." Paley's *Evidences* showed that the evidence of intelligence in producing evil was as credible as the evidence of intelligence in creating good. Of Paley's famous watch analogy leading to the conclusion that there must have been a creator, Ingersoll said: "You know the watch argument was Paley's greatest effort. A man finds a watch and it is so wonderful that he concludes it must have had a maker. Then he finds God, the maker of the man, and he is so much more wonderful than the man that he could *not* have had a maker. This is what the lawyers called a departure in pleading." Jonathan Edwards on *The Will* demonstrated that even though God had exactly predetermined a man's life, God still held him responsible for his conduct and damned or blessed him accordingly. Of both Edwards and Calvin, Ingersoll said: "They were infinitely cruel, their premises infinitely absurd, their God infinitely fiendish, and their logic perfect." However, he went on, "I have kindness and candor enough to say that Calvin and Edwards were both insane." Robert learned from Jenkyn's *On the Atonement*—which he said Jenkyn ought to atone for —"that children could justly be punished for the sins of their ancestors, and that men could, if they had faith, be justly credited with the virtues of others."

Foxe's *Book of Martyrs* with its scenes of torture and bloodshed gave Robert horrible dreams. The work showed him that "Christians had for many centuries imitated the God they worshiped." But Baxter's *Call* failed to frighten him and his *Saints' Rest* with its interminable Sabbaths merely repelled him. In the *Analogy*, Butler, instead of clarifying theological questions, "dug up more snakes than he killed."

And so, said Ingersoll, "all the seeds of Christianity—of superstition, were sown in my mind and cultivated with great diligence and care."

W<small>HEN</small> Robert left Socrates Smith's Academy, his schooling was over. He now had to earn a living. In September, 1852, he moved with his father from Greenville to Mount Vernon in Jefferson County, Illinois, he to find a teaching job, his father to assume a pastorate. Robert's first reaction to Mount Vernon was that it was "a pretty little town of about six or eight hundred inhabitants . . . finely located. . . . I think I shall like to live here."[1] A week later, he was lonesome. The weather was cold, dank, and gloomy giving everyone "the ague and fevers." But Mount Vernon was virgin territory for an ambitious teacher: "every man's name is X in writing."[2]

The afternoon of September 16 Robert went before the Jefferson County board of examiners, consisting of two members, to give evidence of his teaching qualifications. The examiners, he wrote, "considered themselves particularly smart," especially the one who was a teacher. Robert was rather contemptuous of the proceedings. "He asked me all the questions he could think of. I laughed at him and answered them all and asked him if he had any more to ask. He said no and gave me a certificate and then I came away."[3]

Robert began with thirty students on a private subscription basis, each student paying him two dollars and fifty cents per quarter, the quarter consisting of twelve weeks with five teaching days a week. "I am not making money very fast but can manage to get enough to eat and that's all."[4] But he was very popular and fifty students enrolled for his second term. He was not able to complete the term, however, because his father, who had made another move, this time to Marion, Illinois, came down with pneumonia and Robert went to be with him.[5]

It was a great tribulation to the Reverend Ingersoll that he was separated from his children so much. When he was in Cincinnati for a time in 1851, he wrote to John: "O how my dear very dear children are scattered. . . . How afflictive to us all is our present wide dispersion! *O, if we were not so poor!*" And later in the year from Vandalia, Illinois: "But O, the great distance between us! Yet no help for it at present." And from Marion, Illinois, in 1852, came the despairing cry: "God help us, for it is quite too much for me."

When the Reverend became ill, he feared he would not recover. He wanted his children about him. But Ruth was married to a Doctor Carter and living in Erie, Pennsylvania, and John was in Wisconsin. Clark was working in Greenville, he was expected to come and his father was upset that he had not come. But Mary, who taught school in Marion, was with her father. And the Reverend's third wife whom he had married just before his illness was also with him during the critical period. It was Robert, however, who became his father's main prop and chief solace during convalescence. Not that the Reverend's wife was remiss.

"What should you think of me," wrote the Reverend to John early in 1851, "if I should marry the widow Hannium?" Whatever John's reply, the Reverend did not marry the widow. He did marry, late in 1852, Frances Willard, a devout and dutiful woman. She was proud of her husband, of his "piety and talents." "My duty," she wrote, "is to sustain him in every possible way, that his mind may be soothed, that 'the ministry be not blamed.' " She had seen "many clergymen whose influence was lessened by a thoughtless, injudicious, gossiping, or extravagant wife." To help her husband dispel the specter of poverty she took a position as a teacher in a girls' seminary in Mount Vernon. When he fell ill she was able to be with him at the acute stages but not during convalescence. The proprietor of the seminary would not release her unless she forfeited pay in arrears to the amount of seventy dollars. "In our straitened circumstances," she wrote, "it seems too much to relinquish." She was worried lest "those who do not know the *exact* circumstances" would think she was heartless in not going to her husband. "I have not yielded to such a fit of weeping since the death of my mother, now ten years ago."

Thus it devolved upon Robert to be his father's mainstay. Of Robert the stepmother wrote, "He is the 'Benjamin' to Father whose 'heart is bound up in the lad.' "[6] The lad's heart was also bound up in the father.

Robert was resentful at the way his father was treated by the various congregations to which he ministered. The Reverend was a fervent and unrelenting man. He would not temper his abolitionism, for he believed that all men are brothers in the sight of God, and he had taken up Universalism, for he believed that God is love. One or the other of these passionate convictions led to his undoing at the hands of the ruling elements in his pastorates. Finally the Reverend was able to say, "I have learned not to have any *painful* solicitude about staying or not staying in this or in any other place. . . . If my old troubles prove a *serious barrier* to my labors in this village [Greenville, Illinois], I shall *moste likely* give up preaching as my *main* business and try to be useful and happy in some other business."[7] Easier said than done. The Reverend never gave up preaching as his main business. And rebuffs continued to be his lot. Robert did not forget this treatment and later, after he delivered his first anti-religious lecture, in Peoria, he told his wife that he had paid off one of his father's debts.

While in Marion with his father, Robert took employment as assistant to the clerk of the county and circuit courts. In his spare time he started to study law in the offices of the Honorable Willis Allen and his son, William Joshua Allen. Willis Allen was busily engaged, in 1853, in a campaign for reelection as a representative to Congress on the Democratic ticket. Young "Josh" Allen in the absence of his father did the bulk of the legal work for the firm and with him Robert gained most of his early legal experience. "Josh" had another influence upon Robert: he had decidedly liberal leanings in religion, he was spoken of as an atheist. Josh and Robert talked for many hours about religious questions.[8]

Robert's exposure to law and irreligion was interrupted toward the end of 1853 by the decision of his father to go to Tennessee. His father was now in fairly good health but he did not want to make the trip alone. The Reverend had two reasons for going, to preach and to learn first-hand about slavery. He had acquired means of travel, an eighty-five dollar horse and a sixty-five dollar buggy, a "good fit out," said Robert. When they reached Metropolis in Massac County, southern Illinois, Robert wrote to John, "You will likely be surprised to learn that we are in this part of the world, but I don't know why you should, for you know Father intends to see the whole world before many years." Tennessee was not enough for the Reverend, so they went on to Alabama. Several days in Alabama brought forth from the Reverend the comment, "Our sympathies were everywhere strongly excited for the poor slaves and we often expressed our views of slavery even to slaveholders. . . ."

On the way back, in Tennessee, Robert came across a teaching opportunity in Waverley, Humphreys County, which offered him the prospect of clearing about one hundred and fifty dollars a term. This was so attractive that he could not turn it down. His father went back to Marion alone. Robert was not too happy in Waverley: "It is rather lonesome here all alone and in a slave state at that where the very air seems to be chained."[9] The talk was of "niggers, niggers all the time." He saw an auction of slaves and was outraged by the separation of a mother and two children, one two years old, the other, three. The incipient lawyer in him asserted itself and he looked up the law on the subject. He found that no child under eight years of age should be sold or separated from its mother. But "who," he asked, "will prosecute the breakers of the law?" A grand jury would have to bring an indictment and who would constitute the grand jury? The very ones whose interest it was to break the law. Occasionally Robert was asked if he thought slavery was wrong. He would reply, "It is wrong enough to damn the whole of them."[10] But he tempered the remark with good nature for "they take it," he said, "in good part." Robert was not without hope on the question of slavery for he read in the papers that *Uncle Tom's Cabin* was playing to large and enthusiastic audiences in such places as New Orleans, St. Louis, Memphis, and Nashville.

Robert stayed in Waverley until May, 1854, and then went back to Marion. He found his father broken up by the death of his third wife in March. His father had taken out a mortgage on a house in Marion with a view to living there permanently, but this blow caused a change of plans. Also he realized that Clark and Robert had to think of a profession to follow and that meant in all likelihood that they would soon leave Marion. Clark had come to Marion in the early part of 1854 and was in the dry goods business. But he was dissatisfied with it and thought of becoming, like brother John, a physician. When Robert returned, he evidently had some effect on Clark's choice of profession, for the brothers, ever devoted to each other, decided to pursue law together. They had access, as Robert had had, to the legal library of the Allens.

After one month of study they were admitted to the bar in July, 1854, but on an *ex gratia* basis limiting them to minor and routine litigation. Fees soon came in—"our prospects were good," wrote Clark.[11] The brothers continued to prepare themselves for full and official admission to the bar, which took place in Mount Vernon, Illinois, on December 20, 1854. The ceremony of admission consisted of four stages.[12] First, the brothers were requested to submit a certificate of good moral character from a court in some county, which they had secured from Williamson County, where Marion was located. Second, they were required to show competence in the law in an oral examination in open court. This they easily did. Third, they took an oath to uphold the law with all diligence and honesty. And last, but not least, they were required to supply the examiners and the officers of the court with enough food and strong drink to last until midnight.

In 1855 the brothers practiced law together in Marion, where Robert saw a prospect of "considerable money." But then he cast his eyes toward Shawneetown. Shawneetown was seething with activity. It was the salt-producing center of the country. Located on the Ohio River just above Cairo, it was the main port of entry to Illinois for settlers, travelers, and freight coming down the river and it was second only to Cairo as a port for men and goods coming up the Mississippi.[13] It looked as if Shawneetown connected by water with cities like Cleveland and Pittsburgh and New Orleans would displace Chicago as the metropolis of the state. A likely place indeed for an ambitious young lawyer.

Arriving in Shawneetown, Robert looked about for employment to tide him over until his law practice developed. First he worked for a short time in the Federal Land Office and then in the office of John Hall, the clerk of the county and circuit courts. Hall was a leader of the anti-Nebraska men and of the new and rapidly growing Republican party.

It was not a time to take politics lightly. The Irrepressible Conflict was in the air. In 1854, a son of Illinois, "Little Giant" Douglas, had convulsed the nation and his state with his Kansas-Nebraska Act and did much to unite Anti-Nebraska Democrats, Free Soilers, Abolitionists, Know Nothings, and Whigs in the organization of a new party that was to elect another son of Illinois, "Tall Sucker" Lincoln, to the highest office in the land. When Douglas tried to speak in Chicago, a mob howled him down. When he proceeded to stump the state, Abraham Lincoln arose against him: "I have done with this mighty argument of self-government. Go, sacred thing! Go in peace."

Illinoisans grew rabid over events in Kansas. Five thousand armed men went into Kansas to vote for a pro-slavery legislature. They were successful but then anti-slavery men established their own government. On May 21, 1856, a band of pro-slavery men pillaged Lawrence, Kansas. When John Brown of Ossawatomie heard of it, he became the angel of vengeance and caused five men to be slain.

Shawneetown also had its violence and bloodshed. On November 11, 1856, while Robert Ingersoll was at work in the office of his employer, John Hall, one Robert C. Sloo entered, whipped out a gun, and shot John Hall dead. The assassin was the son of Colonel James Sloo, a Douglas man and Hall's most bitter political foe. The son came to avenge reflections upon the good name of his father that Hall had issued for the benefit of the press.

The trial of Sloo lasted forty-two days and gave Ingersoll ample opportunity to observe the methods and tactics of the opposing lawyers. He was particularly impressed with "Black Jack" Logan for the prosecution, the same Logan who later became the Commander-in-Chief of the Grand Army of the Republic. Some said Logan got the name "Black Jack" from his black eyes and his long black hair; others said he got it from his reputation for doing any dirty work that Douglas wanted done. Logan cut a fine figure in the courtroom but he could not prevent Sloo from being acquitted on the grounds of insanity.

In Shawneetown Ingersoll continued the study of law in the office of an eminent lawyer and judge, William G. Bowman. He practiced law too and his business was increasing. He characterized himself, however, as "lazy, careless and fat."[14] But he was comparing himself to his brother Clark who "will always do well and nothing can hinder him. The secret of his success is Energy. He is as energetic as Napoleon ever was." Robert was putting on weight, he now weighed one hundred and eighty pounds—"I never was so large before"—but he could hardly be called fat for he was almost six feet tall. He called himself "sound as a dollar" and was no longer afflicted with the attacks of chills and headache that he had had for five years.

Shawneetown did not satisfy him long. He decided to stay there only until he was sure that he was "a *first-rate* lawyer." Which he decided soon. In February, 1958, he and Clark set up a law firm in Peoria.

Part Two:
PEORIA

"I THINK WE ARE GOING
TO MAKE LOTS OF MONEY"

Peoria in 1858 was a thriving port on the Illinois River. Its population had grown from four thousand people in 1848 to twenty-one thousand in 1858. Like Shawneetown and Cairo, it had had ambitions to become the biggest city in the state. But by 1858 Peoria saw that she had better content herself with being first in Peoria County and second in the state, for Chicago had jumped from thirty thousand people in 1850 to eighty thousand in 1855 and a hundred thousand in 1858.

About the time Ingersoll came to Peoria, river traffic on the Illinois was at its peak. Soon, however, he was to witness, and contribute to, its decline.

Peoria contracted "railroaditis." Litigation was rife over issues of finance and right of way. No sooner had the Ingersoll brothers arrived in Peoria than they were engaged to handle much of the litigation. In the fall of 1857 they lobbied for the railroads at the state legislature.

By February, 1858, the Ingersolls' legal business enabled Robert to write, "Our prospects here are very bright indeed."[1] Clark had preceded Robert to Peoria by a few months and when Robert came he found his brother had "already become acquainted with everybody and all liked him." There were some thirty lawyers in Peoria at the time and so a capacity for being liked was an immediate asset.

The Ingersolls had their office on the second floor of a two-story frame building, No. 4 Adams Street, just across from the Court House. "We have a very nice office," albeit not luxuriously furnished. The sofa served two purposes, by day a place to sit for clients, by night a place to sleep for Robert. Clark had just been married—"If ever I marry I hope I shall be as fortunate"—and the newlyweds were living in comfortable if confined quarters. They were boarding out "at a very nice place," Robert reported, and he himself was boarding "at the finest hotel in the city."

There was one thing about the law office that Robert particularly appreciated; through the civic enterprise of The Peoria Gas Light and Coke Company it was lighted with gas. "Gas you know is an excellent thing in law, in fact indispensable." By March of 1958 the Ingersolls were "getting more and more business" with their future "as bright and flattering as we could ask." Robert reports that the "substantial men" are coming to them now; "by substantial I mean those who have the *spondoolicks*."[2]

The Ingersolls, according to Robert, were also getting most of the criminal practice.[3] One week Robert defended three men on a robbery charge. "Everybody surely thought that they would take a little trip to Alton and seemed surprised that I cleared them." The Ingersolls were not queasy about real guilt or innocence in selecting clients. In May they defended a man indicted for perjury. It was a "hard case," said Robert; but they won it. The man was wealthy and deeded the Ingersolls, as a fee, "six city lots worth at least two hundred and fifty dollars apiece." This fee and their average monthly income prompted Robert to predict, "I think we are going to make lots of money." And why not? "Clark and I have the reputation of being the only criminal lawyers at the bar."

If the Ingersolls were prospering, the country at large was not. Excessive speculation in land and railroads and over-expansion of manufacturing industries had led to an ominous debt structure. On August 24, 1857, the Ohio Life Insurance and Trust Company of Cincinnati and New York failed with liabilities of $7,000,000. Panic seized the New York Stock Exchange. Stocks plummeted, ruining brokers, bankers and manufacturers.

Illinois was hard hit. Within a year, more than two hundred businesses went down in Chicago alone. Many banks closed. Railroads suspended construction because their stocks and bonds lost value and possible investors hoarded their capital. This phase of the depression particularly affected Peoria, second in the state only to Chicago as a center for new railroad projects. Yet Robert Ingersoll was expecting to make "lots of money." Even so, he, too, noted that times were bad: "God knows there can be none *worse.*" But, he wrote to John, "there are better times a coming. . . . so keep your heart whole within you and let the 'wolf' be da——d."

Now as men pondered the emptiness of their pocketbooks, they began to look to their souls. They turned to God. The *New York Times* wrote of "the great awakening." *Harper's Weekly* rhapsodized: "The Christian Churches of the land are now in the midst of an extraordinary awakening. . . . The movement is on so grand a scale that it commands universal attention. It has all the sublimity of vastness. . . . The hymns of the worshiping throngs of Maine are echoed by those of California; the 'daily prayer meeting' girdles the Continent from ocean to ocean." But the Boston *Liberator* termed the revival "an epidemic. . . . Prayer-meetings morning, noon, and night . . . prayer-meetings in town, village, and hamlet, North and South. . . . The whole thing is an emotional contagion without principle. . . ."

It was a contagion to which Robert Ingersoll was immune. "Nothing heard of but prayer meetings," he wrote in May, 1858, "but I have not been to a single one yet."[4] Let economic conditions improve and men would, he said, "stop praying and go to preying." Robert's father was caught up in the excitement and, though sixty and ailing, he was more active than ever going from place to place preaching night and day.[5] Mary Ingersoll became a spiritualist and this bothered her brother. He wrote, "I heard a lady or rather a she-fool lecture on spiritualism this winter and I got enough."

If Robert was out of sympathy with revivalism, he was not as yet a godless man. His letters of the 1857-58 period often indicate a belief in a divinity: "But whether I should ever [see you again] or not my prayer is that God will bless you and protect you all";[6] "May the Good God be with you all is the prayer of Your Aff. Bro."; "God bless you all, the prayer of your brother, Rob G. Ingersoll."[7] But of his church-going Robert wrote, "I have attended church three times in two years." There was no one around who preached a reasonable and humane God. He had heard the other story so often that there was "at least nothing like novelty in it."

ROBERT ENTERS POLITICS

IN the summer and fall of 1858 the eyes of the nation were upon Illinois. Would Stephen A. Douglas be returned to the Senate or would Abraham Lincoln be elected? Douglas was back in favor again. Events in Kansas and Washington attending the operation of the Kansas-Nebraska Act had helped him out. The territorial legislature of Kansas had acted to submit a new pro-slavery constitution to the voters of Kansas. Twice it was submitted and twice it was decisively rejected. But President Buchanan, cowering under the threats of Fire-Eaters from the South that they would rend the Union if he did not support the constitution, persisted in defending it. Infuriated at this betrayal of "the great principle of Popular Sovereignty," Douglas denounced the President.

On his journey back to Illinois from Washington in June, 1858, crowds of people gathered at railroad stations to cheer the Little Giant. He entered Chicago as bands played and cannon boomed. Thirty thousand jubilant people stood in the square in front of the Tremont House to hear him. They roared in approbation when he declared that Lincoln's proposition, "A House Divided against itself cannot stand," meant civil war and Federal despotism, and that Lincoln's attack on the Supreme

Court in respect to the Dred Scott Decision amounted to sub-
mitting questions of constitutionality "to the Republican caucus
sitting in the country" or "to a tumultuous town meeting." They
roared approval again when he declared himself for a government "made by white men, for white men, to be administered
by white men." Thus Douglas pointed the issues for a momentous state election and the exciting Lincoln-Douglas debates.

On August 18, Douglas spoke at a mass meeting in Peoria.
The next day the Republican Convention of the Fifth Congressional District met in Peoria to nominate a representative
to Congress. They nominated Judge William Kellogg, the incumbent, whom two years later Robert Ingersoll would oppose
for the post. Also, on August 19 in Peoria, Lincoln replied to
Douglas. During the remainder of the campaign Lincoln made
five speeches in the Fifth District in behalf of Kellogg, and
Douglas made five for the Democratic nominee, James W.
Davidson.

Robert Ingersoll, who was becoming active in politics,
thought Douglas was right on the "Great Bugger-Boo"—as
Robert called it—of popular sovereignty. Like Douglas, he did
not care whether Kansas became a slave state or not. The point
was, how she became so. He did not want to live in Kansas and,
as he said, "I am not going to bother myself about people
'clothed in the livery of the sun.' "[1]

The campaign of 1858 and the reelection of Douglas fixed
Robert's political loyalty and raised his ambitions. He knew he
was an effective speaker at the bar. He knew that his success at
the bar met the main prerequisite to a career in politics. And he
knew, for sure, what side he was on. He became a leading
figure in the Debating Lyceum which met every two weeks to
discuss the issues of the day. At one of these meetings in late
October, 1859, he participated in heated debate about John
Brown's raid on Harper's Ferry. This, he contended, was the
inevitable outcome of the Black Republicanism of Seward and
Lincoln. This was the consequence of the doctrine, a house divided against itself cannot stand. The only way to forestall
bloody civil strife was to put Douglas in the White House. But

Ingersoll wanted his own position to be clearly understood: he was not for slavery, he was against abolitionism with its inter-ventionist frenzy. Let the law of the land be obeyed, let the states and territories work out their own solution to the slavery problem, and let John Brown swing on the Virginia gallows.

The Ingersoll law office began to be a gathering place for the younger and more ardent Douglasites. The presidential year, 1860, was on their minds, with the South threatening secession if either Seward or Lincoln were elected. The Fifth Congres-sional District of Illinois was a pivotal district between Little Egypt, to the south, fiercely pro-slave by reason of Southern commerce and ancestry, and the districts to the north. It must be made safe for Douglas. How to do this became an engross-ing concern of the Ingersolls and their friends. Who, for in-stance, was to oppose Judge Kellogg for Congress? The talk was that one of the Ingersolls should do it. But which one? The answer came easy—Clark pushed his younger brother. He felt that Robert was better political timber. Robert's repute as an orator was greater and was rapidly growing. He was also very popular.

"The best company and the greatest entertainer I ever saw" was said of Robert by Barrett White, Justice of the Peace in Peoria and one of the Ingersolls' cronies.[2] Another friend, Henry Baldwin, elected mayor of Peoria in 1862, said that Robert had "an inexhaustible supply of brilliant wit." Still an-other friend, John Warner, elected Mayor of Peoria eight times, voted Robert matchless in witty story-telling.

Occasionally the political parleys and the entertainment in the Ingersoll office got out of hand. Once in April the assembled company, abetted by the bottle, decided that it was too late to go to bed and too early to go to work, so they descended to the street, started a bonfire, and held a public meeting. They made impassioned speeches and sang songs, particularly "Annie Laurie." The next morning an irate Peorian appeared in court and signed a complaint alleging that the Ingersolls and others had disturbed the peace. Robert was counsel for the defendants and pleaded not guilty, requesting a jury trial. At the trial he maintained with much eloquence and not a little levity that the issue of civil rights hung precariously in the balance. The jury succumbed and a verdict of acquittal was swiftly reached.

In the last week of April a sad interlude took place. The Reverend John Ingersoll was stricken at Clark's home, where he had been staying since the death of his wife earlier in the year. Before he died, May 1, the Reverend struggled to make clear his thoughts on religion. He had given up the idea of eternal punishment. He now believed in a compassionate God who afforded man, in Robert's words "the eternal opportunity of doing right." He believed that everyone would ultimately be saved. In his last hours he asked Robert to read to him passages from Plato on immortality.

For several years the Reverend had known of Robert's skeptical tendencies but, as his son put it, "He was grand enough to say to me that I had the same right to my opinion that he had to his." In his last hours he did not ask Robert to read the Bible to him nor did he plead with his son to come to terms with God. But he did say over and over that in an after life they would all be together again. He died in Robert's arms.

The son was sustained by the thought that his father was right. He could accept nothing else. The immortality of a loved one was an emotional necessity. It would be years before he could view with equanimity the prospect of an eternal void.

One other thing buoyed Robert up: "I never said to him an unkind word, and in my heart there never was of him an unkind thought."

On August 2, in Peoria, the Democrats at the convention of the Fifth Congressional District nominated Robert for representative to Congress. The chief resolution adopted by the convention stated that Congress should not intervene in "the formation of domestic institutions in states and territories." In his acceptance speech Ingersoll brought down the house with wit and vitriol. Saying of Lincoln that he had "no character—no reputation," he pictured the Republican party as a wet nurse going into the territories with diapers. He declared that the platform drawn up by Republicans of the Fifth

Congressional District lacked even minimum intelligence: look at the grammatical errors in it. The *Transcript,* a Republican paper, was in a high dudgeon: "Bob" should talk; the Democratic party was deficient in literacy, he was deficient in taste. "He was not nominated to be elected, but he was nominated to traverse the counties and create a laugh, tell stories, and please 'the boys' . . . his wit is too deep. He dives so far that he brings up mud with it. It is almost invariably dirty." Ingersoll did deal in mud during this campaign, if not in the quantity suggested by the *Transcript,* but mud was a campaign staple.

Ingersoll and his opponent for Congress, the incumbent Kellogg, scheduled in the manner of Lincoln and Douglas a series of twenty-one debates to be held in the eleven counties of the Fifth Congressional District from August 27 to October 31. Kellogg's arguments in the debates were in the regular Republican vein. He contended that Congress had the power to legislate upon slavery in the territories as recognized in the Northwest Ordinance of 1787 and in the Compromise of 1850. He opposed the extension of slavery but supported the constitutional guaranties of slavery where it existed, including the Fugitive Slave Law. In response Ingersoll departed from the orthodox Douglas line, to the discomfiture of his opponent and the surprise of many of his hearers. Clark Carr, a Republican, relates that he and other members of the party had always looked upon Ingersoll as a pro-slavery Douglas Democrat until they heard him in the debate at Galesburg. Kellogg spoke first, presenting what seemed to be, according to Carr, unanswerable arguments. Then Ingersoll arose. His first two sentences Carr never forgot: "The Fugitive Slave Law is the most infamous enactment that ever disgraced a statute book. The man who approves or apologizes for that infamy is a brute."[3] Ingersoll declared that the Fugitive Slave Law forced the American people to participate in crime, the maintenance of slavery. The very existence of slavery was an abomination. "It may be doubted," writes Carr, "whether there was ever pronounced by any other human being so terrific a philippic against slavery and the Fugitive Slave Law. I myself had heard Beecher and Garrison and

Wendell Phillips and Lovejoy and Giddings, but I had never heard it equalled.

As a rule, Ingersoll was not so vehement against slavery as he was at Galesburg. But Galesburg was a hotbed of abolitionism and an "underground railway" station for fugitive slaves. Ingersoll conducted himself accordingly and said what most of his audience wanted to hear. Not that he had become adroit at speaking out of both sides of his mouth at once. It was not equivocation to denounce slavery and to espouse popular sovereignty in order to keep slavery out of the territories and save the Union. But to get any hearing at all for popular sovereignty in Galesburg one had to make his opposition to slavery strong.

On September 28, a debate was held in Peoria. The *Transcript* said that it was obvious to everybody that Ingersoll was "no match for his competitor in that which goes to make up the public debater and statesman. In the arts and trickery of the politician and demagogue, Ingersoll was at home." However, another Peoria paper, the *Daily Democratic Union,* reported that Ingersoll spoke with "great clearness and precision . . . fortifying every position he took with arguments which could not be and were not refuted." The *Transcript* complained that Ingersoll "dodged nearly all of the great issues" with a "succession of grand splurges without wit or argument." The *Democratic Union* said that Kellogg attempted "to patch together the shreds in which his flimsy framework of principles had been torn by the sledge hammer blows of Bob." On audience reaction to the debaters, the *Transcript* commented, "Judge Kellogg's victory was complete." The *Democratic Union* observed that the "enthusiasm of the Democratic portion of hearers was unbounded."

A debate at Maquon on October 22 furnished the *Transcript* choice material. Someone calling himself "Observer" wrote to the *Transcript* that Ingersoll in the debate was drunk, profane, licentious, and vulgar. Also eight residents of Maquon sent in a signed statement charging that Ingersoll's language "was of the lowest and most filthy character"; that he was so drunk that he "several times fell partially off the stand . . ." and that "the strongest Democrats in town *Declared Him To Be a Perfect*

Nuisance and that they would never vote for such a man." The *Transcript* was inspired by the material and embellished it. It was more than Ingersoll could take. Meeting the editor on the street he had it out with him. The only evidence of the meeting comes from the editor: "The Democratic Candidate for Congressional honors in this district, having exhibited his varied accomplishments during the present canvass, assumed another character yesterday—that of a ruffian and bully. As we came down Main Street, yesterday morning, Ingersoll met us and threatened us with all sorts of vengeance if we alluded to him again in the *Transcript,* saying he would whip us if we opened our mouth to him, ordering us to move on, and applying to us various forcible but we must admit, rather inelegant epithets. Finding that he could not frighten or bully, Ingersoll moved on himself, swearing that if we said anything more about him in the *Transcript* he would cowhide us." There is no evidence that Ingersoll carried out his threats.

At any rate, when the election returns were in, the vote showed that the *Transcript* had not particularly damaged Ingersoll. He lost in the Fifth Congressional District but he won in Peoria City and County. Peoria City and County gave Ingersoll 3754 votes and Kellogg 3550. Douglas also carried the City and County, receiving 3739 votes to Lincoln's 3539. If it means anything, Ingersoll in the City and County received fifteen votes more than Douglas. In the District as a whole Kellogg defeated Ingersoll by a majority of 4500, with Lincoln having about the same majority over Douglas. It was clear that local candidates were less compelling than party affiliation and explosive national issues.

COLONEL INGERSOLL

At 4:30 A.M. on April 12, 1861, the bombardment of Fort Sumter began. The country, North and South, was agog over the reports of an engagement. People stood around telegraph station awaiting the latest news. At Peoria, the night of April 12, a violent storm struck, which interrupted the transmission of telegrams. The delay was almost unbearable. During the afternoon of April 13, when it became known that Fort Sumter was burning, a large crowd gathered at the Court House Square. The National Blues, a Peoria military organization, marched in full uniform to the square, planted a flagstaff fifty-one feet high, and running up the flag, pledged themselves to the Union. The crowd thundered its approval. Soon flags were hoisted on the City Hall and the Engine House. Sunday, April 14, came and the furore gave to solemnity. This was Civil War.

One of the most active Peorians in mobilization efforts was Robert Ingersoll. He was much in demand as a speaker for rallies. On April 22 at a mass meeting he was appointed to a Committee of Safety which had as its main aim the stamping out of what Ingersoll called "treason in our midst." The immediate reason for the meeting was an incident earlier in the day. A boat had gone up the Illinois River, which, rumor had it, was to be loaded with corn for the South. At the meeting it was decided to stop the boat when it returned. A resolution was adopted declaring that from this date no boats carrying provisions or contraband of war would be allowed to go down the river. Ingersoll's speech at the meeting, said the now friendly *Transcript,* "eclipsed, if possible, his former soul-stirring efforts."

Also on April 22, Ingersoll sent this telegram to Governor Yates: "With your permission I will raise a regiment of one thousand men to be ready on call. Will you accept?" The offer was accepted. During the next six months, Ingersoll helped to raise three regiments.

In September, Ingersoll set about raising a regiment of cavalry, first called the McKinstry Guards and later the Eleventh Illinois Cavalry. Judge Basil Meek of Woodford County and Joseph Parrish, a rich Peoria merchant, gave him substantial assistance. Since the cavalry regiments authorized by action of the Illinois Legislature and Governor Yates had already been raised, it was necessary to get authorization from General John C. Frémont then stationed at St. Louis in command of the Western Department. At first, Fremont, under heavy criticism for mismanagement of the Department, was unwilling to approve the undertaking. Then Parrish and Meek appealed to McKinstry, Frémont's Adjutant General and Chief Quartermaster, who, favorable to the project, went to Fremont and pressed for its approval. Frémont was won over and out of gratitude to McKinstry the projectors of the new regiment named it after him. Ingersoll was not with Parrish and Meek in St. Louis during the negotiations but as soon as approval was received Meek telegraphed him to come to St. Louis. Meek felt that because Ingersoll was widely known in central Illinois he should be first in command of the new regiment.

When Ingersoll arrived in St. Louis, he, Meek, and Parrish conferred with McKinstry and Frémont. He was made colonel and Meek lieutenant colonel, although the official commissions did not come through until the middle of October. Terms were worked out for equipping and maintaining the regiment, which was to rendezvous at Camp Lyon on the Peoria Fair Grounds. The terms were published in the *Transcript,* September 16, with the following statement by Ingersoll and Meek: "This regiment is intended to be one of the best in the service."

For a while it looked as though the Eleventh Illinois would escape most of the troubles attendant upon the raising of regiments in the early part of the war, troubles like poor equipment, shoddy clothing, and soldiers' pay in arrears. Then things began to happen. A shipment of overcoats arrived in December that the *Transcript* called "a disgrace to the service"—"The person who sent them ought to have 39 lashes on the bare back." At first Ingersoll refused to accept them but the days were getting colder and no other coats came in, so he had to take them. Then his men's pay was delayed. And no arms arrived. It was a rueful jest that by the time the men got arms their clothes would be worn out.

Growing restless and resentful, the men were now plaguing Peoria with acts of rowdyism. Desertions were mounting. One day an officer went on a tour of the companies to find out how many men from each company "had gone over the fence" which surrounded Camp Lyon. Upon asking the orderly of the company which reputedly had the greatest number of deserters, he was told that none had gone over the fence. "None!" the officer exclaimed. "Why, I believe there are more of your men than of any other company." "Well, I know that," said the orderly, "but they did not go over the fence; they all went under it."

But Ingersoll was by no means discouraged. In the latter part of January, 1862, he went to St. Louis and learned that within a short time his regiment would be ordered to decamp for Benton Barracks, at St. Louis. He was now able to report that the regiment was "fully and perfectly equipped with the exception of arms." It had not been easy. "I never knew what work was before. . . . Something happens every moment—somebody has lost something—broken something—stolen something—something is missing—something has run away—something is bad—something is rotten. The contractors do not feed us—They feed too much—There is not wood and coal enough—There is too much used. Some officer has been insulted. Somebody has the measles—mumps—fever—broken head—black eye—sprained ankle—Somebody is drunk—somebody raising Hell on the general plan. Somebody is sick—wants a furlough—wife about to be confined—two young ones at the point of death. Business must be attended to—wants to go 500 miles—man owes him six bits. The above gives a fair idea of what occurs daily." But "no matter, a light heart and a thin pair of breeches will take any man through the world."[1]

Ingersoll had a special reason for being light-hearted. He was about to be married. The preceding fall he had been counsel for the defendant in a murder case. Some pigs had strayed from the defendant's farm and had been impounded. When the farmer went to get them, the poundmaster resisted and the farmer shot and killed him. "In the echo of that shot," said Ingersoll, "was the cry of my babes." The trial took place in Groveland, Tazewell County. While in Groveland, Ingersoll was invited one day to dinner at the Benjamin Parker mansion. Here he met the Parkers' daughter, Eva, and was immediately smitten. He lost no time, and soon they were engaged. On February 13, nine days before his regiment left for Benton Barracks, they were married. "She is a good natural sweet woman," wrote the bridegroom, "one that loves me and one that I love— that is enough."

Eva came from a family known for unorthodox views on religion. Her grandmother, Sarah Buckman Parker, a woman of vigorous intellect, was an infidel. Her parents were devotees of Paine and Voltaire. Not being emotionally tied to orthodoxy, Eva was a strong influence in her husband's intellectual development. At the time of their marriage he was not free of the God of his childhood. In January he had written John, "I have thrown myself into the great tide of the times, willing to let it bear me wherever it will. . . . And may the same God who watches over you watch over me, if not for my sake, for yours."

On March 9, the day after Robert watched his regiment bid farewell to Illinois and prepare to cross the Mississippi River, he wrote John from Benton Barracks: "When we started the boys gave three cheers for glorious Illinois and our band played 'Sweet Home' and as the sound floated away over the countless waves—I thought—'How many of us will recross—how many again meet father, mother, brother, sister, child, wife?' How many will return to their own firesides, how many be maimed— killed, how long left on the field of battle to suffer and to die? *And then raising my eyes . . . I asked for the blessing and protection of my Father's God.*" (Italics mine.)

If Ingersoll up to the Civil War had wandered from the fold, the War and its perils brought him back.

Had Ingersoll married a devout woman, he might not have wandered again. But Eva Parker was a rationalist. Never caught in the coils of sin-and-hell, her approach to religious questions was emotionally uncomplicated. If she thought of God at all, it was, as a Deist might, of a remote, impersonal force. She could not take seriously the idea of a God made in the image of man, which was the only God her husband could take seriously, either in acceptance or in attack. Agnosticism came easy for her, it came hard for him.

THE ELEVENTH ILLINOIS GOES INTO ACTION

THE Eleventh Illinois was two weeks in going from Peoria to St. Louis. About twelve thousand men were already at Benton Barracks awaiting arms and pay before they went on to zones of active warfare. Ingersoll noticed great military activity with everybody on the alert. "Away they go—regt. after regt., battery after battery. Infantry cavalry and artillery all commingled, going down the great river, covered with transports and those terrible floating forts called gunboats."

Everybody was optimistic. General Burns had taken Roanoke Island in North Carolina and General Grant had forced the surrender of Fort Henry and Fort Donelson. Ingersoll was in General Halleck's office when the news of the fall of Fort Donelson came off the wires. St. Louis, he wrote, "was instantly in commotion. Procession after procession formed and marched through the streets decorated with thousands of flags. And old gray haired men joined with children in singing at the tops of their voices our most stirring and glorious national airs." Thrilled by the celebration and bursting with regional pride over the latest victory, Ingersoll said that the South had found that "Western men are heroes." He was confident that the Army of the West was invincible. He was sure that in a matter of days the Mississippi would again be open to the commerce of the "Grand West." He also had the pleasure of seeing on the St. Louis levee "ten thousand and eight hundred and sixty-five rebel prisoners" from Fort Donelson.[1] Like almost everybody else in the North in the early months of 1862, he thought that the war would soon be over.

"The sooner the war closes the better I shall be pleased," wrote Ingersoll. His wife had come to St. Louis and was staying at the Planters House. Since he was a colonel, he could visit her there often. The prospect of their parting, if only for a short time, was not pleasant. Again, it might not be for a short time, it might be forever. One afternoon Ingersoll visited the graves of soldiers who had died in St. Louis hospitals. In one graveyard alone he counted over 1500 graves. With death so abundant, he could not think himself immune. Particularly since under existing medical and hospital conditions a wound was likely to be fatal. "*Genl. Hospital,*" wrote Ingersoll, "is the most effective officer in the service. Of all things I am going to avoid Hospitals. They are far more dangerous than shot and shell." And also—"I think the army surgeons as a general thing are quacks."[2] Nor did it make Ingersoll feel better that the day he visited the graves he also saw on every hand the harbingers of spring. "The fields are all green again and the trees are budding and some are actually in leaf." The terrible irony of war, that while the earth burgeoned man destroyed, did not escape him.

As of March 20, Ingersoll did not know where or when his regiment was going. His men were eager to get into action. On March 24, the orders to move came. The very next day the regiment embarked on the steamers *Empress, Imperial,* and *Ed Walsh,* bound for Pittsburg Landing to join the Army of the Tennessee under Grant. They were in transit three days. Stopping first at Crump's Landing on the Tennessee River, the Eleventh Illinois was detached of its Third Battalion, which was added to the forces of General Lew Wallace. The First and Second Battalions under Ingersoll went on five miles to Pittsburg Landing to join the Sixth Division under General Prentiss. In all, there were five divisions at Pittsburg Landing when Ingersoll arrived.

Ingersoll was soon informed of the Union strategy. General Buell's Army of the Ohio was scheduled to reach Savannah, nine miles above Pittsburg Landing, where Grant was stationed. This concentration of men was in line with Grant's plan to execute a large-scale offensive action against the Confederates massed in the vicinity of Corinth, Mississippi, under the command of Generals Johnston and Beauregard. Grant assumed that Johnston's Army was still in a state of general demoralization following their retreat from Bowling Green and Columbus in Kentucky. A vigorous offensive would be the coup de grâce.

It did not occur to Grant that Johnston could be planning an offensive himself. When news was brought to him of scouting expeditions being driven back under heavy rebel fire and of pickets seeing the enemy in force two miles away, he still could not believe that Johnston was doing more than sending out raiding parties. On the afternoon of April 5, Grant told a Colonel Ammen who had just arrived in Savannah with a brigade from Buell's army that he need not go on to Pittsburg Landing: ". . . make the troops comfortable. . . . There will be no fight at Pittsburg Landing; we will have to go to Corinth, where the rebels are fortified."[3]

Early Sunday morning, April 6, as Ingersoll and his men were getting ready to go on a scouting mission, the noise of shot and shell suddenly came to their ears, from the direction of Shiloh Church, a little to the southwest of Pittsburg Landing. The noise rapidly increased and everyone soon realized that a major battle was taking shape. Ordering his men to get ready fast, Ingersoll led them toward the battle area. In a matter of minutes they had several skirmishes with advance cavalry contingents and they took a few prisoners.

Ingersoll then advanced with his men through the woods to the edge of an open field where still under partial cover of the woods they formed a battle line. "Shot and shell were tearing through the woods at this point in the most fearful manner," wrote Ingersoll. "Trees as large as my body were shattered in pieces and great limbs came crashing around where we were formed."[4] Since cavalry could be of greatest effectiveness only when the enemy was routed, he was ordered to fall back slowly. "And so all day long we slowly retreated and anxiously watched the greatest battle ever fought on this continent." The line of battle was six to seven miles long, forming a crescent the center of which was directly opposite Pittsburg Landing three miles away. "The roar of the guns was almost deafening. . . . There was no lull, no pause." Back, back, back went Ingersoll and his men, desperately contesting every inch for "twelve dreadful bloody hours." When would Buell come with reinforcements? "All day long thousands of eyes had anxiously looked for the promised coming." Defeat was certain if he did not come soon. Then about five o'clock that afternoon word sped through the Union ranks that Buell was in sight. The cheers of the tired and desperate men arose above the roar and boom of the guns.

Buell's men rushed to support the wavering Union lines. Ingersoll records that "in a few moments the terrible advance of the enemy was stayed." Then "as though by common consent both armies lay down upon the terrible bloody field surrounded by thousands of dead and wounded and slept upon their arms."[5]

Ingersoll could not sleep. "The rain fell all night, slowly and sadly, as though the heavens were weeping for the dead." With his blanket around him he leaned against the trunk of a dead tree and watched the shells of Union gunboats. Precisely every fifteen minutes "would come a flash like heat lightning—then the boom—then the bluish line bending over the distant wood —then the roar of the bursting, and then last of all the double echo gradually dying over the far hills." This continued all night to prevent the Confederates from getting any rest.

Early in the morning, the battle resumed, this time with Grant and Buell on the offensive—"Thank God," said Ingersoll. For two hours the battle raged with all the fury of the day before, neither side advancing perceptibly. Then the Confederates began to give slightly—"the most glorious moment of my life," wrote Ingersoll. But until two o'clock in the afternoon the advance of the Union forces was held in strong check. Then Beauregard issued an order to retire. At four o'clock cheer after cheer arose from the Union lines. "The enemy had not only fallen back, had not only retreated, but were flying in the wildest confusion. The day was ours. The great Battle for the Union had been fought. The greatest, the bloodiest in American history, and had been won by the gallant sons of the Grand West."[6] Although the total Union loss in killed, wounded, and captured or missing was about 13,000, Ingersoll's regiment escaped with four killed and twenty wounded, captured or missing. He himself emerged without a scratch. He was proud of his men. They had shown great pluck. Only a few ran under the first fire of Shiloh.

On the second morning of the battle Ingersoll aided in organizing two new regiments out of the stragglers from the various units of the Union armies. The Peoria *Transcript,* of April 18, presented an interesting version of what took place. It said that on Sunday morning, the first day of the battle, surprised at his toilet, "the Colonel . . . rushed out of the tent in his shirt-sleeves." Whom should he see but "the panic-stricken Ohio troops" (who did not come until the next day) fleeing for safety. "Colonel Ingersoll mounted a 'stump' and harangued them with patriotic eloquence, bringing into play all the powers of his oratorical genius to counteract their fears and inspire them with the terrible consequences resulting from fear at such a moment. He succeeded well, and in a few minutes had the satisfaction of seeing 800 of them reform and return to the ranks." Said Ingersoll of the accounts of his military activities which appeared in the Peoria press, "Ninety-nine hundredths was regular lie and the other hundredth stretched like damnation."[7]

Since the Union forces were exhausted at the end of the Battle of Shiloh, Grant did not order an immediate pursuit of Beauregard but allowed him to retire to Corinth. On April 11, General Halleck arrived at Pittsburg Landing to take charge. He made Grant his second in command and Generals Thomas, Buell, and Pope the commanders, respectively, of the right, center, and left wings of an army that had grown to 100,000 men. General Sherman, thought by many to have made the greatest single contribution to the Union victory at Shiloh, also had an important command. Grant, Sherman, and Pope were for decisive action against Beauregard to force his further retreat and to engage and destroy him. Halleck was of a different mind and commenced instead a slow, cautious advance upon Corinth. On April 17, Ingersoll wrote his brother Clark that a telegram from Beauregard to Jefferson Davis had been intercepted, which read: "Unless I am immediately reinforced I must evacuate Corinth." Surely now there would be a quick assault upon the enemy who was only twenty-three miles away.

But Halleck procrastinated; not all the conditions were favorable. The weather was adverse to an offensive. "It does nothing but rain," Ingersoll noted, on April 19. "The army will be delayed again on account of the everlasting mud." Also, an epidemic of diarrhea struck.

Life in the Union Army was monotonous. Ingersoll appealed to Clark to send some reading material including new publications and a small copy of Shakespeare. On April 27 he wrote, "Write me often. A letter more than anything else kills the monotony of this wretched camp life." On this particular day the weather was delightful: "the skies filled with great slumbering clouds—the air hazy and the woods in full glory of leaf and flower." But it was a brief interlude. During the whole month of April Ingersoll counted but five decent days. It appeared that May would be no different. On May 6 he wrote, "It is now about five o'clock and it is again clouding up. The rain will come again all the blessed night long. The roads already are so bad that another flood could not make them worse. From here [Monterey] to Pittsburg Landing, some twelve or fourteen miles, the road is perfectly blockaded with artillery, baggage, mules, women, niggers and sutlers. Every wagon is in mud to the hubs and there is cussing and swearing enough on that road every fifteen minutes to send a world to hell."[8] Night after night Ingersoll slept on the ground without a dry thread around him, "wet as Jonah in the whale's belly." But his only sickness was diarrhea, which now everybody had.

He was not, however, yearning for a full-scale battle. Shiloh had been quite enough for him. War to him was "horrid beyond the conception of man." But if the war were to be over by summer, something would have to happen soon. On May 6 he thought, mistakenly, that the Confederates were evacuating Corinth and were falling back to Grand Junction. "But I care not where they fall, so they fall somewhere and soon."

On May 22, six weeks after Shiloh, Halleck was two and a half miles from Corinth. "Can see the enemy defenses," wrote Ingersoll. "A battle is expected daily or, rather, hourly."[9] But seven days went by. There was a bloody skirmish or two and Union siege guns threw shells into Corinth, but that was all. On the morning of May 30, Halleck despatched a scouting force to get as close a view as possible of enemy preparations in Corinth. There was nothing to view. During the night the enemy had evacuated. Ingersoll noticed that the Union army reacted with mixed feelings. He himself was pleased. He saw the evacuation as "at least a great moral victory for the North." Surely the South must recognize that she is doomed.

But it was the same story over again. Now they were pursuing the rebels beyond Corinth. General Pope with twenty thousand men, including the Eleventh Illinois, was now in charge. Pope's ineptitude in the chase was soon evident to Ingersoll. During the ten days following the occupation of Corinth, when Pope was reputedly pursuing the enemy with great success, he actually took about fifty prisoners, most of whom came of their own accord and gave themselves up. Said Ingersoll, "A pursuit planned by idiots and carried out by infantry without legs would have been equally successful. In fact, he would have caught them quicker if he had gone the other way."[10]

By July 8 still nothing much had happened. "Will this horrid war ever close?" Ingersoll was asking.[11]

During July and August Ingersoll was in several skirmishes with guerrilla bands. He thought such engagements fruitless. The guerrillas "suddenly appear a hundred or two strong, make a little dash on a bale of cotton or a railroad bridge, then disband, hide their guns, bury their ammunition and thus pretend to be Union men—and we generally believe all they say."[12]

Ingersoll was pleased at one thing and yet displeased. In July General Halleck was called to Washington to become chief military adviser under the title of General-in-Chief. Halleck then promoted Pope to the command in the East of the combined forces of Generals Banks, McDowell, and Frémont. If it pleased Ingersoll that Pope was gone, it displeased him that incompetence should be promoted. Before long he heard what he expected to hear. Outwitted by Lee and Jackson, Pope suffered a humiliating defeat at the second battle of Bull Run. As Ingersoll put it, Pope "lost what cost the Govt. five hundred millions of dollars. He has lost all that we gained in eighteen long dreary toilsome months. He has lost hundreds and hundreds of as brave officers as ever lived and thirty thousand soldiers. He has almost d——d the cause and has totally d——d himself.

"To allow troops to be led by such a jackass is murder."[13]

Ingersoll held Lincoln primarily responsible for the failure of the Union armies in the East. Lincoln, he thought, demonstrated poor judgment in choosing leaders. And maybe something more reprehensible than poor judgment: "When will Mr. Lincoln stop appointing idiots because they come from Illinois or are related to his *charming* wife?" There was, for instance, General Todd who for a time commanded the division to which the Eleventh Illinois was accredited. According to Ingersoll, Todd was "for several years . . . absolutely nothing but a '*Sutler*' in the regular army" and was made a brigadier general because he was Mrs. Lincoln's cousin. "Such appointments would disgrace the Devil himself."[14]

Ingersoll was offered a brigadier-generalship in August, but he refused it. The reason: "I started with the 11th, and am going to see them through."[15]

The failure of Union forces in the East, particularly Pope's defeat, rudely awakened the North from dreams of an early end to the War. The optimism of May and June gave way to gloom in September and October. "Shall we ever meet again?" Ingersoll wrote Clark. "The chances of death, of circumstance, of war almost say, No. . . ." Bothering Ingersoll at this time, the middle of September, was something that happened to a battalion of his regiment, which he had despatched to join a scouting expedition under Colonel McDermott. The battalion was under the command of Major S. D. Puterbaugh. Ingersoll and the rest of his regiment were in Corinth. The scouting force reconnoitered in a region northeast of Corinth and finding no evidence of rebel troops decided to camp for the night along the Hatchee River close to Pocahontas, Tennessee. Some of Puterbaugh's men went in search of forage for their horses, leaving their horses and arms in camp. There was delay in posting pickets. The officers were off by themselves, separated from the men. Twenty minutes after the scouting party arrived at the camp, it happened. As one of the men described it: "We heard a lot of hollering, and saw the dust a-flying, and before we could collect our thoughts and senses, the Rebels were upon us. . . . They came across the bridge like a streak of lightning, with 12 pieces of artillery; they shelled us out of there in a hurry. . . . We had to save our lives by flight."[16] Major Puterbaugh in his report to Ingersoll stated that he tried to rally the men but it was impossible—"the firing, the surprise, the overwhelming force of the enemy and the darkness had thrown everything into confusion."[17] The pell-mell flight of the men became known as the Hatchee-Skedaddle. Most of the battalion left horses, blankets, saddles, carbines, and revolvers behind them. "Thirty men at the bridge," Ingersoll wrote, "could have prevented the whole thing. Five pickets half a mile beyond the bridge and our forces could have retreated in good order." It was most humiliating. "The regiment has enjoyed a fine reputation. . . ." General Lew Wallace referred to the Eleventh Illinois as the "wild-cats."[18] The rebels spoke of it as the "bloody 11th." But "no use crying over spilt milk," said Ingersoll.[19]

Indeed there was little time to cry over spilt milk. The Confederate force that caused the Hatchee-Skedaddle was the vanguard of an army of fifty thousand men under Generals Price and Van Dorn that was coming north from Ripley, Mississippi, to attempt to retake Corinth. By October 1 they were encamped eight miles east and northeast of Corinth. On October 2 they attacked, meeting the Union forces about six miles from town. Outnumbered and in danger of a flanking movement, the Union forces put up a desperate fight but gradually fell back until by night the Confederates were only a mile from Corinth. At four

the next morning, cannonading on both sides recommenced,
continuing until daylight. Then sporadic skirmishing went on.
Finally, at 9:30, General Price led his divisions in a bold
charge on the Union lines and entered Corinth. A rout of the
Union forces seemed inevitable.[20] Then, as a Union soldier
put it, "A prodigious effort was made by our regimental commanders to rally the men and drive back the enemy, which,
fortunately, was successful."[21] As the enemy began retreating,
a heavy fire was poured into them. "They fell like slaughtered
sheep." But the enemy did not flee in disorder. Retreating
southward, they took advantage of a rough, hilly, wooded ter-
rain to slow down their pursuers and harass them with a mur-
derous fire from numerous ambuscades. The Eleventh Illinois
with other cavalry regiments under the command of General
Hurlbut led the pursuit and, Ingersoll noted, "with considerable success." Hundreds of prisoners were taken and great
quantities of arms and stores. The Hatchee-Skedaddle was a
thing of the past, lost to memory in present triumph.

"I HARDLY KNOW WHAT TO THINK"

ON September 10, Illinois Democrats met in convention at
Springfield, the catchword being "the Constitution as it is and
the Union as it was." The convention resolved "that it is the
duty of all good citizens to sustain the President against the
purpose of the *radical Republicans* to induce him to pervert
the efforts to suppress the wicked rebellion into a war for the
emancipation of the slaves and for the overthrow of the Constitution." The convention declared against the importation
of free Negroes into the state, against illegal arrest, and against
interferences with the freedom of speech and press. The resolutions were a threat to the united support that Lincoln needed
to prosecute the war decisively. The War Democrats, however,

did not line up with the regular Democrats and were out of sympathy with the convention and its aims. On September 19, Clark Ingersoll wrote a letter to the *Transcript*, reprinted in the *Chicago Tribune*, in which he denounced the convention and called upon conservative Democrats and Republicans to join in a convention for the purpose of pledging unqualified support of Lincoln and his war measures. On September 22, the day of Lincoln's announcement of the Proclamation of Emancipation but *before* his Proclamation suspending Habeas Corpus, Robert Ingersoll in Corinth read his brother's letter in the *Tribune* and wrote him, "I glory in the position you have taken. . . . The effect of the Springfield Convention is to throw cold water upon the present enthusiasm of the North. . . . It dampens the ardour of the army. . . . The North now has the right and it is her duty to act according to the dictates of humanity, of necessity. She has no right to acknowledge property in man. . . . Slavery is unspeakable, detestable. Destroy it! Our sainted father, if living, would be proud of you. . . ."[2]

On September 24, at Springfield, War Democrats and Republicans joined in the Republican Union Convention and devised a platform which said in effect that Lincoln could do no wrong. The Convention also nominated on the third ballot Clark Ingersoll for Congressman-at-large. Robert was happy that his brother was the nominee: "They could not have made a better choice." On September 29, however, *after* Lincoln's suspension of Habeas Corpus, Robert wrote Clark quite differently than on the 22nd, "For my part I cannot conceive of any possible necessity under any circumstances imaginable for the suppression of that right.

"Better that the Union be divided, better that each state have a separate national existence . . . than to be compelled to assist in trampling into the earth every principle of government made holy by the best blood of the world. . . .

"The Executive has gone too far. . . .

"I know that the platform upon which you run would never make you the slave of oppression, the instrument of torture. . . ."[3]

This letter had little apparent effect on Clark. He continued to profess complete support for the Administration. But to Robert even the Proclamation of Emancipation was a bad measure, though he had written, "Slavery is unspeakable, detestable. Destroy it!" He could not see that the Proclamation would become a boll weevil in the South, boring at a way of life from within. He could not see that ultimately the Proclamation would bring 185,000 Negroes into the Union armies. He did not realize how it would weaken support for the South abroad, how it would inspire the liberal elements of Europe, how it would enlist for the North the active efforts of the factory workers of England, who in their own bondage that was economic, waxed fervent for a government that abolished bondage.

Robert thought the Proclamation would only embitter the South further and would alienate the Border States.[4] And if the slaves do get their freedom suddenly, what will they do? Just before the Battle of Corinth he saw what might happen. In an advance south of Corinth toward Iuka, Alabama, Union troops had seized about one thousand slaves as contraband of war. Then pressed by the Confederates, they retired back to Corinth. "The negroes were terrified beyond description. Some ran to the woods, others pressed on even in advance of our cavalry and several women were seen to abandon their infants—placing the helpless little things down by logs or in the fence corners—regardless of their cries, they fled to the North."[5] The Proclamation of Emancipation would release similar hordes of helpless, irresponsible Negroes upon the North, where they were not wanted.

This was a period of sickness of spirit for Ingersoll. "I hardly know what to think. Does anybody?" He was cynical about efforts to preserve " 'the best government etc.' in the world." Congress was "a collection of fools and knaves." It was no longer an honor "even to be President of the Great Republic." As for the whole business of politics, he advised his brother to get out of it. "You have to be the friend of every booby—to put up with every indignity. You have to be the skillet of grease

in which little hungry puppy editors sop their miserable crusts.
. . ." His brother would be much better off to pursue his own
business and "let the dear people—the garlic-breathed greasy-
capped multitude go to the Devil." For the sake of success
alone he hoped Clark would be elected "but for your own sake
and your own happiness and that of your wife and dear children defeat would be better."[6]

Defeat did come to Clark. He received 119,819 votes; his
opponent, James C. Allen, a regular Democrat, 136,257.[7] Of
the fourteen congressmen elected in Illinois that year, nine
were Democrats. Both houses of the General Assembly of Illinois had Democratic majorities. Thus the voters of Illinois
expressed their displeasure with the Proclamation of Emancipation, the suspension of Habeas Corpus, and the lack of decisive Union victories on the battlefield. Mostly they were displeased with Emancipation. "Shall Illinois be Africanized?"
was the issue.

In December Robert became Chief of Cavalry of the Union
forces under Brigadier General Jeremy Sullivan of the District of Jackson at Jackson, Tennessee. This was to be his headquarters for the winter. But the fortunes of war intervened. In
mid-December news came to Sullivan that a strong rebel cavalry under Brigadier General Forrest had crossed the Tennessee
River and was within thirty miles of Jackson. An attack seemed
imminent. Since only thirteen hundred Union troops were stationed there, the attack would be successful unless reinforcements could arrive. But since the rail line had been cut at several places, it would take at least two days for aid to come.
General Sullivan ordered Ingersoll with six hundred and fifty
men, only one hundred and sixty of whom had ever fired a
gun in earnest, to engage with the enemy however strong and
delay him until Jackson could be reinforced.

They left the night of December 16 and marched all night
to a point six miles beyond Lexington, Tennessee, twenty-five
miles east of Jackson. All day, December 17, they skirmished
with rebel scouting parties. At night they fell back five miles.
"We all slept that night with our eyes open."[8] The next morning

at daylight fighting commenced again. Ingersoll disposed his forces at two bridges over a small stream just outside of Lexington. At one bridge he stationed a detachment of the Seventh Tennessee Cavalry. He himself with companies of the Eleventh Illinois defended the other. "The Tennesseans ran without making any resistance worth speaking of"[9] and the Confederates rushed across the bridge after them.

Ingersoll now had the enemy, twenty-five hundred of them, at his flank at well as in front. More of his men fled so that he had but seventy left. He withdrew them from the bridge he was defending to the road leading into Lexington. He placed his men across and along the road and planted two pieces of artillery in the middle of it and waited. He had not long to wait. "Not less than 10,000 cavalry," said one of his imaginative men, "was bearing down on our handful." Three times they repulsed rebel charges. "The fourth time," Ingersoll wrote, "the enemy ran over us—actually took the rammers out of the men's hands. I was the last to leave the guns. Away I went over a field—and away they went after me. They shot at me it seemed hundreds of times." He came to a high fence. His horse "jumped the fence clear and fine"—but when he came down on the other side his knees gave way and he fell flat—"off I went—and Mr. 'Sesesh' bagged the aforesaid."[10]

Ingersoll was taken for safekeeping to a nearby store, where he stayed four days. Then he was paroled. Several fellow prisoners had various versions of an incident that occurred while he was in custody. One evening he, prisoners, and guards were exchanging yarns and cracking jokes in the store. The laughter drew other Confederates to the store, which became quite crowded, and some stood outside. One prisoner cried to Ingersoll, "Speech! Speech!" "But half my audience can't get in here," said Ingersoll. "Well, let's go outside then," someone said. So outside they went, Rebs and Feds together as if there were no war at all. Ingersoll mounted a box and bantered his audience for a while. Then he became serious, about how reluctantly the North had taken up arms against the South and about the plight of the slaves. He was going along nicely on these matters when up came none other than General Forrest, who listened for a few moments and then shouted, "Here, Ingersoll, stop that speech and I'll exchange you for a government mule."

After his parole Ingersoll went back to Jackson, where General Sullivan told him that he had saved the town.[11] He had delayed Forrest long enough so that reinforcements could come up. Forrest tried to take Jackson but was repulsed with serious losses of men and equipment. On December 24, he retreated across the Tennessee River, burned the bridges, and went on toward Chattanooga.

Ingersoll stayed at Jackson unitl the middle of January. His stay was pleasant, his wife joining him when the safety of Jackson was assured. By the end of January they were in Groveland, Illinois, at the home of his wife's parents, where he awaited orders on his disposition as a parolee. The orders came in March and on the 20th he reported at Benton Barracks where he was put in charge of a company of parolees. He remained in this tedious capacity for three months. On June 18 he petitioned the War Department to allow him to resign his commission, giving as his reason: "My affairs are in such a condition at home, that my presence is absolutely necessary, and by remaining in the service in my present position I should do the government little good, and myself harm."[12] This was his official reason. Another reason was put in a letter to Clark June 26, "Not that I think the rebellion ought not to be squelched. Not that I believe in the craven cowardly peace advocated by the Democracy of the North. Not that I think that Slavery ought for a moment to be preserved or protected. Not that I have come to the conclusion that two nations can exist in peace. Not that I think the North has not the ability to conquer, but because I have seen enough of death and horror. Because I have seen enough of bloodshed and mutilation. . . ."

There was another reason too. He felt he was growing old. He was thirty now. Time was going too fast. "It seems there will scarcely be time to accomplish anything of moment. It is almost too late to begin."[13] He had nothing particular in mind for the future. He would of course go back to the practice of law. Politics? Hardly. Still a sordid business. Aware of his powers as a speaker, he did not discern how he would use them to the fullest. The lecture platform beckoned in a vague sort of way. But it did not occur to him that in the not distant future he would take to the platform in the way that he did.

"COLONEL INGERSOLL FLAYING COPPERHEADISM!"

On June 30, 1863, Ingersoll received his discharge from the army. On July 4 he was in Peoria. The first thing he did was to rent a house. At last he could settle down with the woman whom he loved. "We get along as well as any two ever did in this world." What was more, his wife was an accomplished cook. After twenty months of army fare, he was ready for fresh vegetables and fruits. And he got them, plenty of them, in endless savory combinations. Life was good. In the morning he liked to get up early and take a horseback ride for seven or eight miles. This he called a moderate ride, accustomed as he had been to riding all night, even sleeping on horseback. Moderate riding kept him in condition, made him feel healthy.

Another pleasure was the many evenings he could now spend with Clark. No one of his other brothers and sisters ever meant quite so much to him as Clark. They were about the same age, they had studied law together and were now in the same office, they could tell each other anything and be sure of understanding, they rejoiced in each other's successes, and they had similar views on religion and politics. If Robert still could not quite like Lincoln because of the Habeas Corpus suspension, he was as much a defender of the Administration as Clark. The Union armies in the summer of 1863 restored his faith.

There was the victory at Gettysburg. And especially there was Grant and the taking of Vicksburg. Grant's brilliant leadership in the Vicksburg campaign "smacks of the old Napoleon," wrote Ingersoll. "U.S. Grant is the only General the North has and he is better than the South can boast."[1] The two Union victories in July would "shut the mouths pretty effectively of all the croakers who were asking for the Union as it was and the Constitution as it is."[2]

But Ingersoll was unduly optimistic. In his own state the movement to negotiate a peace with the South was gaining ground. In his own city on August 3, the Democrats, twenty thousand strong, held a convention which declared that the war was a failure and proposed an immediate and unconditional peace with the South. In Illinois, as in other parts of the country, there was bitter opposition to the draft. Fearing disorders in the effort to enforce the draft, Governor Yates asked for five regiments of Federal troops to be stationed at danger points in the state.

By September, Ingersoll saw two great parties forming in the North, anti-slavery and pro-slavery. If the pro-slavery party grew strong, it could mean the actual defeat of the North through internal dissension. It would mean at least a negotiated peace with the South and a return to ante-bellum conditions. This was more than Ingersoll could bear. He had seen the bloodshed that the War had entailed and he could see that the North would win if she were not weakened by enemies behind the lines. The issue had become quite simple. It was whether slavery should be exterminated. This was what had started the war. This was what the war should settle, once and for all. And so as a speaker instead of a soldier Ingersoll resumed his fight for the North. He spoke at a Union mass meeting at Smithville, Illinois, August 31: "There is a gulf between the North and the South as wide as that between Lazarus and the rich man. The very moment the South left the Union we were released from protecting slavery. I am opposed to the Union as it was. . . . I am a free man; I intend to live and die free, nor will I stand between a man and his freedom. I am in favor of the emancipation of the whole world. They may call me abolitionist or anything else they please, it matters not to me. . . .

"In order to have peace with the South you have got to fight them. . . ."[3]

He said he did not care for Lincoln himself, but he was for him altogether in his endeavor to make the country all free. Nor did he agree with Lincoln's plan of emancipation. "I want the negro to be put in a territory by himself." Ingersoll did not make clear where this territory was. Nor did he make it clear in a speech at Pekin, which the Peoria *Transcript* featured under the heading, "Colonel Ingersoll Flaying Copperheadism."[4] The Negroes should not be brought North; they should not remain in the South. They should not come North because they were "a dangerous element." They were "too ignorant and degraded. We have ignorance enough among us. We have already paid dearly for its presence. Give the negro the right of suffrage, make him participate in our elections, and every Copperhead in the North will be running after him hanging to his coat-tail, asking him for his vote." "Great laughter and applause" greeted this statement, reported the *Transcript*. Ingersoll told his hearers what most of them wanted to hear, that the negro should not be saddled on them: "Send him to a country by himself. [Applause] Set off some territory where he can be colonized, where he can have his own schools and churches, his own society and government." Where would that be? Ingersoll did not say. But his audience was with him. And so they were with him when he said: "We are not going to stop this war for the sake of making a disgraceful peace. We have not put a million men into the field and sacrificed 100,000 Northern lives to get down on our knees to the rebels. . . ."

There were, however, a few hecklers in the audience. Said Ingersoll: "I tell you the only way to settle this war is to settle the rebellion—fight until the traitors cry 'Peccavi, We have got enough.' And when you do that everybody will have his rights."

Cried a heckler, "Niggers and all?"

"Yes," said Ingersoll, "the rights of everybody will be respected."

Cried another heckler, a "notorious Copperhead," according to the *Transcript*, "Then what is right?"

"I'll tell you what is right. It is right that you accord to me and to everybody else all the privileges that you claim yourself. That is right." (Great cheering.)

But the second heckler persisted. "Is it right to bring the negroes here?"

"No, I would send them to some country by themselves." Then, perhaps to forestall the question, Where? Ingersoll said, "Now answer me a question; is it right to keep the negro in slavery?"

Heckler evading the question: "It isn't right to bring them to the North and make them citizens."

"Answer my question. Is it right to keep the negro in slavery?"

Heckler (squirming): "It isn't right to make him the equal of the white man." (Cries of "Answer the question" from the audience.)

"Will you answer my question!" demanded Ingersoll.

Came the answer: "It is right to keep him a slave in this country, but to make a freeman of him in Africa." The *Transcript* observed that this answer evoked "evidences of disgust" and that the heckler "beaten, skinned alive, retired to a corner and never uttered another yelp."

"Another drunken copperhead" raised his voice, "Wouldn't you help catch and sell a nigger if you could get half the proceeds?"

Ingersoll's answer produced "immense laughter and uproar:" "If he wouldn't bring any more at auction than you would, it wouldn't pay for the shoe-leather worn out running after him. My friend, *you* had better dry up. If you desire informatiton from me, get Balaam's ass to do your talking. He is smarter than you."

In all his speeches Ingersoll appealed to all former Douglas Democrats "to stand by their country and against Southern treason." Replying to the charge that he had made a political somersault and was now a Republican and an abolitionist, he declared that because he went to war and now supported the President in putting down the Rebellion he could not be said to be in favor of all the President's measures. At Lacon, October 18, he said he needed no introduction to his hearers because he had appeared before them in the days when he was a member of the Democratic party, in the days when that party "carried upon its banners 'War to the Knife against All Oppression—The Union Must and Shall be Preserved.' " He had stayed with the party as long as it clung to that watchword. But when it changed to "The Union as It Was—the Constitution as It Is" after the Rebellion started, he had left the party. All true Democrats had left it just as Douglas would have. A follower of Douglas could be no other than a supporter of the Administration and a war man through and through. He would do nothing to give aid and comfort to Jeff Davis and the rebels.[5]

In 1864 Ingersoll's war efforts increased. He was outraged that his own Peoria should have so many advocates of an immediate peace, so many who were outright Southern sympathizers. One day in March the sheriff of Peoria County came into his office on legal business. There were several persons present and they were discussing the war. The sheriff noting the trend of the discussion which was heatedly pro-Administration interspersed dissenting remarks, one to the effect that the Administration was carrying on the war solely to liberate the Negroes. Ingersoll countered that the negroes were as much entitled to freedom as the sheriff or any other man. The sheriff then shouted, "It's a God damned lie!"[6] Ingersoll grabbed a chair and struck at the sheriff but did not really hit him, according to witnesses who quickly intervened. The sheriff contended that Ingersoll did hit him and brought charges of assault and battery. The case was tried March 14. The jury deliberated three hours and reported that they were deadlocked in disagreement. The jury was discharged and presumably the matter was ended. But the sheriff demanded a new trial. "The Copperheads," said the *Transcript,* "went to work to get up another jury—one that would be 'sure fire.' " Ingersoll objected to the new trial on the ground of double jeopardy. The court sustained his objection and dismissed the case.

In May Ingersoll had a special reason for pro-Administration speeches in Peoria County and other counties of the Fifth Congressional District. His brother was chosen by a Republican Convention to fill out the unexpired term in Congress of the deceased Owen Lovejoy. Owen was the brother of Elijah, the abolitionist editor, who in November, 1837, had been killed at Alton, Illinois, by a pro-slavery mob. Owen was a Congregational minister in Princeton, Illinois, at the same time that the Reverend Ingersoll, who admired him greatly, was in nearby Greenville. Owen had preached against the sin of slavery before his brother's martyrdom; after it his wrath knew no bounds. When Owen went to Congress in 1862, a "Radical" or "Black" Republican, he inveighed against Lincoln for temporizing with Evil. Destroy slavery now. Cease truckling to the Devil. It was a demanding role which Clark Ingersoll took over. And there was the coming regular election in the fall. Clark would have little time to make a name for himself in Congress before the District Republican Convention in August.

At this point Robert, who was now a recognized full-fledged Republican, became Clark's campaign manager. He worked hard that summer of 1864 to secure Clark's nomination. In his numerous speeches he unequivocally endorsed Lincoln. There was no chance for any suspicious Republican to decide that Robert was still a Democrat at heart. Late in July he reported to Clark, who was in Washington, "I have just returned from Stark, Penn Township. Had a large meeting, three thousand at least were present. Everything went off in fine style, and every Union man was pleased to death by my speech." About the prospects for his brother's nomination Robert said, "I think there is no danger. Knox and Peoria [counties] are certain. We must look after Bureau" [Lovejoy's county].

When the August Republican Convention came around, Bureau County was satisfied and cast her votes for Clark, as did the other counties of the Fifth Congressional District. The day after the Convention Robert wrote him, "The Convention passed a very complimentary resolution setting forth that the overcoat of the afflicted Lovejoy has fallen upon your shoul-

ders, together with a large share of his underclothing, including socks and suspenders."

The nomination out of the way, a hotly contested campaign
followed, which reflected the course of political events in the
nation at large. August was a month of gloom in the country.
The Union armies had not lived up to expectations. Suffering
heavy losses in the Virginia campaign, Grant had still not
reached Richmond. Sherman was not yet in Atlanta. While
the Confederates under General Early were at the very portals
of Washington, Lincoln darkened the picture with a call for
500,000 volunteers. The national credit was at its lowest ebb.
A dollar in paper was worthy fifty cents in gold. Horace Greeley
demanded that Lincoln "inaugurate or invite proposals of
peace forthwith." Republican leaders despaired of victory in
the coming election. Raymond, editor of the *New York Times,*
wrote Lincoln: "The tide is setting strong against us." Lincoln
himself was pessimistic, signing a memorandum on August 23,
which read in part: "This morning, as for some days past, it
seems exceedingly probable that the Administration will not be
reelected."

In Chicago the Democratic National Convention assembled
on August 29 and nominated George B. McClelland for President and George H. Pendleton for Vice President. A resolution provided "that this Convention does explicitly declare,
as the sense of the American people, that after four years of
failure to restore the Union by the experiment of war, . . . justice, humanity, liberty and the public welfare demand that immediate efforts be made for a cessation of hostilities. . . ." The
platform charged that Lincoln had violated the Constitution
by trampling upon the rights of States, by suppressing freedom
of speech and press, and by depriving citizens of their legal
rights through resort to the arbitrary procedures of military
law.

The platform and the candidates were acclaimed all over
the country, including Peoria and the Fifth Congressional District of Illinois. Earlier in August the Democrats of the District had demonstrated impressive strength at a mass meeting

in Peoria. Thousands had marched in a procession, with banners proclaiming "Give Me Liberty or Give Me Death." "Usurpation Unchecked is Despotism Accepted," "Lincoln Inaugurated the Reign of Terror," "Ours is a White Man's Government—Defile it Not with Miscegenation." While Robert Ingersoll himself once subscribed to these sentiments, now he utterly repudiated them. The Chicago platform he condemned "as a cheat, a delusion, and a lie." Far from the war being a failure, the Union was on the verge of a glorious success.

Happily, September bore out Ingersoll's prediction. Farragut's victory, in late August, over the Confederate fleet at Mobile Bay and the consequent capitulation of Forts Gaines and Morgan had caused little rejoicing in the North. But when, on September 2, Sherman took Atlanta and in mid-September Sheridan defeated Early at Winchester and Fisher's Hill in the Shenandoah Valley, the North exulted. Who said the war was a failure! On September 14, even before Sheridan's victories, Secretary Seward in a speech at Washington declared: "Sherman and Farragut have knocked the bottom out of the Chicago nominations." The New York *Tribune* announced that it would "henceforth fly the banner of Abraham Lincoln for the next president." Ex-Secretary of the Treasury, Salmon P. Chase, who had resigned from the Cabinet because of unhappy relations with the President, now took to the stump for Lincoln.

So did Representative Benjamin F. Wade, who only in August had joined with Representative Henry W. Davis in a manifesto "To the Supporters of the Government" bitterly criticizing Lincoln and his Amnesty Proclamation of December, 1863.

The concrete campaign material of Farragut, Sherman, and Sheridan resulted in a decisive victory for Lincoln, who carried every state in the Union except New Jersey, Delaware, and Kentucky. In Illinois, Clark Ingersoll won over his Democratic opponent by a vote of 18,152 to 11,282.[7] His campaign manager had done a good job. Clark had not gone home to campaign since Congress was in session. But in June, by his efforts in the House in behalf of a joint resolution which later became

the Thirteenth Amendment, he had given his constituency
ample assurance that he was following in the footsteps of Owen
Lovejoy. When on January 31, 1865, the House gave the
amendment the necessary two-thirds majority, it was Clark
who rose and said: "Mr. Speaker, in honor of this immortal
and sublime event, I move this house do now adjourn."[8]

THE DEIST EMERGES

O N March 17, 1865, Robert wrote to his brother John, "I
have been reading this winter Buckle's 'History of Civilization
in England' and I think it is the greatest work I ever read. He
was a man of vast learning, and had the clearest and most
logical head in the world." Buckle's main concern was with
the growth of the rational and scientific attitude in Europe and
the decline in the political and spiritual powers of king and
church. The sooner science won undisputed mastery the better.
The church kept men in ignorance and superstition and per-
petrated the grossest cruelties upon its critics. Buckle believed
in a deity whom he referred to as an "All-Wise Being," "the
great Architect of the Universe," "the Creator and Designer
of all existing things," "the Infinite Wisdom," "The Divine Om-
niscience." This deity does not interfere with the works of man
and the operations of nature because perfect law reigns in a
perfect universe.

Ingersoll had encountered a similar view of God in Paine's
Age of Reason. But there was one basic difference. Paine believed in personal revelation, every man communing with God
in his own way; Buckle held that deity was utterly impersonal,
utterly unresponsive to man, and that the only possible rational
attitude toward deity was recognition of and admiration for the
eternal scheme of things. When Ingersoll first read Paine, in
his early twenties, he was not ready for even Paine's brand of
deism. He was still too close to his penates. But the *Age of Rea-*

son raised questions and started thoughts. That Ingersoll was ready for Buckle in 1865 was because Paine had helped prepare the ground.

During 1865-1866, Ingersoll also read John Draper, Auguste Comte, and Voltaire. Draper, the great American doctor and medical educator, in his *History of the Intellectual Development of Europe* demonstrated that society developed by the same scientific principles that governed the human body, "that the civilization of Europe has not taken place fortuitously, but in a definite manner, and under the control of natural law." A Supreme Power has set in motion the laws of individual and social development but never interrupts their operation, a conception of God like that of Buckle. In his first iconoclastic lecture, "Progress" (1866), Ingersoll borrowed generously from Draper's work.

Ingersoll was greatly indebted to Voltaire. He often mentioned or quoted Voltaire in his lectures and beginning in 1894 he presented a lecture entitled "Voltaire." The *Philosophical Dictionary* made a strong impression on him with its erudition and its derisive attacks upon theology and the church. If the later Ingersoll could not accept Voltaire's axiom that God is a logical necessity, the earlier one saw nothing to object to and was taken with the rational approach. The later Ingersoll, the agnostic, found the evidence of a God inadequate; the earlier, the deist, agreed with Voltaire that the evidence of no-God was inadequate. In July, 1866, Robert wrote Clark that he was reading Voltaire and reacting as follows: "I am steadfast in the faith and enjoying myself hugely. And feeling *infinitely* free. I feel as though I could exist without God just as well as he could exist without me. And I also feel that if there must be an orthodox God in Heaven I am in favor of electing him ourselves.

"I am as much opposed to an autocrat hereafter as now."

Auguste Comte, whom Ingersoll was also reading, was a long step beyond Voltaire in rationalism. The chief exponent of Positivism, Comte held that all pheonomena result from natural causes only. As man's knowledge increases, theological

and metaphysical explanations of phenomena are seen to be
invalid. Forget about such unknowables as God or Vegetative
Soul or Vital Principle or Essence or Inherent Virtue or Nature. Concentrate on the knowables.

The iconoclastic tendencies at work in Ingersoll's mind were
at first reflected little in his public utterances.

A man in politics could ill afford to offend most of the electorate, namely, the orthodox. On April 19, 1865, at a ceremony in tribute to Abraham Lincoln, Ingersoll addressed a
saddened throng of twenty thousand people in Peoria. His religious references were unexceptionable by anyone's criteria.
Speaking of the terms of surrender that Lincoln had offered the
South, Ingersoll said, "Shall we offer them the same terms?
Forbid it, Almighty God." At another point he said, "Assassination is contrary to the will and express command of the
most high." And again, "The principles of the Almighty are
eternal, they govern the universe."[1]

In a speech at Peoria, August 29, on the anniversary of the
86th Illinois Regiment, his sentiments were quite acceptable:
"From being slaves of the devil, we have become co-workers
with the Infinite Father of all;" "and in the name of the Infinite
we thank you again and again;" "the eyes of the Omnipotent
are upon us;" "Man makes parties—God makes principle." He
even said: "We thank you . . . that the spires of our churches
still point to the skies" and "If ever I vote to make them [lead-
ers of Confederacy] citizens of this great republic . . . may the
Almighty in the morning of the resurrection forget my soul.
. . ."[2]

But some Peorians must have doubted Ingersoll's sincerity.
They knew that he never went to church. They had heard about
gatherings in Breed and Murray's drugstore on Main Street,
where two or three nights a week Ingersoll and his cronies
would get together to discuss all manner of topics. It had got
about town that blasphemy was a staple of the talk, with Ingersoll the chief dispenser. If what he said was anything like what
he said in a letter to Clark, March 13, 1865, the report was
well based: *"Bob Cassell has got religion and has joined the*

Campbellite Church! ! ! 'Jim Perry,' the circuit clerk, has joined the *Baptist Church,* and old *Welcome* P. Brown, the enlightened atty at law, has experienced a *new-birth* and has joined the Methodist denomination of *true believing.*

"There has been an *outpouring* of the Holy Ghost in Metamora [close to Peoria]. I suppose from that that the *Holy Ghost* is a *liquid substance.* Everybody over that way is coming to a knowledge of the truth as it is in the aforesaid '*J. Christ.*' "

Yet this same man could write reverently of sacred things, as in a letter to his brother John, on the death of John's younger child, a son named Robert: "Only a few days and we will have to join the dear ones on the other side. Another voice is calling you to heaven. You have one reason less for wishing to live. . . . Think of little Robby as being with our father and mother. Never think of him as dead—He has only ceased to be mortal."[3] Ingersoll still clung to a personal immortality. It was intolerable that "dear ones" should be extinguished forever.

On the night of May 14, 1866, Ingersoll delivered *Progress* in Peoria, his first lecture that could be called iconoclastic.[4] Ten days earlier he had written Clark, who was in Washington, that he was working at the lecture and that he wished Clark were there to advise him. The problem was, how could Robert say what he wanted to say and not lose political good will for himself and his brother. The gist of the lecture was that the church had attempted to enslave the mind of man and had almost succeeded, that consequently the progress of mankind had been slow, had been stopped in fact for centuries. If the church did not stand in the way, it was the king. "War and theology were the business of mankind."

Ingersoll's hearers were not disturbed by such statements as: "In the sixteenth century a man was burned in France because he refused to kneel to a procession of dirty monks" or "The histories were all written by the monks and bishops, all of whom were intensely superstitious, and equally dishonest" or "Credulity occupied the throne of reason and faith put out the eyes of the soul." Such statements dealt with an era long passed. A few hearers—there were few Catholics in Peoria—may have resented his saying, "It was discovered that a man could be healthy without being a Catholic." Most of his hearers would enjoy digs at Catholics. So far, so good. Ingersoll was politically on safe ground. But then he left the past for the present: "True religion is a subordination of the passions and interests to the perceptions of the intellect;" "The rush of the ship, the scream of the locomotive, and the electric flash have frightened the monsters of ignorance from the world, and have left nothing above us but the heaven's eternal blue, filled with glittering planets wheeling through immensity in accordance with *Law.*" Well, this was hardly orthodox. God in the image of man was out of his heaven.

The Peoria *National Democrat* had little use for the Ingersolls, because they were "nigger lover," anti-Johnson Republicans. It thought little of Robert's lecture—"People tried to keep awake, and we saw several who were wide awake. . . ."[5] The Peoria *Transcript,* however, now that Robert was in the right political camp, said that the capacity house "listened attentively" to the "eloquent" speaker and applauded him "enthusiastically."[6] Neither paper made anything of the possible political detriment of the speech.

"STAND BY PRINCIPLES, OLD BOY"

R OBERT was in close communication with Clark in Washington, advising him on his Congressional speeches and his political strategy. At home he saw to it that Clark's activities did not go unnoticed. And he was not without efforts in his own behalf. "I have been very busy for the last few months and travelling all over the country," he wrote his brother John, in March, 1865. Busy at politics, "a low dirty scramble, through misrepresentation, slander, falsehood, and filth, and success brings nothing but annoyance and fear of defeat next time, and yet if one gets started in that kind of business, it is very hard to get out. I find myself scheming all the time, thinking what I will try for, and calculating the chances."[1] Robert had just returned from Springfield, where he had attended a session of the legislature. "A more scaly set of one-horse thieves and low lived political tricksters never assembled on the earth." As a result, Robert was losing his respect for the "thing called *law*" and he wondered if Congress were any better than the legislature.

But he was not so disillusioned with the processes of government as to despair of the solution of the problems of reconstruction. In a letter to Clark, March 8, 1865, he declared that the session of Congress which had just closed "will be long remembered. It has I think in the interest of Freedom immortalized itself. The glorious resolution that slavery shall be eradicated, destroyed and utterly abolished forever is the grandest resolution ever passed by that body." Clark had given a speech for the resolution. Said Robert, "I am proud too that your name is so well connected with that great measure of Liberty." Clark had also spoken for the repudiation of the Confederate debt, on which Robert commented, "What you say . . . is manly—strong—rings like a trumpet. I will have it inserted in the *Transcript*. Your reputation is getting better every day."[2] Robert also wrote, "I am thinking of you constantly." They had been together so much, had shared so much of hope and sorrow—would that they could "finish the journey of life together." Robert was anxious for Clark to come home so that they could explore "the great questions that now and soon will be asked by the people, and which soon must be answered. We could greatly help one another. . . ."

As Robert saw reconstruction, the issue was "whether the country and liberty are to be preserved or whether the Confederate Army with ballots instead of bayonets, with Genl Andy Johnson at the head, will conquer at last." Clark Ingersoll took an active part in the Congressional debates on reconstruction and Robert sent him many letters of advice and encouragement. "Stand by principles, old boy," he wrote on March 1, 1866, "let every office in the district go to pot. Stand firm by the idea that every vestige of slavery must perish before reconstruction is possible or even *desirable*."

The statement "let every office in the district go to pot" was not mere rhetoric. A particular office was meant, that of the collector of internal revenue in the Fifth Congressional District. It was one of the richest spoils of a victorious candidate for Congress and would of course go to the person who had aided the candidate the most. Next to Robert Ingersoll, that person was a Henry Sanderson. Clark recommended Sanderson for the office shortly after Johnson became President and Johnson gave his approval. The man replaced was John Bryant, brother of William Cullen Bryant. But with Clark's opposition in Congress to Johnson's Reconstruction program and Robert's opposition in central Illinois, the President rescinded Sanderson's appointment and reappointed John Bryant.

Johnson's action upset Robert. "I am afraid," he wrote to Clark, "that knocks all my aspiration for the state at large right square in the head. Well, you know that is my luck."[3] Robert was aiming at the nomination for Congressman-at-large on the Republican or Union ticket. The Union ticket would be a fusion of Republicans and War Democrats. But Robert was afraid that the War Democrats would follow the lead of Johnson, also a War Democrat, and become Peace Democrats. As a result the Johnson forces would carry the state in the 1866 elections unless, as Robert put it, "great exertions are made."[4]

Nor would Clark's reelection be easy. His chief opponent for the nomination was Thomas J. Henderson, a Johnson supporter. "He can't beat you," wrote Robert, "but he will make us rather active." First off, Robert advised, Clark should come home at the earliest opportunity and speak in defense of his record as a Congressman. Clark took the advice and during the last week of March made a quick tour of the District. In a speech in Rouse's Hall, Peoria, he delighted the Radical Republicans with an uninhibited attack on Johnson's reconstruction policy. "Adopt it and we give up all. Restore the rebels to Congress and them and the Copperheads to power, and they would pull down the flag of the Union from the dome of the Capitol and trample it in the dust." At one point in the speech Robert interrupted Clark to ask him to comment on the rumors going about that he (Robert) had been enabled by Clark's efforts to "swindle the U.S. Treasury of several hundred thousand dollars" through manipulation of whiskey revenues. Absolute lies, complete fictions, said Clark. He challenged the defamers to appeal directly to Secretary of Treasury McCulloch. Or "let them go to Mr. T. C. Moore, the U.S. Assessor, or Mr. Chase, Deputy Collector. I will ask a Congressional investigation, if those making the charges would bring them out in the open to Washington." Clark also answered other charges relative to chicanery in the use of his office. When he finished the speech, he received an ovation.

Clark's speech was not soon forgotten in Peoria. Robert wrote him after he returned to Washington to make a similar speech in Congress. "I want to impress upon your mind the necessity of your making a *speech* as is a *speech*. I want you to give your *entire* attention to that for at least a week or ten days. And I know that you can make immense capital. Take about the same ground that you did in your effort at Rouse's Hall. There has not been as good a speech upon reconstruction etc. published."[5] Clark took Robert's advice and on May 5 in the House he flayed Johnson's policies and Johnson, the man. It was too much "that we should be afflicted with the rinderpest, the trichina, the cholera and Andrew Johnson all in the same year."[6] The speech attracted national attention. On May 9, Wendell Phillips referred to it in an address to the American Anti-Slavery Society in New York City: "It is only now and then a party man reaches that absolute forgetfulness of party as to rise into full manhood. Ben Wade has it; Thaddeus Stevens has it; and Ingersoll, of Illinois, got it." Back home in Peoria Robert read the speech with pride and elation. "The strongest speech in Congress," he wrote. "You proved that Johnson is an impudent boaster, an egotistical ass, a shallow hypocrite, and a malicious impostor.

"You have not only taken the bull by the horns but the ass by the ears."[7]

Clark's prestige was now greatly enhanced in his Congressional District. He could not leave Congress to campaign at home during May, June, and July, but that speech compensated for his absence. Then, too, there was his brother's zeal in his behalf.

The Republican Convention of the Fifth Congressional District was to be held in Peoria July 18. Before that time the townships of the counties would hold meetings to select delegates to the county conventions and then the county conventions would select delegates for the district convention. During May, June, and the first two weeks of July, Robert thoroughly stumped the District.

By July 14, four days before the District Convention, it was clear that Clark had carried not only every county but every township in the District: "Your triumph has been without precedent." On July 18 the Convention echoing the unanimous township vote nominated Clark by acclamation. The Peoria *National Democrat* ruefully recorded the proceedings as follows: ". . . the convention for the benefit of the Ingersoll family met yesterday in the Court House. . . . Col. Bob Ingersoll, of the Ingersoll family, read a letter from 'my brother,' thanking the Convention for nominating him. (He did not explain how he came to get the letter so soon after the nomination.)"

". . . THE BREAD AND BUTTER BRIGADE . . ."

S HORTLY before the District Convention, Clark wrote Robert urging him to run for Congress at large. Robert replied that he was certain he would be nominated if he were to run but he did not want to run for several reasons. To begin with, there was the possible detriment to his brother's career. Then the state was to be re-districted at the next meeting of the legislature in January, which would mean according to a stipulation in the re-districting plan that if he were elected he could hold office for only one term. Again, since it would be quite an undertaking to canvass the state, his law practice would suffer too much. And, he said, "office is the end of home." He had two daughters now, Eva, born September 22, 1863, and Maud, born November 4, 1864. Both daughters, incidentally, had the middle name Robert.

There were other reasons that he gave for shunning a political career: "I would have then to stick to politics for a living. Would have to join the bread and butter brigade sure enough—study the art of navigation and trim my little sails to catch the breath of ignorant admiration and paid flattery. And then you know, dear Bro., politicians all have a great trick of committing suicide or 'hara-kiri.' Look at Seward. He is a political corpse today. . . . Webster died on his knees, asking to be president. . . . Douglas went away repeating a senseless prayer after an ignorant priest. Calhoun became infamous while living and infinitely more so after death. Benton lived to be laughed at . . . . Look at poor Buchanan. Contemplate Franklin Pierce. . . . Pity Harrison. Drop a tear for *honest* Zachary Taylor. . . . I care very little for political preferment."[1] If Robert did not desire preferment, he acted like someone who did. In 1866, while he was campaigning for his brother, he somehow found time to stump the state of Indiana for the Union ticket, which was made up of Radical Republicans.

In January and February, 1867, Robert attended the session of the Illinois legislature, in Springfield. He did not propose to be involved in the first business of the session which was the election of a United States Senator. He disliked the chief contender, the incumbent, Lyman Trumbull. His man was John C. Palmer but he said, "I believe that the people of the state want Trumbull and . . . I have no interest in thwarting the plebs." Trumbull was elected.

The election over, the legislature got down to the business of legislation. As Robert was attorney for the Peoria and Rock

Island Railroad, of which he later became president, he was particularly interested in several railroad bills on franchises, financing, and rights of way but he was afraid that the bills were "in the tomb of the '*Capulets*' with no Romeo to open the door." Another bill of consequence to Robert came up before the legislature in February. It provided for the re-creation of the office of attorney-general which had not existed since 1846. The bill became a law with the approval of Governor Richard Oglesby on February 27. The office was appointive for the first term of two years; thereafter it was to be elective at each gubernatorial election. Immediately upon approval of the bill Governor Oglesby appointed Robert to the post. All reason for shunning political preferment now evaporated. Robert accepted the position the day it was tendered.

One of Robert's reasons had been that a career in politics would be "the end of home." Now he was required to keep an office in Springfield and attend all sessions of the Illinois Supreme Court. Another reason had been that his law practice would suffer. Now, while he did not have to give up private practice, the new post would take most of his time. Now he was a member of that "bread and butter brigade."

In April Robert asked Clark whether he should move his family to Springfield. He raised three questions about the move: "its effect upon me as a lawyer? And upon my prospects in politics? Also what effect it might have upon your chances in the Fifth district?" Whatever Clark's reply, Robert's family stayed in Peoria.

If generally Robert was in good spirits, he fell prey to melancholy as he thought of the evanescence of life and the inevitable parting from loved ones. It was hard enough in Peoria to be separated from his brother: "the town is lonesome without you. And the old lonely feeling that I am only a passenger in this world comes over me."[2] And again, "It makes me shudder to think how old we are growing. . . . Our lives are touching the confines of the sombre. . . ." In Springfield, with neither his brother nor his family, it was worse: "I am afraid of the land of shadows—the dim 'Beyond' is filled with frightful shapes or appears perfectly empty which is still more frightful."[3] But these lugubrious periods were few. Robert was too busy for morbidity to become chronic.

Robert was following avidly the progress of events in Washington and his brother's part in them. The Fourteenth Amendment which had been passed in April, 1866, had been rejected by all the Southern States except Tennessee; and Tennessee had ratified it without enfranchising the freedom. Robert counselled Clark to take the position that every state that rejected the Fourteenth Amendment should be reduced to territorial status. In June, 1867, he wrote Clark: "I want you to prepare a speech for the July session. Take the time to do it. Drop everything else. Read carefully and review scathingly the Atty Genl's opinion on your Reconstruction Act. Take the most radical ground as to the power of Congress over the whole matter. You can make the best speech of the session just as well as not and I want you to do it. Now do attend to this and get yourself before the country again in splendid shape. Every speech you have made so far has been a 'palpable hit' and I want you to repeat . . . ."

Clark followed orders. He excoriated the rulings of the Attorney General. He decried the usurpation of the powers of Congress. He denounced Kentucky for her traitorous conduct in electing a slate of nine Democratic representatives to the Fortieth Congress. Having read Clark's speech and the speeches of other congressmen in the *Congressional Globe,* Robert pronounced his brother's to be "altogether the best." He would have it published in the Peoria *Transcript.* He knew that it would "meet with the hearty and cordial approval of the Union men" in the Fifth District. "A few more speeches of that kind and your political fortune is made, and assured beyond chance. . . ."

Robert's legal activities now took most of his time. He found that an attorney-general had to do much more than counsel the legislature and the Governor and prepare and present cases for the state. He was beset with requests for legal advice from all manner of people—justices of the peace, town clerks, constables, "and men too poor to employ a lawyer." Also carrying on a limited private practice, particularly as a defender of railroads in property damage cases, he represented the Chicago and Rock Island Railroad; the Logansport, Peoria and Burlington; the Toledo, Peoria and Warsaw; and the Illinois Central.

Robert was relishing life. "I never was so well situated before, and was never so happy in my life. . . ."[4] The contrast between his present and his not-remote past was made vivid for him by a business trip to Mount Vernon. "This morning I arrived at this ancient and decaying town. I feel that I am again in heathen lands. A vision rises before me. I see shapeless felt hats, surmounting heads covered with long lank 'yeller' hair— the hair falling down upon a shirt open in front showing a breast covered with dirty frowsy moss . . . . I see sore eyes, and long flabby breasts hanging down upon leathery bellies— the bellies supported by dirty legs . . . . I hear people say 'I have saw,' and 'I've hearn,' and 'I seed.' They talk about his'n and her'n and your'n. I see meetinghouses without fences— dooryards without grass—without vines, without flowers . . . . I see young men without an aspiration and old men without a hope.

"A little while ago I saw the house where I used to live. May God spare me a second sight."[5]

Busy as he was, Ingersoll found time for wide reading. He often made trips to Chicago and there he liked to scout around for books. And he would go to the theater if a travelling company happened to be in town. On one trip he and Governor Oglesby saw the great Italian actress, Ristori, in three plays, *Elizabeth, Judith,* and *Mary Stuart.* "I want to talk to you about a week on the Ristori subject when we meet," he wrote Clark. Ristori acted only in Italian but Ingersoll was enraptured. He and Oglesby sat in a lower box and were able to see every expression of her face—"her face is the miraculous thing about her." After one of the performances they went to Ristori's dressing-room. They were vivaciously received, she talking in Italian, they in English, through an interpreter. They talked of the Italian struggle for liberty. Ingersoll said that any nation capable of producing a Ristori would of necessity become free. He also said, "Italy has furnished America with its first and last sensation—*Columbus* and *Ristori.*"[6] What a to-do there was then—kisses, tears, and ecstatic wringing of Ingersoll's hand.

HE WOULD LIKE TO BE GOVERNOR

On May 31, 1867, the Peoria *National Democrat* stated, in a vein not unusual: "In the year Anno Domini 1867, the Republican party of Peoria consists of the Ingersoll family, Enoch Emery, and a few head of cattle." The day before, the paper mentioned the *Transcript* as the "mouth-piece," the "cellar organ" of "a corrupt clique, who are a stench in the nostrils of all honest Republicans as well as Democrats." The "Ingersoll family," according to the *Democrat,* consisted of the two brothers plus Robert's law partners, S.D. Puterbaugh and Eugene McCune, and Captain George Puterbaugh. All five of these worthies had wickedly contrived against the public good by getting themselves into office. One was in Congress, another was attorney-general, S.D. Puterbaugh was a circuit judge, McCune was the Peoria prosecuting attorney, and Captain Puterbaugh was the city attorney. The time had come to throw the rascals out. To top it all, the ringleader of this outfit was a *"shameless* disciple of infidelity."

Robert was undecided about running for attorney-general in 1868. As of January, 1868, he considered the office "not worth canvassing the state for." He was in low spirits: "I am pretty much tired of everything and feel as though the whole thing was a farce—but not one to be laughed at."[1] Yet he planned to be active in organizing Grant clubs throughout Illinois. The Republican State Convention was to meet in Peoria on May 6; this, he felt, would neither help nor hurt him.

He noted with some satisfaction that the Republican campaign, both state and national, was starting early—a good thing because "we will have plenty to do to get the party of God and humanity through the wilderness." And there would be plenty to do for Clark who was up for reelection.

Late in February, however, Robert himself became the central figure of a developing political drama. The denouement determined his career. It had been suggested to him by various people that he ought to run for governor. But he shrugged the suggestions off as being insincere or impractical until the Grant Club of Peoria passed a resolution to the effect that Robert Ingersoll was their choice for governor. Immediately Robert wrote to Clark, "What effect would my running for gov. have upon your prospects in this district? I don't think it would hurt you. Tell me your idea."[2] Clark urged him to run. On March 6, Robert wrote, "I have not yet said that I would be a candidate. I am merely looking." Governor Oglesby was urging him to run, "in fact all I have talked with." On March 8 he was in Chicago trying to gauge the support that he could count on from politicians, press, and public. He found the Chicago *Tribune* noncommittal but the Chicago *Journal* "very zealous."[3] After a week in Chicago he felt that his chances for election were good. He decided to declare himself a candidate.

The *Democrat* now got out its choicest weapons of defamation. It had heard that Governor Oglesby was reported to have said "in a private conversation" that the governorship was worth $20,000 any year and that "if properly managed during the erection of the new state house, it would be worth $25,000 per year. This is probably the reason the 'family' have such a willingness for one of their members to serve the dear people in that capacity." In the same issue, March 18, 1868, the *Democrat* charged that one of the partners of Ingersoll as a sutler during the war had sold rotten peaches and stale oysters to the soldiers. On March 24, the paper reported that it had heard that due to the stoppage of the distilleries in Peoria, the " 'family' are about 'out of soap.' " On April 7, there was merriment over an announcement Ingersoll had sent to a political meeting stating that he was unable to attend: " 'Announces his inability.' Grant called it 'a load'; some people denominate it the 'pickled cabbage disease'; other plain people call it 'intoxication.' 'Inability' is a good term." Ingersoll's advocacy of suffrage for the Negroes provoked the *Democrat* to call him the "miscegen candidate" who was even in favor of "practical amalgamation"—"How will the soldiers who went into the ranks to fight the rebels and preserve the Union like thus to be told that doing battle for the Union was all a humbug, and that they were all the time fighting for the negro?"

In fact, Ingersoll did not want suffrage for the Negroes in Illinois until they were enfranchised in the South. In this he differed with his brother who felt that the Northern states should immediately grant the Negro the vote. Clark urged Robert to push Negro suffrage in Illinois but Robert demurred on the ground that if the Negroes could not vote in the South but could vote in Illinois "they would come here in droves."[4]

Another problem on which the two brothers differed was the retiring of the Federal debt. Clark supported the redemption of government bonds in greenbacks without specie backing. Robert said that this was nothing more or less than repudiation. He did not expressly say that Clark's stand on the question might be politically embarrassing to the brothers in Illinois but he did say that Joseph Medill of the Chicago *Tribune* had denounced Clark and in the same article had praised Robert. In a letter to Medill Robert made it clear that he would not accept the support of the *Tribune* if this invidious comparison were continued. "I told Medill," wrote Robert, "that I could not respect myself if I would allow it." As a result, he was sure that Medill would turn against him too but "God damn him! Let him howl. I can beat him at his own game."[5]

The impeachment of Andrew Johnson was still another matter on which the brothers did not agree. "I am afraid that the great impeachment doings is after all a little premature," wrote Robert to Clark, who supported impeachment, "I am afraid that the Congress assembled will hit a sawyer . . . ."[6] Robert held that the Tenure of Office Act which Johnson had allegedly violated did not apply to the appointees of Lincoln and that Johnson was within his rights in removing Stanton as Secretary of War. Certainly the removal fell far short of the alleged "high crime." And Robert did not approve of the tactics of some of Johnson's accusers who were using every possible means to get the two-thirds vote in the Senate necessary to convict.

The impeachment business was one more strong reason for a sensible man to eschew politics. So ruminated Robert. On March 25, however, he informed Clark that his prospects for the governorship "appear to be very good indeed . . . . I am quite confident of success." And he would "bet his ears" that if nominated he would be elected and that he would break into the Senate in 1871. He asked Clark to write some letters for him, "a hundred or so . . . . Write to the old chaps in the country—they feel honored and flattered . . . . not just to the acknowledged politicians but to those who are not expecting a letter."[7]

Ingersoll's main opponent for the nomination had seemed to be John M. Palmer until Palmer wired him in the first week of April: "I am not and will not be a candidate for governor." But on April 29, a week before the Republican State Convention, Robert wrote to Clark, "It looks now as though Palmer really wanted to be Governor after all . . . . If he allows himself to run, he will simply prove himself to be a dirty dog."[8] Robert feared that he had little chance to beat Palmer but he was going "to fight it out to the bitter end." This was the crisis in his political career: if he were beaten now, it would end him politically—"I will then have been whipped too often" [Actually only once before, in 1860, as Democratic candidate for Congress]. Robert complained that the people did not seem to know him, really know him. They were his friends when he was helping them, "but when I want anything they generally prefer another man . . . ." No, his party did not appreciate him and he was "heartily disgusted." And after the Convention he would have "to settle down to the practice of that miserable profession known as the *law,* and bid goodbye to all political aspiration."[9]

The *Democrat* in its report of the Republican State Convention that assembled on May 6 in Peoria stated that the "jacobin convention" opened "with prayer, and the first man put in nomination . . . was Robert G. Ingersoll, an avowed infidel. That's consistency for you." The *Democrat* thus took note of a matter which worried many of the delegates. If Ingersoll were nominated, the ensuing campaign might be fought on only one issue, his infidelity. On the other hand the delegates had the impression that Palmer, the only other strong contender, would decline the nomination. They had sent him a telegram the night before the Convention inquiring as to his availability. His reply was: "Do not permit me to be nominated. I cannot accept the nomination."[10]

Palmer's message caused much confusion. The situation was made to order for a political coup. A Mr. Chesley of Vermillion moved that Ingersoll be nominated by acclamation. But another delegate instantly forestalled such action by nominating S. W. Moulton. Then Palmer and a Mr. Dubois were nominated. On an informal ballot the voting was as follows: Palmer, 263; Ingersoll, 117; Moulton, 82; Dubois, 42. The vote needed to nominate was 254.

Then occurred what the Palmer forces must have planned all along. Since it was now clear that Palmer could have the nomination if he wanted it, a supporter, F. A. Eastman, of Chicago, arose and read a letter from Palmer, dated April 11, to Horace White of the Chicago *Tribune,* in which Palmer stated in classical political vein that if nominated he would be governed "by the duty of the hour." Anyone versed in politics would know that this was the lucid language of acceptance.

The convention, now in no doubt as to Palmer's intention, proceeded to a formal ballot. The result: Palmer, 317; Ingersoll, 118; Moulton, 52; Dubois, 17. Palmer's nomination was then made unanimous.

Palmer, of course, accepted the nomination. He intoned to the Peoria *Transcript* that he had not wanted it but "it appears, however, that it is the deliberate judgment of the Republican party of this state, that the duty of making this canvass shall be assigned to me, and I accept that judgment as conclusive . . . ."[11] The *Gazette* of Waukegan deplored Palmer's coquetry with the nomination.[12] While Ingersoll followed "a frank and honorable course," Palmer "played 'fast and loose,' 'open and shut,' for the purpose of having the office seek him, at the same time waiting and expecting the nomination."[13]

Ingersoll was dejected at his political setback. That he dearly wanted the governorship and saw himself rising still higher in the political firmament could hardly be made plainer than in these words to Clark: "I am thinking of bidding a long farewell to all my greatness."[14]

How Robert needed now the companionship of his brother! "When you are away there is no one for me to talk to—no one that is capable of understanding me." Then from Clark came a long letter of praise and consolation. Robert had done a magnificent thing in refusing to sacrifice his convictions for political reward. And he wanted Robert to remember how immensely grateful he was to him for his devotion, his counsel, his inspiration. "What would I be without you, my dear brother? When I think, you and I are thinking—when I speak, you and I are speaking—without you I would be but half a man. The world will hear from you soon—on that I stake everything I possess." Robert was deeply moved by the letter: "Of one thing dear brother you may rest assured and that is—that you can not admire me as much as I do you—that you can never be as proud of me as I am of you, and that you can never love me any more than I love you.

Thanking you for the happy tears you make me shed . . . ."

Immediately after the Peoria convention, Robert resolved to foreswear politics forever. But two weeks after the convention his resolution relaxed enough to let him attend the Republican National Convention in Chicago, which unanimously nominated Grant for president on the first ballot and nominated Schuyler Colfax of Indiana, Speaker of the House of Representatives, for vice-president on the sixth ballot. To Ingersoll,

Colfax was "the strong man on the ticket" and would attract more votes for Grant than Grant would for him. He was pleased with Colfax's letter of acceptance, a forthright statement of principle,[15] but with Grant's "Let us have peace" letter he felt nothing but disgust. Grant endorsed the platform adopted at the convention but declared that he would always heed the will of the people, that he knew no law higher than the will of the people, and that, therefore should the time come that the people wanted a change of policy from that contemplated in the platform he would deem it his duty to reflect their wishes. It was "a poor dirty letter," wrote Ingersoll, "written by a man destitute of principle and devoid of enthusiasm. If there is a contemptible demagogue in the world, it is the man who says that he has no opinions of his own—that he wishes only to carry out the ideas of the people."[16]

Three weeks after the Chicago convention Ingersoll observed that as a consequence of Grant's lack of color and conviction the Republican Party was in the grip of universal apathy. Peoria, for instance, was unable to muster enough enthusiasm to hold a ratification meeting. "There have been very few [meetings] anywhere" in Grant's home state, and not even in Indiana, where Colfax was held in high esteem."[17] "I feel blue about the situation," wrote Robert to Clark. "I wish I could see you and talk with you for days."

By the middle of July Robert's disdain of Grant had abated but little. But who else was there? He could not support the Democratic ticket, Governor Horatio Seymour of New York for president and Major-General Frank P. Blair of Missouri for vice-president, for while he put Seymour above Grant he considered the Democratic platform an outrage. The platform condemned the reconstruction policy of the Republicans as "unconstitutional, revolutionary, and void." On the payment of war bonds, the platform declared that if such bonds did not specifically provide for payment "in coin," they should be made redeemable in "lawful money." This to Ingersoll meant depreciated greenbacks and repudiation. And so although he regarded Grant as "pretty dry fodder," he thought he might be able to "choke it down."

Whatever resolve Ingersoll may have had to retire from politice, he could not remain heedless of a siren call from the State of Maine. His eloquence on the hustings had come to the attention of Representative James G. Blaine of that state. Blaine invited him to spend a couple weeks in Maine to make "a few speeches." Ingersoll accepted, and his tour was a major triumph. Of his first speech at Portland, on September 6, Blaine said to him that "it was incomparably the greatest speech he ever heard" and Senator Fessenden of Ohio said, "That is the best speech I ever heard . . ."[18] and he urged Ingersoll to stump his state. The Portland *Press* reported: "Take him all in all, we shall probably never see his like again. . . . Nearly all the time that he was speaking, the applause was like a continuous roar of thunder." It was the same thing at Augusta. Governor Harrison of New Hampshire heard him there and said, "Ingersoll, as an orator you are infinite."[19] Both Senator Wilson of Massachusetts and Representative Canness of Maine were scheduled to speak on the same program at Augusta but, wrote Ingersoll, "both refused to speak, saying to the crowd that no man could follow me."[20] Senator Fessenden, who "Seems to have taken a wonderful fancy to me," heard him again and said "that he would like to hear me every day until election." The *Augusta Journal* commented that "it is the universal testimony of all who listened to Col. Robert G. Ingersoll that he is the leading stump orator of the country."

What a conversion Ulysses S. Grant underwent from the image Robert conveyed to his brother to that he presented to the public! Now Grant was the very nonpareil of character, a giant in the public good—"this hero of the Rebellion, who accomplished at Shiloh what Napoleon endeavored at Waterloo; who captured Vicksburg by a series of victories unsurpassed . . . . , who, having been summoned from the deathbed of rebellion in the West, marched like an athlete from the Potomac to the James, the grandest march in the history of the world. This was all done without the least flourish upon his part. No talk about destiny—without faith in a star—with the simple remark that he would 'fight it out on that line', without a boast, modest to bashfulness, yet brave to audacity, simple as duty, firm as war, direct as truth—this hero, with so much common sense that he is the most uncommon man of his time . . . ."[21]

Ingersoll returned to Peoria on September 15, where four days later he spoke in Rouse's Hall to a wildly cheering packed house who had gathered to welcome back their 'Bob.' They had read that their 'Bob' had taken the state of Maine by storm.

Overnight Ingersoll had become a national figure. From all over the North invitations to speak poured in. But he was still attorney-general of Illinois; that and his own law practice forced him to decline most of these invitations. He did find time to go into adjacent Indiana, where the story of his successes was like that of Maine.

The man should be a senator they were saying here and there in Illinois. The Peoria *Transcript* referred to him as "Our Next Senator." On October 19, "The Largest Political Procession Ever Seen in This City," according to the *Transcript,* held high the banners and the signs proclaiming the names of Grant and Colfax, and John Logan, the candidate for congress at large, and Clark Ingersoll, again the nominee of the Fifth Congressional District, and "Col. R. G. Ingersoll, Our Next Senator."

In the election of 1868 Illinois joined twenty-five other states to give Grant a landslide electoral vote, 214 to 80. Clark Ingersoll defeated his Democratic opponent, John M. Neglas, by a vote of 20,991 to 13,686.[22] The election over, Robert sought an appointment as district attorney. He had withdrawn his candidacy for attorney-general at the time of his bid for the gubernatorial nomination. In December he wrote to Clark that his "prospects for the Dist. Atty. business look bright enough." He asked Clark to obtain the assistance in his behalf of the vice-president elect, Schuyler Colfax. In January, 1869, Robert was in Chicago trying railroad cases and he said that he was having a number of Chicago men write for him. He was being urged by "a great many of the best men in Chicago"[23] to move to that city, and he was tempted.

Several times Robert had thought of leaving Peoria for grass that seemed greener. In one letter to Clark he said of Peoria, "All things considered Peoria is the meanest town in the United States." Peorians were "envious, jealous, and hateful." He would "go where the people will be proud, instead of envious, of a man of sense." This was in July, 1867, soon after he had been appointed attorney-general, when he was thinking of moving to Springfield, the state capital. He decided then to stay in Peoria because he figured that both he and his brother would be better off politically. But now, in January, 1869, he was persuasively told that Chicago was the place in which his political and legal talents could flourish. Peoria, he wrote, is a "small and pinched up town." In Peoria the average run of litigation was inconsequential and without challenge and the legal fees that could be charged were small—"The whole practice of law here is simply odious to me." Again, however, Robert decided not to move. Peoria, he calculated, was still the best base for political operations.

In March Robert wrote to President Grant about the district attorney appointment and he asked Clark to take the matter up with Senator Wilson of Massachusetts, Representatives Blaine and Canness of Maine, and other Eastern congressmen. Clark was as assiduous for Robert in Washington as Robert had been for Clark in Peoria and the Fifth Congressional District. But someone else got the appointment. No reason was specifically given and Robert was at a loss except to conjecture that his reputation as an infidel stood in the way.

Well, now he really was through with politics! "I shall take no more interest," he wrote to Clark, "except to give you a lift now and then."[24]

THE INFIDEL UNFOLDS

FOR several days prior to July 4, 1869, Ingersoll was the cause of a fine to-do in and around Peoria when it became known that he was to address on the holiday a gathering of Germans at nearby Sulphur Springs. The Fourth of July fell on the Sabbath. It was bad enough that those beery, atheistic Germans proposed to desecrate the day with their kind of celebration, but it was evil compounded that they should invite a notorious infidel to speak to them. The churches pleaded with their constituents to shun the occasion. Ingersoll's old enemy, the *Democrat,* and his old friend, the *Transcript,* descanted on the abomination. And Mayor Brotherson chimed in with them. When Ingersoll was importuned not to make the speech, the *Democrat* reported his answer as follows: "Bob says that he will make the talk if there is anyone to talk to and he don't care whether the Presbyterian, Methodist, Baptist, Episcopalian, or any other church denomination likes it or not. . . ." The result of the outcry was great interest in the event and an impressive parade of celebrants headed by Spencer's Light Guard Band proceeded through Peoria to Sulphur Springs.

Ingersoll chose as his theme the struggle of early Americans for religious and political liberty. From what he said no one could say he was an unbeliever: "Every man on earth, under the Creator, has every right any other man can have. . . ." Nor could one say that he was out of sympathy with church and clergy: "Hell ain't as hot as it used to be. . . . Now our God is one of infinite mercy and tenderness. . . . The church will grow. There are grand men in the church and they are growing stronger every day. . . ." Spoken like a politician, like a man who was aware that he was still talked about as "our next senator."

On the observance of the Sabbath, he thanked the Germans "for teaching us something new. . . . I was educated on a different plan. I was not allowed to chew gum on Sunday. I was not allowed to crack hickory nuts. If I was caught chewing gum, it was only another evidence of the total depravity of the human heart. . . ."

On religious liberty he said, "Come. Wear your hair as you please. I say, Liberty to all. If I want to go to church, I'll go. If I want to hear a Calvinist preach, I will go—but I don't think I'll go this year. Let everybody do what he wants to do. It won't be long until the joss house will be built by the side of the churches. . . ."[1] Outspoken but not really offensive.

The furore before the occasion was not matched after it. In fact, there was a kind of embarrassed silence. The ardent critics before the event were rendered noncommittal by his unexpected restraint.

Ingersoll's popularity was now so great with the Germans of the Peoria community that they asked him to speak to them again, this time on the occasion of unveiling in Peoria a statue of Alexander Friedrich Heinrich von Humboldt, the great German naturalist, in commemoration of his birthday September 14, 1769. Ingersoll presented a lecture, which reviewed the life and achievements of the naturalist with particular emphasis on his scientific investigations demonstrating "the sublimest of truths—'The Universe is Governed by Law!' " In this lecture Ingersoll put aside political caution. He said that one of Humboldt's greatest accomplishments was "to do away with that splendid delusion called special providence." He charged that "all religions are inconsistent with mental freedom." The idea of creation was founded on the ignorance and credulity that religions foster.

Ingersoll delivered "Humboldt" in Cincinnati two weeks later. The Cincinnati *Times* reported that "Robinson's Opera House was crowded last evening. . . . The renowned lecturer Col. R. G. Ingersoll . . . was escorted to the stage by a number of prominent citizens and introduced to the audience by the Mayor." The Mayor said: "A brilliant, genial gentleman; a man of brains, a man greatly respected and admired by all who know him, and greatly detested by many of those who do not agree with him in opinion. . . ."[2] "Applause and cheers," according to the *Times,* broke out frequently during the lecture.

Something had happened in the country that an audience could applaud and cheer an infidel, a blasphemer. If he had given such a lecture ten years before, he would have been mobbed. It was a change not confined to a particular locality. The philosopher John Fiske noted what happened to the Harvard mentality in just eight years. In 1861, as a student at

Harvard, he was threatened with expulsion if he continued to disseminate his ideas on evolution; yet in 1869 he was invited by Harvard to deliver a series of lectures on Positivism in, of all places, Holden Chapel.[3]

The intellectual upheaval was the outcome of many circumstances and forces: the frontier psychology that made men self-reliant and daring; the rapid advance of practical science that could make a heaven on earth; free thought from Germany that examined the origins of religion; unitarianism and transcendentalism that challenged sacerdotal authority; the Civil War that uprooted men and morals; the dawning of the Gilded Age with its worship of Mammon; and Evolution that struck directly at divine creation and the infallibility of the Bible. Traditions and patterns of conduct crumbled. As never before, people were susceptible to new ideas. "The world is beginning to change," said Ingersoll in "Humboldt," "because the people are beginning to think."

"Humboldt" was a sign that Ingersoll had forsworn elective office. It was an infidel's clear manifesto. If he had been elected governor, he could not have delivered it—that is, if he wanted a second term. Again, if he had been elected governor, a thirty-year career as a fearless foe of Bible and theology, church and clergy would not have materialized. Tasting the sweets of elective victory and avid for office, he would have chosen the calling of politics. He could not have served both anti-God and Mammon. He could not have run down the deities of the electorate. Which is what he did do in "Humboldt."

The die was cast. Not again would he make obeisance to the electorate as indeed he had done in his Fourth of July address, two months before "Humboldt." Not again would he utter such words as "Now our God is one of infinite mercy and tenderness" or "There are grand men in the church and they are growing stronger every day." He was done with temporizing. "Humboldt" crystallized his convictions. The reception to "Humboldt" crystallized his career. The infidel overcame the office seeker.

Eʟᴀʀʟʏ in 1870, Ingersoll took up the cudgels for woman
suffrage. On March 15, a convention was held in Peoria for the
purpose of forming a county Woman Suffrage Association.
Susan B. Anthony, who together with Elizabeth Cady Stanton
led a national crusade for the cause, was one of the speakers,
the others being a Rev. R. H. Pullman and Ingersoll. Ingersoll
offered a resolution to the convention, which was passed unanimously: "That we pledge ourselves, irrespective of party, to use
all honorable means to make the women of America the equals
of men before the law." In his speech he advocated that the
sense of the resolution should be incorporated in an amendment to the Federal Constitution. He decried the fact that
women had been declared unable to act as notary publics or
practicing attorneys.

On April 29 the Peoria County Woman Suffrage Association held its first quarterly meeting. Ingersoll and a Miss Emily
L. Balchwin were chosen as delegates to the national Convention of the American Woman Franchise Association. In his address to the county suffragettes he showed in considerable detail
that the oppression of women had its roots in the Bible.

The Peoria *Transcript* was displeased with Ingersoll, not because he had vented criticisms of the Bible but because he, who
should know better, had committed himself to a weak cause.
The paper noted with satisfaction that he lectured on "Woman"
"to the smallest audience the Colonel ever addressed in Peoria";
Ingersoll should know that "a good cause is quite as requisite
as a good speaker."[1] Women are weak and liberty would corrupt them; women, God forbid, would become constables and
jurors; women if they had any more privileges would tend to
free love. Do women serve in the army? Why then should they
vote?

On May 3, Ingersoll's reply appeared in the *Transcript*. "According to your doctrine," he said, "the rights of a human being depend upon the strength of that being. On the contrary, I assert that the rights of human beings do not depend upon strength. Justice is not a matter of weight. . . . If the right of self-government is not a natural right, our government is based on an infinitely insecure foundation. . . .

This was a cause dear to Ingersoll's heart. Out of no abstract and legalistic concepts came his passionate espousal of suffrage for women. It came from his deep devotion to human liberty and his adoration of his wife and two daughters. "Tell them," he wrote when he was away for a few days, "that they are my Holy Trinity comprising the only Deity I worship."

In 1870, though his brother was up for reelection, Robert was not an active campaigner. Now and then he appeared on the platform with Clark, who came home in August to battle for renomination in the primary, but he seldom spoke. He was still disaffected with politics. And he realized that his inconoclasm was a political liability. Repeatedly the press of the Fifth District carried comments like this bit in the *Republican* of Bureau: "If in our own district those who dislike E. C. Ingersoll and his vulgar brother and his insolent set, who suspect his integrity and want of religious principle . . . can see no better way to break his power than to vote for a democrat . . . why, a thousand times better to do this than suffer the ring to triumph again. . . ."

The opposition to Clark on religious and moral grounds came to a head in October when after a narrow margin of victory in the primary he became the target of a circular prepared by members of the clergy. The circular was in the form of a letter from J. M. Caldwell, pastor of the Methodist Episcopal Church of Princeton, countersigned by five other clergymen and church officials, to a clerical colleague, J. G. Evans. The letter said: "The Christian people of this city, almost to a man, feel that the honor, purity, and security of the republican party, and the interests of Christianity, imperatively demand the defeat of Mr. Ingersoll . . . . a thoroughly corrupt man, devoid of moral principle, profane, atheistic. . . ." All good Christians were called upon to support his Democratic opponent, B. N. Stevens, "a thoroughly conscientious and liberal minded Christian *gentleman. . . .*" The letter also urged voters not to throw away votes on F. B. Ives, the candidate of the Prohibition Party. He had not the slightest chance of being elected and to vote for him would be to reduce the vote for Stevens. Besides, although Ives was himself a preacher in nearby Tiskilwa, he was a man with "defective moral perceptions, and destitute of the experience and strength of character essential to represent us properly in Congress."

Thirty-seven men of Tiskilwa—called by Caldwell "an infidel representative of Ingersoll men"—arose to the defense of Ives and Ingersoll, and replied in the *Transcript* that the charges against the two were baseless, the "mere assertions of a lot of disaffected, disappointed political and moral leaders." Ives also replied announcing that in view of the Caldwell "network of falsehoods" and in view of those who now wished to vote for their second choice, Ingersoll, he was releasing from their pledges those who had promised to support him. But the damage had been done. The Caldwell circular was distributed in various churches of the Fifth District and contributed materially to the defeat of Clark Ingersoll on November 8. He received 9,963 votes; Stevens, 11,579; and Ives, 868.[2] Clark then transferred his residence to Washington, D. C., where he engaged in the practice of law.

Robert was tempted to move to Washington too—"I am here living with fools"—but he was prospering in Peoria. His legal business was big and was increasing. And he was involved in various railroad projects in addition to his acting as counsel for a number of roads. He had been elected to the board of directors of the Peoria, Atlanta and Decatur Railroad Company and the Peoria and Springfield Railway Company and he was enmeshed in the financial operations of the Peoria and Rock Island Railway Company, himself holding a $50,000 chattel mortgage on it. As attorney for the Peoria and Rock Island he fought several legal battles in 1871 in the endeavor to save the road from bankruptcy. One battle created quite a stir, as it dealt with an issue crucial to the financial status of many railroads—could subscribers to a railroad company be compelled to pay their subscriptions? Ingersoll won the case. On one occasion he went with a delegation of Peorians to Fairview, Illinois, to try to persuade the representatives of the Pekin and Mississippi Railroad to put Peoria on their route rather than a rival claimant, Canton. The *Canton Register* was irate: "R. G. Ingersoll, Messrs. Lindsay, Emery and others, proceeded to indulge in much wind, coupled with sneering allusions to Springfield and Canton. . . . Canton gave Peoria to understand that Canton was there for business not bluster or brag or harangues and at the proper time would make her offers and pledges."[3]

Ingersoll's business frequently took him away from home for three or four days at a time. This he did not like because the trips usually meant poor food and dreary lodging as well as separation from his loved ones. Once he had to stay in Monmouth, Illinois, trying what he called "a long and tedious case." Life was "too short to be wasted in this way," he wrote to Clark. "A good dinner lost is gone forever. A poor night's rest can never be made up." At times he worried that he was indulging too much in creature comforts and the pleasant little vices of tobacco and spirits. He was watching his weight, 227 pounds, for a while in 1871. He gave up tea, coffee, spirits, and tobacco, both smoking and chewing. "I am going to continue in the good cause until I satisfy myself whether the effect upon me is good or bad." The effect was bad.

"Total abstinence," he wrote, "has killed thousands."

Here was a man who delighted in the things of the world, and yet, keenly aware of the sorrow that would end them, he often fell prey to mournful thoughts. The happier he was, the more he felt that life was tragic. The beauty of a day in June put him in mind of the fewness of the days of man: "that the happiest life ends in a grave and that the better we are the more tears will be shed when we die." One day in November, Ingersoll, from a warm and happy house, saw the dead and fallen leaves: "Nothing is sadder than the leafless trees, except, it may be, the treeless leaves." On such a day he longed to see his brother. The winter of life was coming and he and his brother would soon be parted forever: "Life is too short to waste it away from each other." On such a day, too, what a refuge from his thoughts his home was. Here was his wife, Eva, a pleasure to the eyes, a balm to his soul, and a genius with boiler and roaster. She was a strikingly handsome woman with a clear-cut, strong face, a quick smile, bright and candid eyes, and smooth black hair. Here were his two little daughters whom he loved to tickle and nuzzle and hoist in the air. Their laughter was a pure delight to him. It was monstrous that theologians should sit around and discuss the question whether an infant sans baptism would go to hell. "Do not, I pray you, soil the minds of your children with this dogma. . . ."[4]

"IMPIOUS POPE BOB"

O N January 29, 1871, the 134th anniversary of Thomas Paine's birth, Ingersoll delivered the lecture, "Thomas Paine," at Fairbury, Illinois, at a ceremony dedicating the newly completed Fairbury Hall to Free Thought. It was in "the palmy days of Free Thought in this city," said the *Fairbury Blade*. A large number of boldly thinking people dominated the Fairbury citizenry and were making things hum in the realm of unorthodoxy. As they were building the hall, in 1870, they determined to make clear what the main purpose of it was to be, and so they inlaid the number 94 in the center of the arch over the stage, the 94 signifying that they computed time not according to B.C. or A.D. but D.I., that is, the year of the signing of the Declaration of Independence. At the dedication ceremonies "the hall was packed to the doors and many people were unable to get inside."

Ingersoll reviewed Paine's life and his fight for political and religious freedom. *Common Sense* "aroused our fathers, like a blast;" the *Crisis* "was a cloud by day and a pillar of fire by night, leading the way to freedom, honor, and glory;" *The Rights of Man* was "a magazine of political wisdom, an arsenal of ideas, and an honor, not only to Thomas Paine, but to human nature itself." Then came the *Age of Reason,* and Paine, the esteemed patriot, became a thing to be shunned, a pestilence, a moral plague, "and at the bare mention of his name the bloody hands of the church were raised in horror." His crime: he demonstrated that a revelation that comes to us second-hand, either verbally or in writing, is a contradiction in terms; he denied the divine origin of Christ; he attacked the doctrine of eternal damnation; "he believed that murder, massacre, and indiscriminate slaughter had never been commanded by the deity."[1]

The *Age of Reason* was the immediate inspiration of Ingersoll's next lecture, "The Gods." On December 20, 1871, he wrote to Clark that he was working on "The Gods" and that as soon as he finished it he would send it to him to get his reaction "as to the propriety of its publication." It is a vast subject, he said, and "requires a good deal more learning than I have." He wished it were possible for him to do research in the Library of Congress, but he was too busy to go to Washington.

On January 29, 1872, Parker Pillsbury, a Boston free thinker, and Ingersoll lectured at Fairbury on the first anniversary of the dedication of Fairbury Hall. Pillsbury talked on Paine. Ingersoll gave "The Gods." A special train from Peoria brought Peorians and stopped at other points along the line to Fairbury. By the time it reached Fairbury it was full. The Peoria *Democrat,* loth to say a kind word for a home town Republican, reported that while Pillsbury "addressed the crowd in his sincere, solid and sober manner," Ingersoll was "showy."

Ingersoll was invited to deliver "The Gods" in Peoria on February 23. Again the *Democrat* found no good in him: "he seeks to overthrow the very foundations upon which rest our entire system of morals . . . . he is an enemy of man as well as God. . . ." The theme of the lecture was its very first sentence: "An honest God is the noblest work of man." Peoples make

Gods in their own likenesses. "The negroes represented their
deities with black skins and curly hair. The Mongolian gave to
his a yellow complexion and dark almond-shaped eyes. The
Jews were not allowed to paint theirs, or we should have seen
Jehovah with a full beard, an oval face, and an aquiline nose.
Zeus was a perfect Greek, and Jove looked as though a member of the Roman Senate. The gods of Egypt had the patient
face and placid look of the loving people who made them. . . .
The gods of India were often mounted upon elephants . . . and
the deities of the Arctic zone were passionately fond of whale's
blubber. . . ."[2]

Ingersoll had a great talent at reducing the miraculous and
the solemn to the racy terms of everyday experience. He was
also expert with the anecdote. Here is the way he disposed of
the idea that a loving God takes care of all his creatures: "a devout clergyman, happening one day to see a crane wading in
quest of food, pointed out to his son the perfect adaptation of
the crane to get his living in that manner. 'See,' said he, 'how his
legs are formed for wading! What a long slender bill he has!
Observe how nicely he folds his feet when putting them in or
drawing them out of the water! He does not cause the slightest
ripple. He is thus enabled to approach the fish without giving
them any notice of his arrival. My son,' said he, 'it is impossible
to look at that bird without recognizing the design, as well as
the goodness of God, in thus providing the means of subsist-
ence.' 'Yes,' replied the boy, 'I think I see the goodness of God,
at least so far as the crane is concerned; but after all, father,
don't you think the arrangement a little tough on the fish?' "[3]

But levity could quickly fade away and a grimmer form of
irony would take its place reinforced by another of Ingersoll's
talents, that for vivid imagery: did it ever occur to the exponents of the design of a loving God that "a cancer is as beautiful in its development as is the reddest rose? That what they
are pleased to call the adaptation of means to ends, is as apparent in the cancer as in April rain? How beautiful the process
of congestion! By what ingenious methods the blood is poi-
soned so that the cancer shall have food! By what wonderful

contrivances the entire system of man is made to pay tribute to this divine and charming cancer! See by what admirable instrumentalities it feeds itself from the surrounding quivering, dainty flesh! . . . ."[4]

And now a would-be David arose in Illinois and ventured to tackle this Goliath of infidelity. He was Professor Clark Braden, a Campbellite minister and erstwhile president of Southern Illinois College, a quiet little man, youngish looking though grandly moustachioed and bearded. He came to Peoria to give seven free lectures, April 22-28, on revelation, evolution, theism, and Ingersoll. But his sling was out of whack and Goliath won the day. Sticking close to his manuscript, Braden spoke in a monotonous voice and with little gesticulation. The result, according to none other than the Peoria *Democrat,* was that Braden drew small audiences and "no one seemed to be particularly interested in what he said,"[5] while Ingersoll pulling all the stops of an accomplished orator packed them in from far and near.

Although Braden seemed to be an innocuous and academic sort of man, he had vitriol in his veins. For years after his appearance in Peoria he spiced his lectures with instances of Ingersoll's depravity. In 1881 he published a pamphlet, *Ingersoll Unmasked,* based on alleged affidavits and statements of reputable people—"forged," wrote Judge S. D. Puterbaugh of Peoria. Typical charges in *Ingersoll Unmasked*:

> II. He once stopped his Father, in prayer, in family worship, at the home of a stranger, and assailed what he was uttering.
> V. In Marian, Illinois, he undertook to clean out a grog-shop, and had his ear torn loose from his head by a tumbler hurled by the grog-seller.
> XII. In a drunken row, in a den of infamy in Peoria, he had his scalp cut open by a beer mug, in the hands of a prostitute.
> XVI. In his own parlor, he insulted a lady guest, by tossing off a bumper of wine, with the blasphemous toast: 'Here's to Jesus Christ.'
> XVIII. At Maquon, he was so drunk that as he rushed through a store he fell into a tub of butter.

XXVII. It is common for him to speak of the son of God as "J. Christ," "Mr. Christ," and "Mr. J. Christ."

Braden wrote to the Peoria *Transcript* stating that *Ingersoll Unmasked* was based on facts which he defied Ingersoll and anyone else to deny. "If they are denied, I will furnish the proof. . . ." The *Transcript* refused to go into the matter, branding the charges as baseless, ridiculous, and vicious.

In 1873 and 1874, Ingersoll added to his repertoire of lectures "Voltaire," "Individuality," and "Heretics and Heresies." He first lectured on Voltaire, at Fairbury, Illinois, on February 20, 1873, the 179th anniversary of Voltaire's birth. Again, a special train from Peoria and from intermediate points carried a capacity load of Ingersollites to Fairbury. An incredible thing, commented the Peoria *Democrat,* that a special train should be hired and filled by men and women who are "to feast and hear eulogiums" in honor of Voltaire. What had Voltaire done "to earn the admiration of the honest people living on the prairies of Illinois?"[6] For two hours and a half Ingersoll told his hearers at Fairbury what Voltaire had done. Voltaire "mocked kings that were unjust . . . the titled fools . . . the corruption of courts . . . popes and cardinals and bishops and priests, and all the hypocrites on the earth . . . the haters of liberty, the persecutors of their fellow-men. . . . Voltaire . . . examined the Bible for himself, advocated intellectual liberty, struck from the brain the fetters of an arrogant faith. . . ."[7]

On September 1, 1873, Ingersoll delivered "Individuality" at a picnic on the Peoria fair grounds sponsored by the Free Congregational Society of Bloomington, Illinois. Everyone was invited. The occasion drew a large crowd—and much criticism. First, it was the Sabbath; second, beer and wine were dispensed; third, "pernicious doctrines" were disseminated. The devil is loose among us, cried the *Democrat,* "knocking the props from under the Christian Church." The devil delivered a lecture remarkable for "rhetorical beauty and symmetry," but the ideas and sentiments of the speech were "not beautiful or noble in the least." It was a pity that Peoria's fame should rest on being the stronghold of atheism. "In no other city in the west, scarcely in the Union, has atheism had the prominence given it that it has in Peoria."[8]

In December, 1873, "Impious Pope Bob" (Chicago *Times*) delivered "Individuality" before the Chicago Free Religious Society. Again it was on a Sunday and that was bad enough. But that Ingersoll should flay Christianity and the church for so-called crimes against the individual was "monstrous and shocking."[9]

In April, 1874, Ingersoll first delivered "Heretics and Heresy," also before the Chicago Free Religious Society. Pointing to the horrors of the Inquisition, to the ferocity of the religious wars, to John Calvin's grim theocracy, and to the witch-hunting of the Puritans, he proclaimed "that the spirit of persecution still lingers in the church." The Presbytery of Chicago was about to try for heresy the powerful and popular preacher, David Swing, who, said Ingersoll, "has been enjoying the luxury of a little honest thought and the real rapture of expressing it." Was it possible that this trial was to take place in Chicago, "in this city of pluck and progress—this marvel of energy—this miracle of nerve!"[10]

Ingersoll answered the charges against Swing one by one, using all his resources of irony, humor, and emotional appeal. A typical answer: "If this doctrine (the 'call') is true, God, to say the least of it, is an exceedingly poor judge of human nature. It is more than a century since a man of true genius has been found in an orthodox pulpit. Every minister is heretical just to the extent that his intelligence is above average. The Lord seems to be satisfied with mediocrity. The people are not." Ingersoll told the story of an old deacon who wanted to get rid of an unpopular preacher. To the deacon's suggestion that he quit the ministry and go into something else, the minister replied that he could not conscientiously leave the ministry as he had had the 'call'. Said the deacon, 'That may be so, but it's unfortunate for you, that when God called you to preach, he forgot to call anybody to hear you.' "

As Ingersoll was proceeding through all the heresy charges,

the members of the Chicago Free Religious Society often in-terrupted him with cheers and laughs, hand-clapping and knee-whacking. It was not only the substance and words but also the physical aspect, the personality, and the delivery of the man. Generously fleshed but well-informed, he had a large, shapely head, a full, mobile face, and eyes, deep-set and glow-ing; he was cut out for the business of oratory. Imaginative and emotional, he could be innocent and sweet, bland, fierce, tear-ful, rapt, jolly, buffoonish. And he had a resonant voice of re-markable range and flexibility.

In 1874 Ingersoll had his first volume of lectures published, containing "The Gods," "Humboldt," "Thomas Paine," "In-dividuality," and "Heretics and Heresy." It was a handsome volume, "one of the handsomest ever issued in the west," said the Chicago *Times* in its review of July 5. The book would have been met by "a howl of execration but a simple ten years ago;" It marked "an epoch in the world of thought, a new birth." The *Chicago Evening Journal* said that it was probably "the most radical book to be found in the whole range of theology," the writer carrying the philosophy of rationalism "to its extremest logical sequence."

But to judge by an experience which he had in February, 1874, Ingersoll was not yet the complete rationalist. He and his wife were in New York City on business and pleasure and one night they decided to amuse themselves by visiting a Dr. H. Slade, a noted spiritualist, to see what communications they could get from the other worlds. In Slade's office, at 413 Fourth Avenue, they sat down at a small, plain walnut table in a room well-lighted with gas burners. The Doctor showed them two slates, a double one which opened like a book and a single one.

"Very well, we will take this double slate and clean it with this wet cloth—you see the two surfaces are now absolutely clean. Now we put this little bit of plain pencil between the leaves of the slate. Let us now close the slate and put it right here in the middle of this walnut table and we will leave it here for a few minutes and we shall stay right here too." Wonder of wonders, the pencil commenced writing. "We could hear it," wrote Robert to Clark, "scratching away as lively as you please—crossing the t's and punctuating like a schoolmaster."[11] Robert said he listened with a lawyer's mind and checked all possible details. It was a perfect hoax—ridiculous! insane!— and he and Eva started to laugh and then they got up and left without waiting to read the pencil's message. And yet maybe, maybe there was something to it. Well, they would try it again, if Slade who had been miffed by their reaction would let them.

The next day, about noon, they went back taking with them a Colonel Ralph Plumb of Illinois. Slade was not at all unwilling to solicit another communication for them. This time Ingersoll applied what be called "various tests and precautions." Then the pencil wrote again. The message was: "The soul of man can never die.—signed F. Plumb." Incredulous, the Ingersolls turned to Colonel Plumb, also incredulous. Plumb said that F. was his daughter who had died the year before, that once when Ingersoll was visiting at the Plumb home she had heard him say he did not believe in immortality, and that in her last sickness she had talked about what he had said and wondered how a person could be so wrong. " 'I suppose she has taken this opportunity of setting you right,' " Plumb added.[12]

Ingersoll was impressed. "I want you to go to 413 4th Avenue, New York, Dr. Slade, and see what you can make of it," he wrote Clark. "It appears so utterly impossible that I doubt my own senses. My *reason* refuses to believe my eyes and ears. I neither believe nor disbelieve; but I am stumped. . . .

"I really want you to go to New York simply to investigate the thing—If it does not happen just as I have described— draw on me for time, trouble, and expenses."[13]

If Clark did as his brother requested, he too was stumped. Years later, in 1893, Robert stated that at one time he had paid some attention to Spiritualism and he had attended a number of séances, the most notable being that of Dr. H. Slade. The Slade feat had never been explained to him. "At the same time, I do not believe that there is anything supernatural in the universe."[14] In other words, in 1893 Ingersoll was sure that the spiritualists were mistaken, in 1874 he was not so sure.

While Ingersoll's various activities, law, lectures, and railroads, kept him very busy, he found enough time to take his family on substantial vacations. In July and August, 1874, they were at the famous New Jersey resort, Long Branch, which in the years following they frequently visited. A vacation to Ingersoll was a time also for respite from dietary restrictions which with some success he otherwise tried to follow. "I don't wish to trifle with your feelings," he wrote to Clint and Sue Farrell, Mrs. Ingersoll's sister, "but we had a few dozen Blue Point oysters raw last night for lunch and fried oysters and clams for breakfast. Wipe your mouths and forget this as soon as you can." Ingersoll went bathing occasionally but he knew he did not appear to best advantage in a bathing suit, resembling nothing so much as a "stack of hay struggling with the waves."

In September, 1875, the Ingersolls went abroad for a couple months. His diary of the sojourn has a number of interesting entries of which here are a few:

> September 7—"The French have a most wonderful art of hiding dirt."
>
> September 8—"Over the grave of Voltaire the priests are mumbling, while idiots kneel in prayer."
>
> [At the Cathedral of Notre Dame:]
> "saw the confessional and a few fools with clasped hands adoring a stone Jesus in the arms of a marble virgin."
>
> September 22—"Today my darling Eva is twelve years old. We all gave her twelve kisses a piece and one to grow on. We gave her the same number of slaps and told her how dearly we loved her."
>
> October 1—[Expecting a cablegram from one R.G.H. conveying a sorely needed large sum of money:] "Went to Charing Cross. Nothing. Damn RGH."
>
> October 2—"Went to Charing X. No dispatch—Nothing. Damn RGH."
>
> October 3—"Went to Charing X. Damn RGH."
>
> October 4—"Went to Charing X—no dispatch. Damn RGH."

October 5—"Went to Charing Cross. No message. G.D. R.G.H. All felt homesick."

October 8—[On seeing a copy of Adam Krafft's painting, *Descent from the Cross,* in the South Kensington Museum:] "Mary Magdalen lets the head of Christ fall upon her lips. Her face up-turned in a kind of rapture, the most loving and affectionate thing I saw in all the Christ business."

The Ingersolls visited all the places which American tourists in the British Isles and France were supposed to visit. At Castle Blarney, however, Ingersoll did not kiss the Blarney Stone because he said he was quite aware that he in particular did not have to. When they were being taken through St. Paul's Cathedral in London, the guide of course paused here and there to make a speech on points of special interest. At the sarcophagus of Wellington, the guide told of the ponderous masonry of the foundation, of the immense block of granite scooped out for the remains, of the heavy iron coffin in an oak box banded with iron, and finally of the massive slab that was cemented on top of the sarcophagus. "By Jove," exclaimed Ingersoll, "You've got him! If he ever gets out, just telegraph R. G. Ingersoll, at Peoria, Illinois."

Visiting the Tower of London, Ingersoll was particularly impressed with the old instruments of torture and the block upon which heads were chopped off. Later he vividly depicted these memorabilia of a cruel past in his lecture, "The Liberty of Man, Woman and Child." "I saw the Rack. This was a box like the bed of a wagon, with a windlass at each end, with levers, and ratchets to prevent slipping; over each windlass went chains; some were fastened to the ankles of the sufferer; others to his wrists. And then priests, clergymen, divines, saints, began turning these windlasses, and kept turning, until the ankles, the knees, the hips, the shoulders, the elbows, the wrists of the victim were all dislocated, and the sufferer was wet with the sweat of agony. And they had standing by a physician to feel his pulse. What for? To save his life? Yes. In Mercy? No; simply that they might rack him once again.

"This was done, remember, in the name of civilization; in

the name of law and order; in the name of mercy; in the name of the most merciful Christ."

"THE PLUMED KNIGHT SPEECH"

INGERSOLL did not participate in the campaign of 1872. He announced that "he has quit politics entirely." He had gone all out for Grant in 1868 and had gotten nothing. "For some reason," he wrote, "the leaders in politics are not my friends ... The American people have lost the power to confer honor."[1]

But the situation changed by 1876. A chief contender for the Republican nomination for president was Ingersoll's friend Senator James G. Blaine. Others in the running were Senator Oliver Morton of Indiana, also his friend; Senator Roscoe Conkling of New Jersey; Secretary of the Treasury, Benjamin H. Bristow of Kentucky; Elihu B. Washburne of Illinois, minister to France under Grant; and Governor Rutherford B. Hayes of Ohio. The Republican National Convention assembled in Cincinnati in mid-June.

A few days prior to the convention, Blaine had played the leading role in a stirring drama in the House of Representatives. On April 24, before the House he had denied charges that in a deal involving his interest in railroad bonds he had allowed the Union Pacific and two other roads to expect legislative favors. But the House, which was Democratic, ordered an investigation. The most damaging evidence against Blaine was in certain letters which he had written to Warren Fisher and which James Mulligan of Boston, Fisher's bookkeeper, had in his possession. Blaine persuaded Mulligan to give him the letters with the promise that he would return them. But he did not return them and upon the advice of his attorneys he refused to let the investigating committee see them. Instead he appeared before the House and holding the package of letters aloft he pointed to them and said, "I invite the confidence of forty-four millions of my countrymen while I read these letters from this desk!"

And how he read them! Reading only parts of some of the letters and omitting some letters altogether, he executed, as the New York *World* put it, "a *coup de théatre.*" When the performance was over, he received a thunderous ovation.

But Blaine, some thought, was done for politically. On June 5, the New York *Herald* stated, "He will hereafter belong to the invalid corps of the Republican Party." But on June 12, the *Herald* reported that the Blaine men were asking all good Republicans a ticklish question: "Are you prepared to admit that the investigations and alleged developments made by the Democratic House of Representatives have been made in good faith, and that they are justified by the results?" Of course they were not ready to admit that the Democrats had exposed Republican corruption. There was no doubt about it, there was a Democratic plot to destroy the Republican Party and put the secessionists in power. By June 14, the first day of the convention, the *Herald* did a complete turnabout on Blaine—"even his opponents acknowledge that he has the first chance of a nomination." He would be nominated on the second or third ballot.

A few days before the convention, Ingersoll was urged by Judge Drummond, of Indianapolis, to support Washburne for the nomination. "I hate him as strongly as I like you," replied Ingersoll. When Washburne had run for the Senate against Richard Yates, Ingersoll said he had worked for him with all his might even to the point of alienating old friends. In return, Washburne did him all the injury he could: "He told about me what he knew to be untrue. And always exhibited the utmost bitterness." But Blaine—"He is my friend, and I am his. . . . You would like him if you knew him. He is a splendid man . . . blessed with a big brain and a big heart." He would surely get the nomination.

Ingersoll's services were also requested for another candidate, by the candidate himself, Senator Morton. He had often spoken from the same platform with Morton in Indiana and

Illinois during the elections of 1866 and 1868. They were on very friendly terms. But he had to tell Morton that although he would like to place his name in nomination he would have to follow the wishes of the Illinois delegation of which he was chairman and which seemed to be strongly for Blaine.

On June 13 the Illinois delegation held a caucus. Both Congressman John A. Logan and Ingersoll pleaded the merits of Blaine. The vote was Blaine, 34; Bristow, 4; and Washburne, 2. The night of June 14 at a conclave of Blaine moguls Ingersoll was selected to put Blaine in nomination the next day. This was hardly enough time to prepare a proper speech.

About midnight Ingersoll and his brother retired to their hotel room. Clark was pretty anxious about the speech and said to Robert, "You have a big man to enter the lists with, and you ought to be well prepared." Robert assured Clark that he would be and then to the consternation of his brother promptly went to bed and soon was asleep. About three in the morning he awakened, quietly got out of bed, found a piece of common wrapping paper, and started writing. One hour later he was in bed again. When Clark awoke, it was broad daylight and there was his brother deep in slumber. He shook him, "My God, what about your speech!" "There it is," said Robert laughing and pointed to the wrapping paper. "Well, I'll be God damned!" said Clark.

There was some mighty eloquence during that day in Exposition Hall as various nominations, chiefly of favorite sons, were made and seconded. The day was coming to a close when the convention clerk reached the state of Maine, Blaine's state. The applause and cheers so far had been desultory and sectional. Now from every part of the house, from all but a few of the six thousand people present, came a "simultaneous, thunderous outburst." A man arose from an obscure corner and advanced to the central stage. It was Ingersoll. The convention became "a bedlam of rapturous delirium,"[2] and remained in that condition for ten minutes. Finally Ingersoll, who had stood the while "with wonderful presence," was able to begin his speech.

Blaine was "the grandest combination of heart, conscience, and brain beneath the flag." Blaine was sound on the public debt: "The Republicans of the United States demand a man who knows that prosperity and resumption, when they come, must come together; that when they come, they will come hand in hand through the golden harvest fields; hand in hand by the whirling spindles and the turning wheels; hand in hand past the open furnace doors. . . ." Blaine was sound on reconstruction: "the people call for the man who has preserved in Congress what our soldiers won upon the field; . . . for the man who has snatched the mask of Democracy from the hideous face of rebellion. . . ." Blaine exposed the Democratic plot to besmirch him: "Like an armed warrior, like a plumed knight, James G. Blaine marched down the halls of the American Congress and threw his shining lance full and fair against the brazen foreheads of the defamers of his country and the maligners of his honor."[3]

The conclusion of the speech, the "bloody flag" waving, keynoted the ensuing Republican campaign: "Gentlemen of the convention, in the name of the great Republic, the only Republic that ever existed upon this earth; in the name of all her defenders and supporters; in the name of all her soldiers living; in the name of all her soldiers dead upon the field of battle, and in the name of those who perished in the skeleton clutch of famine at Andersonville and Libby, whose sufferings he so vividly remembers, Illinois—Illinois nominates for the next President of this Country, that prince of parliamentarians —that leader of leaders—James G. Blaine."

Pandemonium took over. The effect of the speech, said the Chicago *Times,* "was indescribable. The coolest-headed in the hall were stirred to the wildest expression. . . . Words can do but meagre justice to the wizard power of this extraordinary man."[4] The New York *Herald* reported that Ingersoll easily took all the oratorical honors; the Chicago *Tribune* that he "swept the whole body like a tumultuous flood;" the Philadelphia *Record* that "no similar effort had produced a similar enthusiasm within our recollection."

Had the convention not adjourned, Blaine, many thought, would have been nominated at once. But it was 5:15 P.M. and the shades of dusk were gathering fast in Exposition Hall, which had no lighting facilities. So Macpherson, the presiding officer, pounded his gavel as though to break it, and declared the convention adjourned. Shelby M. Cullom, one-time Representative from Illinois, who was sitting behind Macpherson at the time, stated, that if he had had the gavel "there would have been no adjournment and James G. Blaine would have been nominated." A London *Times* correspondent wrote that Ingersoll's speech was "one blaze of rhetoric" which "completely carried the convention away with it" and that it would have changed the nomination if balloting had started immediately.

As it was, Blaine had a commanding lead in the balloting which commenced the next morning and he held it for six ballots. On the sixth ballot Hayes who had been gaining slowly had but 113 votes to Blaine's 308. Bristow was third with 111. Necessary to nominate, 379. On the next ballot Hayes polled 384 votes, Blaine 351. Thereupon the convention made the nomination unanimous.

The fame which the "Plumed Knight" speech brought Ingersoll increased with his speeches in the campaign that followed. Republican leaders beseeched his aid. On August 5, Blaine wired him to come to Maine: "No exaggeration to say that your coming may be turning point in national fight." On August 8, Hayes also wired Ingersoll to go to Maine. Carl Schurz wanted him in St. Louis. William Wheeler, nominee for vice-president, wanted him in his state, New York. The Chicago *Evening Journal* said that "never in the history of politics was there such a demand for any one speaker as there is . . . for Robert G. Ingersoll."[5]

Ingersoll went to Maine in August, his wife with him. For almost three weeks he stumped the state. "I have had," he wrote, "a continual and continuous ovation in Maine."[6]

The speech at Bangor, August 20, including the circumstances under which it was delivered and the response to it, was typical of the series. He arrived at Bangor about 3 P.M. in the company of Blaine, Governor Connor, and C. A. Boutells, the chairman of the Republican State Committee. They proceeded immediately to the grounds where Ingersoll was to speak. He usually spoke outdoors to accommodate the thousands who wanted to hear him. With him on the platform, constructed for the occasion, were his wife and the Republican elite of the state and community. Governor Connor introduced him. He waited out the usual ovation and then began to speak in an easy, cordial, conversational vein about the Republican party, the party of humanity, freedom, and progress. With gathering vehemence he itemized the deeds of the Republicans since 1860 and the misdeeds of the Democrats. He rapturously told of the Republican party during the Civil War, "hopeful in defeat, confident in disaster, merciful in victory. . . ." He raged as he told of the enormities of the Democrats of the North during the war. They "formed secret societies to burn cities—to release prisoners. They shot down officers who were enforcing the draft; they declared the war unconstitutional; . . . they were the friends and allies of persons who regarded yellow fever and smallpox as weapons of civilized warfare."

Similarly, he contrasted the two parties up to 1876, scattering witticisms and anecdotes as he went. He vilified Samuel J. Tilden, the Democratic nominee for president. Tilden, an attorney, was "a kind of legal spider, watching in a web of technicalities for victims. He is a compound of cunning and heartlessness—of beak, claw, and fang. He is one of the few men who can grab a railroad and hide the deep cuts, tunnels and culverts in a single night. . . . He was never married. The Democratic Party has satisfied the longings of his heart. . . . He has courted men because women cannot vote. . . . He is a New York Democrat." The men who run New York City, "the worst governed city in the world," where "political influence is bought and sold like stocks and bonds, where nearly every contract is larceny in disguise," these are the men who have befriended and nurtured Samuel J. Tilden.[7]

Ingersoll's audience frequently interrupted him with cheers and gales of laughter. "Go on," they clamored, "Go on! More!

More!" When he finished his speech, which lasted two hours, again they cried, "More! More!" The Bangor *Whig and Courier* was unable to find words to describe the speech and its effect: "Such a speech by such a man—if there is another—must be heard; the magnetism of the speaker must be felt; the indescribable influence must be experienced, in order to appreciate his wonderful power."[8] With extraordinary versatility in emotional appeal and delivery, "he held the assemblage by a spell more potent than that of any man we have ever heard speak."

On his way back to Peoria, Ingersoll spoke at Worcester, Massachusetts, New York, Philadelphia, Pittsburgh, Columbus, and Indianapolis. Whenever he appeared, the tribute of press and audience was extravagant. When he spoke on September 10 at Cooper Union in New York, not only was the main hall filled but also the corridors and every possible room that his voice might reach. Not since the war had there been such a crush in Cooper Union. Again he spoke for two hours and again, when he was done, "there were loud calls and appeals to him to go on."[9] Chauncey Depew said that it was the greatest speech he ever heard.[10] He said later that by all odds Ingersoll was the most effective orator of the campaign.[11]

Ingersoll said in New York substantially what he said in Bangor. But in New York he paid more attention to the charge of the Democrats that the chief spokesman of the Republicans was an enemy of Christianity. His audience howled with glee when he declared: "I tell you, my friends, you do not know how easy it is to shock the religious sentiments of the Democratic Party; there is a deep and pure vein of piety running through that organization; it has been for years 'spiritually' inclined. . . . You have no idea how sorry I am that I hurt their feelings so upon the subject of religion. Why, I did not suppose that they cared anything about Christianity, but I have been deceived. I now find that they do, and I have done what no other man in the United States ever did—I have made the Democratic Party come to the defence of Christianity. I have made the Democratic party use what time they could spare between drinks in quoting Scripture. . . ."[12]

In Philadelphia, Pittsburgh, Columbus, and Indianapolis, the story was the same, tremendously enthusiastic audiences. At Indianapolis, on September 20, he spoke to Civil War veterans. A passage in this speech known as the "Vision of War" was soon to be found in most collections of readings and declamations. "The past rises before me like a dream. Again we are in the great struggle for national life. We hear the sounds of preparation—the music of boisterous drums—the silver voices of heroic bugles. . . . We see the pale cheeks of women, and the flushed faces of men; and in those assemblages we see all the dead whose dust we have covered with flowers. . . . We see them part with those they love. . . . We see the wife standing in the door with the babe in her arms—standing in the sunlight sobbing. . . . He is gone, and forever. . . .

"We see them all as they march proudly away under the flaunting flags, keeping time to the grand, wild music of war. . . .

"We are by their side on all the glory fields—in all the hospitals of pain—on all the weary marches. . . .

"We are at home when the news comes that they are dead. . . .

"The past rises before us, and we see four millions of human beings governed by the lash . . . we see the hounds tracking women through tangled swamps. . . .

"The past rises before us. . . . The broken fetters fall. . . . The wand of progress touches the auction-block. . . .

"These heroes are dead. . . . They sleep in the land they made free, under the flag they rendered stainless, under the solemn pines, the sad hemlocks, the tearful willows, and the embracing vines. . . ."[13]

From Indianapolis Ingersoll returned to Peoria, where on September 22 he was tendered the reception of a conquering hero. But he was not home long. In response to numerous requests he spoke all over Illinois, then back to Indiana, then in Ohio, Missouri, Iowa, and Wisconsin. On October 20, he spoke in Chicago, in the Exposition Building, to 10,000 people while 40,000 milled around outside. Every possible vantage point in the Exposition Building was preempted, the aisles, the frame of the huge elevator, the organ loft, even the girders. It was the largest audience that ever greeted a speaker in Chicago. Not only that, commented the Chicago *Tribune*, "such another attendance of ladies has never been known at a political meeting in Chicago."[14]

A few days after the Chicago speech, Blaine, who was campaigning in the mid-West, and his wife, Harriet, visited the Ingersolls in Peoria. The Ingersolls had recently moved into the so-called Cockle mansion which had taken two years and $50,000 to build. Of brick and stone, the house had four stories and a basement and was heated throughout with steam. It was considered the outstanding private residence in Peoria. Harriet Blaine was much impressed with the house and its appointments, but "it was as the small dust in the balance," she wrote," compared to the hospitality which was lavished upon us." She had never felt so welcome anywhere in her life.

The Ingersoll household comprised, in addition to the immediate family, Mrs. Ingersoll's mother, her sister and brother-in-law, Sue and Clinton Farrell, and their daughter, and Susan Sharkey, who had come to take care of the two Ingersoll daughters, Eva and Maud, when they were babies, and had stayed on to become a factotum about the house. It was "a varied and agreeable family," said Mrs. Blaine.

The Blaines arrived in Peoria from Chicago about six in the morning. They were met by Peoria notables and Mrs. Ingersoll, who, Harriet observed, was "dressed beautifully in a brown silk costume." Ingersoll was not in the welcoming group because he was late in returning from a speaking engagement. Breakfast was to be at seven, but it was put off until the host should come. After two hours he had not come; the breakfast, however, had, and a plenteous one it was—"three kinds of meat," reports Harriet, "not to mention fried oysters, potatoes in different styles, cakes, etc." A problem arose as to who should preside at the servings since Ingersoll was not there; Clint Farrell was supposed to, but he was taken with a fit of nervousness and fled. Blaine was asked to take over, but he said he never served at home and anyhow he was so hungry he was sure he could not hold out for more than three or four plates. Enough of this nonsense, was the response of Susan Sharkey, who took over in no uncertain fashion, piling every plate high with portions of everything without asking for preferences. As they were finishing breakfast, Ingersoll arrived. "Nothing," said Harriet, "could exceed the warmth of his welcome."

All day the house was thronged with people and every man who came in wanted to be introduced to Harriet. In the evening a great crowd gathered in front of the house and serenaded the Blaines. James went out on the veranda and acknowledged the demonstration; Harriet was called for, but in spite of Ingersoll's urging to make an appearance, she would not do so, "I need not say that for this I was too modest."[15] Ingersoll appeared for her.

"HAYES IS A COWARD . . ."

THE campaign of 1876 was one of the most exciting and bitterly fought contests in the history of American politics.

The day after the election, November 8, was a day filled with conflicting reports of the outcome. Most of the morning newspapers announced a Tilden victory; a few, including the *New York Times* and the New York *Herald,* said the result was in doubt. While Tilden had a majority of 250,000 in the popular vote, he might lose in the electoral count. In the morning the *Times* gave Tilden 184 electoral votes and Hayes 181, with Florida (4 votes) doubtful. In the afternoon the *Times* added Florida to the Hayes column. That night the Republican National Committee announced the election of Hayes by a majority of one electoral vote. This count included for Hayes Florida, South Carolina, and Louisiana. But the Democrats claimed these states for Tilden. Soon complete returns for South Carolina gave the state clearly to Hayes. Florida and Louisiana, however, appeared to have gone for Tilden. Then the Republican controlled canvassing boards in Florida and Louisiana, alleging frauds and irregularities, threw out votes for Tilden and produced majorities for Hayes. Oregon also came into the picture, one man, it was contended, having been illegally designated an elector.

For four months the dispute raged, the country actually on the verge of civil war. Finally an Electoral Commission composed of five senators, five representatives, and five supreme court justices—eight Republicans and seven Democrats—voted eight to seven in each case that the disputed electoral votes of South Carolina, Florida, Louisiana, and Oregon belonged to Hayes. Thus, at four o'clock the morning of March 2, the President of the Senate made ready to announce to a joint meeting of both houses of Congress that Hayes had been declared President of the United States.

No one was happier at the outcome than Robert Ingersoll. He sought and expected either an appointment to the Cabinet or to a ministerial post. He and his wife had arrived in Washington January 14 and stayed there, at Clark's home, until the first week of April. Every so often they would go up to the Capitol to see how the election proceedings were going. On February 20, both Ingersoll families were in the House gallery when the decision of the Electoral Commission on Louisiana was announced. They could hardly keep from jumping up and down and proposing three cheers.[1] But it was a sobering thought that Florida and Oregon were yet to be considered by the Commission. Ingersoll wrote, "In a certain sense my future is all depending upon what will happen in the next few days."[2]

Ingersoll also pondered the possibility that Hayes, if he were declared elected, would ignore him altogether because the religious people could be counted on to do their utmost "to block the wheels of Fortune's car."[3] If that should happen, well, he would take it without a whimper. By March 3 he still had no inkling of what Hayes might do for him, or, indeed, for anyone except Senator John Sherman of Ohio, who had just been appointed Secretary of the Treasury. Ingersoll was not too happy about his own efforts for office because, as he put it, "Washington is filled with gentlemen willing to take any office within the gift of the President."[4] But he was aiming high, the post of minister to England or something comparable. March 8 found Ingersoll in the doldrums because Hayes seemed about to ignore for Cabinet positions "all his real friends" in favor of Democrats, and Southern Democrats at that, and even worse, Southern Democrats who had served in the Confederate armies, men like General Joseph E. Johnston of Virginia and David M. Key of Tennessee.[5] Blaine and Morton were also upset over the situation and asked Ingersoll to call on Hayes to see what was up. He did have a conference with Hayes and "advised him to be their friend."[6] He urged him to forget the past, that is, Blaine's dubious role as a broker in the Little Rock and Fort Smith Railroad fiasco. Hayes "pretended to accede," said Ingersoll, but the next day reliable reports had it that the President was still bent on appointing Democrats. "Well, just my luck! It always was that way."[7]

Ingersoll bitterly ruminated that it would have been much better if Tilden had been elected, at least he could not have destroyed the cohesion of the Republican party, a thing that Hayes was evidently going to do. The more Ingersoll thought about the situation, the angrier he got, so angry in fact that he resolved to give a lecture in New York on March 14, in which he would take sides against Hayes and "denounce the whole thing." The New York papers got wind of Ingersoll's intention and gave him a great deal of publicity, favorable and unfavorable. Hayes and his advisers were worried and Ingersoll was requested to see the President again. This time Ingersoll was persuaded that the President did not mean to form "an alliance with the rebels at the expense of his friends," that if he appointed a Southern Democrat or two, it was for the sole purpose of taking a step toward the reconciliation of the South and the North.[8] Thus the lecture, "Eight to Seven," which Ingersoll delivered in New York was in support of the Administration.

Ingersoll still expected a good appointment. Some concrete recognition of his services was due. Hayes considered appointing him to the important Louisiana commission which was to go to Louisiana to try to settle the acute differences between the people of the state and the carpetbagger-Negro regime. But he thought better of it when he began to receive letters like this one, from William D. Porter of the law firm of Porter and Bainbridge: "I believe the appointment of such a man, who disregards and scoffs at the most sacred things, would shake the confidence of all Christian men in your Administration of which we now have such great hopes, and, for which we offer such fervent prayers."[9] Hayes was a religious and a politic man. He decided not to offend the Christians.

Later in the year, in November, Ingersoll was under consideration for the German mission. Hayes and Secretary of State William Evarts had invited the Illinois Republican members in Congress to submit their choice for the post. Unanimously the Illinois Congressmen chose Ingersoll.[10] When asked if he would consent to have his name proposed for the mission, he said, yes. At the time he was touring the East with his lectures, "Progress," "The Liberty of Man, Woman and Child," and "Ghosts" and was causing hubbub among the orthodox. Therefore, since Hayes had turned him down before on religious grounds, Ingersoll was pretty sure that he would not dare give him the Berlin post now. Very well, if the price of saying what he thought was to lose the appointment, he would gladly pay it. On November 11 Ingersoll wrote that he was going to give his scheduled lectures in Utica, Syracuse, and Albany before he went to Washington to see the President or the Secretary of State. By the time he reached Washington, November 16, the press both lay and religious had denounced the proposed appointment. The New York correspondent of the Montreal *Witness,* calling Ingersoll "the blatant and offensive atheist," asked the people to think of the "deep, deep disgrace of being represented in the German Empire" by him. "A great disgrace" threatened the country was the echo of the Brooklyn *Catholic World.* The Boston *Congregationalist* thought Ingersoll was "one of the last men to be appointed to any such representative position." The Boston *Post* said: "The religious community rises as one man to demand that he shall not be sent to Berlin to represent a Christian people."

The day after his arrival in Washington, Ingersoll, with Senator Oglesby of Illinois, went to see Secretary Evarts. Evarts was cold and evasive, or, in Ingersoll's words, he was "A dirty dog, without even good manners."[11] With much circumlocution he merely gave Ingersoll to understand that he was "under consideration" for the Berlin post. "Under consideration" was he? Well, Evarts could take someone else "under consideration." Wrote Ingersoll, "Hayes is a coward, and most of his cabinet are like him."[12] If only Blaine had been elected president, things would have been different. Only Blaine could destroy the incubus of hypocrisy and cant which had settled upon the Administration. Wait until 1880.

"MY REVIEWERS REVIEWED"

RETURNING to Peoria in April, 1877, Ingersoll set about arranging the itinerary of his first transcontinental lecture tour. At this time he was his own manager. He prepared his own advertising materials and negotiated lecture contracts. He did, however, have an advance agent who perfected arrangements along the scheduled itinerary. If the contract stipulated a flat rate for a lecture, the minimum was $200; the rate above this depended on the number of people in a locality. But Ingersoll usually allowed the other contracting party to choose between a flat rate and a percentage of the gross receipts. He always stipulated that the admission fee should be not less than fifty cents. When he was on tour he lectured at least three times a week, making in the early years of his career $200 to $2400 an appearance, in the later years, $400 to $7000. The famous impresario of the lecture platform, James Redpath, later one of Ingersoll's managers, once said that Ingersoll was the "best card in America."

The tour of 1877 began in the Mid-West states of Missouri,

Iowa, and Wisconsin and went west to California by way of Nebraska, Kansas, Colorado, Wyoming, and Nevada; then back by roughly the same route, a different lecture at a second appearance, to Illinois, thence through Indiana and Ohio to New York and New England states. Mainly, Ingersoll presented "The Liberty of Man, Woman and Child" or "Ghosts"; occasionally, "Progress" or "8 to 7." The political lecture aroused less enthusiasm than the others. The San Francisco *Chronicle,* for instance, noted after Ingersoll had given "8 to 7" on June 14 that the reception accorded him "was not so hearty as on his last appearance . . . the applause not being so enthusiastic or frequent as on the occasion of his irreverent utterances."

While the press generally ascribed Ingersoll's drawing power on this his first tour to his "plumed knight" speech and campaign speeches, it was also aware of another reason for his popularity. An amazing change had come over the people. They were tolerant of ideas which ten years back they would have abominated. The *Daily Evening Post* of San Francisco commented that the crush to hear Ingersoll was indisputable evidence that the people had become liberal in their thinking.[1] "Whither are we drifting?" asked the San Francisco *Daily Examiner* as it pondered the popularity of a heretic lecturer.[2] The people "have been exposed to the prevalent skeptical atmosphere of the age," said the Sacramento *Daily Union,* and Ingersoll "has organized and formulated their drifting doubts."[3]

Of Ingersoll's lectures up to this time, "Ghosts" was the boldest attack upon religion. Although "The Liberty of Man, Woman and Child" was a step beyond "Progress" in assailing orthodoxy, it contained much matter, devoid of religious bearing, on the proper relations of husband and wife, mother and father and children. Even the orthodox could listen to "Liberty" with little distress of conscience. Who could object to Ingersoll's strictures on "the cross man," "the stingy man," "the boss," in the family? Who could not forget what he said about religion when he said: "Think of making your wife a beggar! Think of her having to ask you every day for a dollar, or for two dollars, or for fifty cents! . . . Oh, I tell you if you have but a dollar in the world, and you have got to spend it, spend it like a king; spend it as though it were a dry leaf and you the owner of unbounded forests! I had rather be a beggar and spend my last dollar like a king, than be a king and spend my money like a beggar."

"Ghosts" was another matter. It was an unrelieved assault upon past and present faith in the ghosts of the unknown and the unknowable and upon the church that infallibly made known the messages of the ghosts. This was "terribly shocking,"[4] said the Des Moines *Leader;* "a nauseous dose," the San Francisco *Mail;*[5] "obnoxious . . . blood-curdling," the Cheyenne *Daily Leader.*[6] Yet when Ingersoll lectured in Des Moines "the most orthodox" by the amount of their applause,[7] seemed to be on his side; he was "tumultously applauded" in San Francisco;[8] he had "charm . . . indescribable" in Cheyenne.[9]

In explaining Ingersoll's power, the press commented much on his qualities as a speaker. His physical appearance: "He is of splendid figure, open countenance and honest expression"—Denver *Tribune;*[10] "He is in the full prime and vigor of life, with a ruddy complexion, a keen sparkling eye, broad high forehead, made higher by partial baldness, a smoothshaven face and an open, frank countenance."—The *Daily Nonpareil,* Council Bluffs, Iowa.[11]

His delivery: "a genial smile, a voice of great compass . . . fine intonations . . . graceful, yet emphatic gestures."—*Evening Wisconsin,* Milwaukee.[12] "He is offhand, informal, old-fashioned, but full of surprises. He starts in a capering boyishness, gamboling and cavorting, to end in a burst of fiery earnestness." —*The Inter Ocean,* Chicago.[13] "He bubbles over and gushes, and faints and thunders; arpeggio, mezzo, pianissimo, mezzo profundo—staccato!"—The *Daily Leader,* Cheyenne.[14]

His sincerity: "We believe that every person, last night, feels in his heart that the speaker believed it was true."[15]—*Gazette,* Burlington, Iowa. He has "impregnable firmness of conviction."[16]—*The Sentinel,* Milwaukee.

His humor: "The incisiveness of his wit, the irresistible ludicrousness of his similes. . . . We have never heard a speaker who could so easily excite his audience to laughter."—Sacramento *Daily Union*.[17] He was so full of fun that "one laughed in spite of himself" at "the irreverent way he treated the holy things of our mind."—Des Moines *Leader*.[18]

His language and fluency: At times there is "such a Southern love air in the poetic peopling of the fellow's worlds, that men's judgments are ravished and the harem-like honey of his words melt them into forgiveness or lull them to forgetfulness."[19]—Des Moines *Leader*. "One great secret of Ingersoll's success is that he does not aim too high. He said not a word that was not perfectly intelligible to the great mass of the audience. He is eminently simple, direct and straightforward with the dash of humor and flavor of quaint idiom which are always popular with American audiences."—Boston *Traveller*.[20]

Naturally Ingersoll provoked a strong reaction in religious circles. The clergy could not ignore an infidel lecturer who was so popular. The *California Christian Advocate* lamented that pulpit and press had to give Ingersoll so much attention, but under the circumstances, the magazine conceded, what else could they do?

Ingersoll no sooner arrived in San Francisco, the morning of May 19, than reporters and photographers streamed into his hotel room. And delegations from other California towns were there with invitations to lecture. He stayed in California six weeks. At the end of the first week he wrote, "I have stirred up a hornet's nest on this Coast. And the preachers are making mince meat of me. The vials of wrath are being poured out and all I can say is 'Let 'em pour.' "[21] By the end of the fourth week, so many of the clergy had poured out their wrath that he got up a special lecture, "My Reviewers Reviewed," which he first delivered in San Francisco, June 27. A sell-out audience in the Grand Opera House listened to him for two hours and forty minutes and netted him $2300. The following day Ingersoll wrote, "We had a magnificent meeting last night. . . . I made it hot for the dear old stupid theologians. I never made a better speech in my life."[22]

One part of "My Reviewers Reviewed" prompted the New

York *Observer,* a Presbyterian organ, to challenge Ingersoll to put up or shut up. A San Francisco minister had said that the grand test of the principles of infidels and atheists was the deathbed, that both Voltaire and Paine had failed miserably to pass the test, their last days being "too harrowing for recital." In reply, Ingersoll offered any clergyman in San Francisco one thousand dollars in gold if he could prove "that the death of Voltaire was not as peaceful as the coming of the dawn" and another thousand if he could prove that Paine died in spiritual agony, "frightened to death by God." On July 19, the editor of the *Observer,* Irenaeus Prime, wrote: "Let the Colonel deposit the money with any honest man, and the absurd story, as he terms it, shall be shown to be an ower true tale. But he won't do it. His talk is Infidel, 'buncombe' and nothing more."[23] Ingersoll answered that he would deposit the money, subject to Prime's order, in the First National Bank of Peoria if Prime agreed to present his evidence as to Paine at the end of ninety days giving prior notice of the time and place of taking depositions. Ingersoll would agree to the same conditions and, further, would allow Prime an extra thirty days to prepare the last say. The evidence was to be presented before an arbitration board of three members, one to be selected by Prime, one by Ingersoll, and the third by the two already selected. Their decision would be final. Each party should deposit a bond in the amount of two thousand dollars to guarantee the payment of the victor's expenses. Ingersoll made a separate but identical proposition on Voltaire. The *Observer,* however, limited itself to Paine.

In the issue of September 27, the *Observer* stated that they had not challenged Ingersoll on the grounds specified in his formal proposition, which were: Did Paine in his last days (1) admit the Bible to be an inspired book, (2) or recant his infidel opinions, (3) or regret that he had repudiated the Bible, (4) or call upon Jesus Christ in any sense whatsoever. They had challenged him on what he had said in San Francisco. Ingersoll now charged the *Observer* with evading the issue because his utterances in "My Reviewers Reviewed" had the same sense as the stated grounds of his proposition. The *Observer* asserted that they would prove "not only that Tom Paine died a drunken, cowardly, and beastly death, but that for many years previous, and up to that event he lived a drunken and beastly life." They would also prove that Paine, wrecked in mind and body, was ready one minute to call upon God and Christ for mercy and the next to blaspheme. The *Observer* introduced much testimony of witnesses who had visited or attended Paine during his last days.

The lawyer in Ingersoll now came to the fore. He discredited the *Observer's* witnesses and cited fifteen of his own, including Paine himself, to prove that Paine did not change his views and that he died in tranquillity. In a rejoinder, November 1, the *Observer* stated that they had gone into the details of the unpleasant subject because of the numerous calls for information from all over the country and because of the attempts of infidels like Ingersoll and certain Unitarian ministers of New York and Brooklyn "to revive and honor the memory of one whose friends would honor him most by suffering his name to sink into oblivion." The *Observer* brought in additional evidence, not to show that Paine recanted—that they had never held—but that he was a shameless sot, a moral degenerate, a stranger to soap and water, who died as he had lived, uttering blasphemies and abandoned of God. The new evidence in a sense was just what Ingersoll wanted; it proved conclusively that Paine on his deathbed did not recant.

In his final letter on the subject Ingersoll upbraided the *Observer* for failing to adhere to the issues that had started the dispute and for flagrantly slandering the defenseless dead, but he was gratified that the *Observer* had been compelled to say, "Paine died a blaspheming infidel." The *Observer* did not reply.

Part Three:
WASHINGTON

WASHINGTON

INGERSOLL'S visits to Washington, in 1877, made him consider living there. He had gone as far as he could in Peoria, where "too much has to be done for too little money." Washing offered advantages in law and business that Peoria could not approach, to say nothing of advantages political. Besides, and this influenced him greatly, his beloved brother lived in Washington.

There were several other aspects of the city which appealed to Ingersoll. "The streets are smooth as floors and clean as parlors," he wrote. Also there was a great deal of social activity; and people appeared to be enjoying themselves. His wife and daughters, who were with him on his visits to Washington, were made much of at festivities in their honor.

In mid-December Ingersoll decided to move to Washington. He wrote Clint and Sue Farrell of his decision and urged them to come along. He advised Clint to give up his spice business in Peoria, which was not doing too well and had no future. Clint could work for him in Washington as a kind of secretarial partner who among other things would take charge of the publication and distribution of his lectures. Ingersoll had no doubt of his own money-making prospects; he would make enough to take care of everybody and assure Clint of a good future. Sell the spice business and become known as the "Infidel Bookseller."[1]

In January, 1878, the Ingersolls found a house easily large enough to accommodate themselves, the Farrells, Mrs. Ingersoll's mother, and Susan Sharkey. It was close to the White

House, on Lafayette Square. Recently constructed, of brick and brownstone, the house had four stories and a basement and large, square rooms. Plenty of room for everybody. Maud, the younger Ingersoll daughter, now thirteen, and Eva, fourteen, could sing and play the Steinway all day long if they wanted to and not bother anybody. The little girl of the Farrells could have her own playroom. And Grandmother Parker could have her own room too; "I want to take care of her," said Ingersoll, "I want to make her life happy and sweet."

Meanwhile, for legal services rendered, Ingersoll was given a pass by the Cunard Line which was good for a round-trip to Europe for both the Ingersoll and Farrell families. The Farrells could not go, the Ingersolls went in August. They stayed about a month in the British Isles and France. Ingersoll noted that the Royal Family treated them with utmost coolness— "They pretend not to know that we are in town."[2] And no wonder. He had denounced king as much as bishop and priest for attempting to shackle the minds of men. In speaking of "crowned mediocrity" in "The Liberty of Man, Woman and Child" he had compared George Eliot and Queen Victoria as follows: "The Queen is clothed in garments given her by blind fortune and unreasoning chance, while George Eliot wears robes of glory woven in the loom of her own genius." But Ingersoll was miffed by the Royal indifference and said, "All right! we will get even with them when we get home."

The main attractions of their stay in the British Isles were Shakespeare, Ingersoll's "Bible," and Burns, his "hymn-book." They visited every possible point associated with the two. With particular tenderness and reverence Ingersoll wandered over the Burns region. Burns, too, had castigated orthodoxy and political and religious tyranny; he, too, had exalted human love and the home. When Ingersoll stood in the humble cottage at Ayr, where Burns was born, he was moved to write a poem of tribute. A photographic enlarged copy of the original with marginal portraits of Ingersoll and Burns hangs in the cottage. The following is the first of three stanzas:

Though Scotland boasts a thousand names,
  Of patriot, king and peer,
The noblest, grandest of them all,
  Was loved and cradled here.
Here lived the gentle peasant-prince,
  The loving cotter-king,
Compared with whom the greatest lord
  Is but a titled thing.

When Ingersoll returned to the United States he added a lecture on Burns to his repertoire.

From the fall of 1878 to the late spring of 1879, he did little else but lecture. He left the law business to his brother, with whom he was in partnership. In addition to "Robert Burns" he had four other new lectures, "Skulls," "Hell," "Some Mistakes of Moses," and "Hard Times and the Way Out." The least popular of these was "Robert Burns." The Cincinnati *Daily Enquirer* commented, "The fact of the matter is that people want to hear Bob prove that there is no hell."[3] They were not interested in a relatively innocuous panegyric of a poet. But they packed Pike's Opera House in Cincinnati when "Hell" was the subject and thundered their approval. Ingersoll got the same response in New York when, as he put it, he "gave hell hell."[4] One hour before the time set for his appearance in Chickering Hall there was standing room only and ticket speculators outside "got any price they chose to ask."

The lecture "Skulls" contained about the same matter as "The Liberty of Man, Woman and Child." The title came from a row of skulls, which Ingersoll had seen, showing man's evolution from the Neanderthal age to the present. "Hell" was a variation of "My Reviewers Reviewed" with the names of the California "reviewers" largely omitted. It was the nucleus of one of Ingersoll's most famous lectures, "Some Mistakes of Moses." This was an exhaustive, satirical treatment of the Biblical story of the creation, of Noah and the Flood, of the trials and tribulations of Moses and the Children of Israel, and of the morality of Jehovah as recorded in the Pentateuch.

Ingersoll was at times criticized for stressing in his attacks the literal interpretation of the Bible and for ignoring the view that the Bible was the record of the religious experience of a people advancing to higher concepts of morality and deity. A long time elapsed between the Decalogue and the Beatitudes. But the men who made this criticism were exponents of the so-called "higher criticism" which was a virtual novelty in theology.

When Ingersoll delivered "Some Mistakes of Moses" in Chicago, the clergy swarmed to the attack, hardly indicative that he was striking at a dead theology. Of the few who thought he was, Robert Collyer was a Unitarian whom the Chicago Presbytery pronounced a heretic. And David Swing was tried by that Presbytery for heresy. Swing charged Ingersoll with "concentrations upon minor points" yet such points were major in his own heresy. That Collyer would misread the pertinence of Ingersoll's attacks might be expected from his statement, "I look upon the Old Testament as a rotting tree."[5] Few clergymen could say that. The Reverend Dr. Ryder even as he attacked Ingersoll for a narrow interpretation of the Bible admitted that that kind of interpretation abounded in the church.[6] Dr. Thomas, a Methodist minister, said, "It may be that we have claimed too much for the Bible, and thereby given not a little occasion for such men as Mr. Ingersoll to appear at the other extreme, denying too much."[7]

Dr. Thomas' statement aptly puts the case for and against Ingersoll. He did go to extremes. He did go over the Bible with a fine-toothed comb and treat his findings as he did the miracle of the manna in the wilderness: "This manna was a very popular thing. It would melt in the sun, and yet they could cook it by seething and baking. One would as soon think of frying snow or of boiling icicles. But this manna had another remarkable quality. No matter how much or little any person gathered, he would have an exact omer; if he gathered more, it would shrink to that amount, and if he gathered less, it would swell to that amount. What a magnificent substance manna would be with which to make a currency—shrinking and swelling according to the great laws of supply and demand."[8] But if Ingersoll searched the Bible for inaccuracies and oddities and railed at the letter of it, the point remains he was not attacking straw men. Literalism in theology was the rule, not the exception.

"THE WORLD LOOKS DARK TO ME"

A RELENTLESS leitmotiv in the temperament of Ingersoll was an intense, even morbid, awareness of death. When he was but twenty-four he wrote to John, "It is very strange how long we have been permitted to live and I am almost afraid to open every letter I get for fear it say that some one of us is dead. . . ."[1] He had had little of the stable home life that gives to children a sense of security. Never for long in one place until he moved to Peoria and with little financial prospect until Shawneetown, he had had good reason to suppose that the hazards of life outweighed the supports. Basically insecure, he became particularly sensitive to the ultimate insecurity, death. Even after he was married and was established professionally and financially, he would often write as he did on January 1, 1868, to Clark: "I cannot bear to think of another year gone, that I am one year nearer, *nothing!* One year nearer the end. One year nearer some great sorrow. One year nearer the death of the ones I love. One year nearer all that I dread. . . . One year nearer the horrible—the terrible—the *Unknown.*"

At 1:30 A.M., May 31, 1879, death hit Ingersoll hard. About 9:30 P.M., May 30, Clark was stricken with a heart attack. Robert reached his bedside at ten. For two hours Clark was in great agony. Then he said, as the pain ebbed, "I am better now." And he died. "He, as the rest of us," wrote Robert to John on June 1, "mistook the approach of death for the return of health." On June 3, the day after the funeral, Robert wrote the Farrells, "The curtain has fallen on the deepest tragedy of my life."

The funeral aroused intense public interest because of the prominence of the Ingersolls and because of the character of the obsequies. Robert conducted the services. He and Clark had decided that upon the death of one, the other should officiate at the funeral. The ceremony took place at Clark's residence in the late afternoon of June 2. It was noted by the Chicago *Tribune* that more distinguished people were present than at any other similar occasion since the obsequies of Salmon P. Chase, Secretary of the Treasury under Lincoln. But the absence of the clergy gave the occasion a "special desolation." Everyone wondered what Ingersoll would say and how he would act. The ceremony was simply his reading of his tribute to Clark. As he began to read, his eyes filled with tears. He tried to hide the tears by putting on his glasses. He said a few words more and then broke down bowing his head upon Clark's coffin. Only after several minutes passed was he able to continue and then his voice was so choked with emotion that he could hardly be heard. He finished the eulogy sobbing.

He said: "The loved and loving brother, husband, father, friend, died where manhood's morning almost touches noon, and while the shadows still were falling toward the west. . . . While yet in love with life and raptured with the world, he passed to silence and pathetic dust. . . . He climbed the heights, and left all superstitions far below. . . . He loved the beautiful . . . sided with the weak. . . . He was a worshiper of liberty. . . . He believed that happiness is the only good. . . .

Life is a narrow vale between the cold and barren peaks of two eternities. . . . From the voiceless lips of the unreplying dead there comes no word; but in the night of death hope sees a star and listening love can hear the rustle of a wing. . . ."[2]

"Pagan Eloquence" was what the Washington *Star* called it in an editorial on the subject, which drew so many reactions that the *Star* wrote another. The pith of the editorials was that Christianity so glorifies death that after a man dies his influence upon the living continues unabated. But death to the Pagan means that the memory and influence of the deceased "have only the life of the reflected rays of the sun that has set."

Many thought that Ingersoll's tribute at one point contained an intimation of a belief in immortality: "but in the night of death hope sees a star and listening love can hear the rustle of a wing." These were the words of Ingersoll's agony. He may have found relief in the phantasm of the words but only while he said them. The day after Clark's funeral he wrote, "My poor brother lies asleep in that silent chamber that has no window toward the East."[3]

Henry Ward Beecher read the funeral speech to his congregation at Plymouth Church, Brooklyn. He called it "one of the most exquisite yet one of the most sad and mournful sermons that I ever read." But he had no doubt that Ingersoll's brother now "saw in the eternal world things which he had counted but shadow there."

When Clark died, he left much legal business unfinished, which Robert had to attend to. Like Robert he made plenty of money but, like him too, he spent plenty; he left his family in straitened circumstances. Robert came to their rescue not only by turning over to them the fees from the litigation which he finished but also by his own regular contributions which he kept up for years.

There were many other instances of Ingersoll's generosity. He helped his brother John, who was practicing medicine in Wisconsin but not doing too well, and when John died, he helped his children. He often rendered legal service to the needy free of charge. He gave benefit lectures for a variety of causes: the G.A.R., the Hebrew Orphan's Asylum of San Francisco, kindergartens in Harlem, the Actor's Fund, the relief of tornado-stricken Fort Smith, Arkansas, and for two children left orphans. He gave freely of his time and money to such organizations as the New York State Freethinkers' Association, the Manhattan Liberal Club, the American Secular Union, and the Ethical Society. For years his charities ran from $25,000 to $40,000 annually.

By 1879 many organizations of liberals and freethinkers had come into being. The National Liberal League, of which Ingersoll became vice-president in 1877, held its first convention, in Philadelphia, in July, 1876. The goal was the complete secularization of the state. To attain it, the League sought to abolish Sunday laws, civil recognition of feast days and thanksgivings, religious worship in public institutions, and teaching the Bible in public schools. It championed universal education, universal suffrage, and equal civil rights for all. At the second convention of the League in Rochester, New York, in October, 1877, which was the first Ingersoll attended and at which he was elected vice-president, the same platform was enunciated. The following year, at Syracuse, the Liberal Leaguers scrutinized the Comstock laws which prohibited the circulation through the mails of immoral and obscene matter. The majority were in favor of a resolution to demand the repeal of the laws but a vigorous minority, of which Ingersoll was one, favored only an amendment to the laws to protect from arrest and punishment those who expressed honest and conscientious opinions. Earlier in the year Ingersoll's name was first on a petition having 70,000 signers which asked for repeal or modification, but he signed it with the express understanding that he was for modification only. He and the other minority members at Syracuse were against repeal because they were for the outlawry of immoral and obscene matter, though they recognized the problem of defining such matter. After heated sessions, the convention decided not to take a stand on the issue at that time but to wait until the next year.

Anthony Comstock, however, had no trouble in defining immoral and obscene matter. It included advertisements of abortions, contraceptive information, erotic pictures and stories, serious but unconventional treatments of sex, love, and marriage, and free-thought materials. This sin-conscious man had zealously lobbied through Congress the postal laws of 1873, which strengthened the laws of 1865 and 1872. Even under the old laws, as chief scavenger of the Committee for the Suppression of Vice under the auspices of the Y.M.C.A., he had caused many a trafficker in dubious literature to be brought before the bar of justice. With the passage of the new laws he was appointed Special Agent of the Post Office and then indeed he became a man to reckon with.

In November, 1877, armed with warrants, Comstock arrested two freethinkers, Ezra Harvey Heywood and De Robigne M. Bennett, on the charge of sending obscene matter through the mails. Heywood, who lived in Princeton, Massachusetts, had been a fervent abolitionist and later he devoted himself to labor reform, temperance, and woman suffrage. Though married, he advocated free love. From his press in Princeton he issued a wide assortment of pamphlets. Bennett lived in New York, wrote prolifically, and founded and edited *The Truth Seeker,* a free-thought weekly.

Specifically, Heywood was arrested for mailing his pamphlet, *Cupid's Yokes,* and a medical book, Trall's *Sexual Physiology;* Bennet, for mailing his tract, *An Open Letter to Jesus Christ,* and a scientific treatise, *How Do Marsupials Propagate?,* by H. B. Bradford, a clergyman of Enon Valley, Pennsylvania. On December 15, 1877 Ingersoll wrote to Postmaster General McKay protesting Bennett's arrest. He enclosed the two publications in question and insisted that while there might be an offense of good taste there was no obscenity. He also questioned the propriety of allowing agents like Comstock to go around in the name of morality harassing and arresting whomever they wished. Comstock had visited Bennett's printers, threatening them with arrest if they continued to print *The Truth Seeker.* And he had tried to coerce the American News Company to stop selling it. Largely through Ingersoll's efforts, the case against Bennett was dismissed.

The case against Heywood took a different course. To begin with, the title of his pamphlet, *Cupid's Yokes,* was unfortunate; then there were the many rugged phrases about love and marriage such as "legalized prostitution" and "relics of barbarism." The work was written with utmost sincerity. To Comstock it was "too foul for description;" to Ingersoll, who had no use for free love tenets, it was "not obscene, but simply silly."[1] In June, 1878, Heywood was convicted and sentenced to prison for two years. Ingersoll was not party to the ensuing agitation to secure a presidential pardon—which was granted—because Heywood's views on love and marriage were so far from his that despite the principle at stake he could not rise to the man's defense.

When the Liberal League met again, in September, 1879, in Cincinnati, they had provocation aplenty to deplore the Comstock laws. Bennett had been arrested again, in December, 1878, for mailing obscene matter. The following March he was convicted and sentenced to thirteen months hard labor in the Albany Penitentiary. Bennett had been ardent in the pages of *The Truth Seeker* for the repeal of the Comstock laws and the pardon of Heywood. He had also been extremely caustic with Comstock. What anguish it was to Comstock that Bennett had escaped justice once. And then to be made a fool of by the scoundrel! In desperation Comstock devised a stratagem. He wrote Bennett an illiterate letter, signed "G. Brackett," asking him, for the enclosed three and a half dollars, to send several tracts, one of which was "Cupid's something or other."[2] Bennett complied, and his arrest followed.

The trial was held in the United States Circuit Court of New York City, Judge Charles L. Benedict presiding. After the verdict, Bennett appealed to the District Court, but the conviction was sustained. In June he began serving his sentence. It was then that he asked Ingersoll to intercede for him with President Hayes. Ingersoll said he would. Much as he disapproved of *Cupid's Yoke,* he saw no obscenity in it. Moreover, Bennett himself had stated that he did not endorse its ideas. Again, Bennett was convinced, and so was Ingersoll, that the real cause of the persecution was Bennett's theological views which "do not harmonize with current opinions."[3]

One happening, however, almost put an end to Ingersoll's intervention. An indignation meeting on the Bennett case was held in Boston, in June. Ingersoll had been consulted about having the meeting and he had opposed it. He knew that among the people who would attend would be many with whom he did not care to identify himself, the free lovers and those whose actual business was in pornography. But the projectors of the meeting went ahead with their plans. The day after it, Ingersoll noticed in a newspaper account that a letter had been read, purporting to have been written by him. Angrily he wrote T. B. Wakeman, a prominent New York freethinker and Bennett's attorney, asking about the letter and stating, "If that matter cannot be set right by those who put the false statement afloat, I must correct it myself, whatever the effect on Mr. Bennett may be."[4] He also stated, "I dislike to be mixed or classed with persons whose ideas and principles do not in any way accord with mine." Wakeman's explanation, not known, must have been satisfactory, for Ingersoll replied, "All right about the letter."[5]

This matter cleared up, Ingersoll went to see Hayes. He had a long talk with him and told him that he could not afford to endorse the outrage of Bennett's conviction and imprisonment and that he must issue a pardon. Hayes refused to interfere. Ingersoll was positive that Hayes himself did not consider *Cupid's Yokes* an obscene pamphlet but that he would not act because (1) five Federal judges of the District Court of New York had ruled on the appeal of Bennett that the pamphlet was obscene and because (2) he was being flooded with letters and telegrams from clergymen, church members, and Sunday School pupils protesting a pardon.[6]

Ingersoll now decided to go into the case intensively. The trial of Bennett had had several questionable aspects. Judge Benedict had ruled out the testimony of certain scholars and authors who found no obscenity in *Cupid's Yokes*. He had also ruled out the similar testimony of publishers and bookdealers. Again, although the pamphlet as an entirety was the basis of the indictment, the court ruled that the whole of it was not at issue and allowed the prosecuting attorney to confine the attention of the jury to certain marked sections. The court's definition of obscenity as anything that tended to excite impure thoughts in the minds of the young and the inexperienced was to Ingersoll ridiculously vague, applying with equal force to the Bible, Shakespeare, and *Cupid's Yokes.* It was also Ingersoll's opinion that when the Judge upon request sent this definition to the jury room he should have seen to it that the initials of the respective attorneys thereon did not convey the impression to the jury that the defense attorney accepted the definition.

Ingersoll laid these features of the trial before the President. He also made the point that the trial should have been held in the Federal District Court rather than in the Circuit Court.[7] Thus the case might have come up before the United States Supreme Court. As it was, the Circuit Court of Appeals could, and did, refuse to allow the case to go to the highest tribunal. Ingersoll also presented the President a brief on the law of pardons.

For a while Ingersoll was confident that Bennett would receive a pardon. But a talk he had with the President, on July 22, set him right. He began to think that he was not the best man to represent Bennett. More than ever, Hayes was being pressed by the religious people not to grant a pardon. Mrs. Hayes was under pressure too. Ingersoll wrote to Bennett, "A great many ladies have written to Mrs. Hayes setting forth that you are an extremely bad man."[8] And it did not help that the man who was Bennett's advocate was the nation's top infidel, as odious to most of the letter writers as Bennett himself. But Hayes was embarrassed. He had pardoned Heywood, who both wrote and mailed *Cupid's Yokes;* he could hardly do less for the man who only mailed it. He remembered, however, the storm of protest in the wake of Heywood's pardon. He was accused of capitulating to liberals, infidels, free lovers, and smut dealers.

One of the chief sources of pressure upon Hayes was the powerful Society for the Suppression of Vice. It narrowly averted deep disgrace, however, when information came to light that its president, Samuel Colgate, of soap and Vaseline fame, had published and mailed a pamphlet which, in extolling the virtues of Vaseline, called attention to its value as a contraceptive. Bennett's *Truth Seeker* exposed the horror. Ingersoll wrote to Bennett for the evidence so that he could give it to Hayes.[9] It was given to Hayes, but not before Colgate and Company withdrew the pamphlet. This indication of Colgate's right thinking was enough to save the day for the forces of purity.

The case for Bennett now took a distinctly bad turn. Comstock got hold of some indiscreet letters which Bennett, long married, had written a woman. These letters greatly disturbed Ingersoll. He wrote to Elizur Wright, the president of the National Liberal League, that he hoped Bennett could satisfactorily account for the letters; "if he cannot, had he as many mouths as Hydra, that corruption will shut them all."[10] And Ingersoll wanted no truck with a man who held marriage lightly. He wrote Francis Abbot, president of the Liberal League before Wright, that Bennett was no friend of his, that they had not even been on good terms in business matters affecting the publication of Ingersoll's lectures, and that the only reason he had entered the case was his conviction that Bennett had been wronged.[11] Now he was not so sure. In an interview in the Chicago *Times* he stated that if Bennett actually wrote the letters, "I am wasting my sympathy on the wrong man."[12] In another interview, in the Pittsburgh *Dispatch,* he said that if Bennett wrote them, "I shall be sorry from the bottom of my heart."[13] No denial came from Bennett. No further support came from Ingersoll. Hayes washed his hands of the whole affair and Bennett served his entire sentence.

Comstockery was a crucial issue at the fourth annual meeting of the National Liberal League, in Cincinnati, in September, 1879. Prior to the meeting, Ingersoll, Wright, Wakeman, Abbot, and others were busy with plans to make the meeting the occasion for calling a national convention of all liberals for the purpose of taking political action. Ingersoll favored the formation of a new party, the Liberal Party, dedicated to the complete secularization of the state.[14] The new party should not nominate its own candidates for federal and state offices but should support those candidates of the other parties who were closest to its objectives. Ingersoll held that the new party should never give a blanket endorsement of another party. It would be unthinkable to come out for the Democratic party, for the Catholic Church controlled it. It would be equally unthinkable to come out against the Republican party merely because Comstockery flourished under it.

Ingersoll also wanted to be sure that the free lovers and their kind would not be in the party; "Let them spend their time in examining each other's sexual organs, and in letting ours alone."[15] With regard to freedom of religion the question was raised as to the position the party should take on polygamy for the Mormons. "Why should that ulcer be solved by us?" asked Ingersoll. Nor did he want the Bennett case to dominate the proceedings at Cincinnati. The Liberals had a noble work to do: "Let us to this high calling be infinitely true. Let us occupy the heights."

The first day of the Cincinnati meeting September 13, was devoted to the transactions of the Liberal League itself. Ingersoll was chairman of the Committee on Action which brought in three resolutions on unfinished business and three on the formation of a political party. Those on unfinished business dealt with the Comstock laws, which the League the previous year, at Syracuse, had wrangled over to the conclusion "to inform themselves." The resolutions now stated that "we are utterly opposed to the dissemination through the mails, or by any other means, of obscene literature, whether "inspired" or uninspired; that we call upon the Christian world to expunge from the so called "sacred" Bible every passage that cannot be read without covering the cheek of modesty with the blush of shame, and until such passages are expunged, we demand that the laws against dissemination of obscene literature be impartially enforced; that we are in favor of such postal laws as will allow the free transportation through the mails of the United States of all books, pamphlets, and papers irrespective of the religious, irreligious, political, and scientific views they may contain, so that the literature of science may be placed upon an equality with that of superstition."[16] The resolutions pleased everybody. The advocates of repeal of the Comstock laws liked the stress on the applicability of the laws to the Bible; those for modification of the laws liked the strong words against obscene matter; both liked the demands for the free circulation of matter not obscene. The resolutions were passed unanimously. And so were those on political action, aimed at the secularization of the state.

The second day of the meeting, the Liberal League joined with other groups to form the National Liberal Party. Ingersoll headed the committee to draw up a platform. The committee brought in a platform the same as the resolutions of the Liberal League the previous day. The platform was adopted unanimously. As the day drew to a close, a clamor arose in the assembly! "Ingersoll—Ingersoll—a speech from Ingersoll!" He responded with a short, impassioned address keynoted by his opening statement: "Allow me to say that the cause nearest my heart, and to which I am willing to devote the remainder of my life, is the absolute, the *absolute,* enfranchisement of the human mind." He closed by saying: "There is no office I want in this world. I will make up my mind as to the next when I get there, because my motto is . . . My motto is: One world at a time!" And thus the meeting ended, with everybody in a happy mood.

But in the months that followed, discord arose. One problem had to do with the independence of the new party. Ingersoll felt that the party should not put forth a separate slate of candidates. On the other hand, T. B. Wakeman led a group of enthusiasts who felt that the party should go all the way. Why, it was possible to elect their own President of the United States! Another cause of dissension was the Bennett affair. Some of the Liberals were intent on making it the spearhead of a crusade. Not Ingersoll. He was done with Bennett. He would resign as vice-president of the National Liberal League if the Bennett case were not dropped. Francis Abbot and A. L. Rawson, the secretary of the League, led the movement to get behind Bennett. "I wish," wrote Ingersoll to Elizur Wright, "that

Bennett and Rawson had their necks broke, and that Abbot
was in the same condition."[17] Wright was also threatening to
resign as president of the League. Both officers, however, decided to wait a year to see what would happen.

In September, 1880, the League met in Chicago. This time
Wakeman was Chairman of the Committee on Resolutions.
One of the resolutions announced a plan to establish an independent party which should put up its own state and congressional tickets and in four years a presidential ticket. Ingersoll
did not object to this resolution because it also contained a
provision that such tickets were contingent on the strength of
the party and that in the meantime there should be support, if
warranted, for the candidates of the other parties. But he objected strongly to two resolutions which urged the repeal of the
Comstock laws and the defense of all persons indicted under
those laws. He proposed two substitute resolutions: that the
League should set up a committee "to examine said laws and
report to a future Congress wherein they should be amended
so that perfect freedom of the press and of conscience shall
not be endangered;" and that the League set up a committee
of defense to investigate the cases of all persons indicted under
the Comstock laws and if it were found that such persons were
in the "honest exercise of the freedom of thought and expression" it should be the duty of the committee to defend them if
they did not have the means of defending themselves.

All afternoon and all evening, of September 17, the delegates
bitterly debated the resolutions, with Ingersoll talking often.
Repeatedly he implored the delegates to realize that if they
passed Wakeman's resolutions the charge would be hurled at
them that they favored the dissemination of immoral and obscene matter.[18] He insisted that those parts of the Comstock
laws prohibiting the mailing of smut must be retained. Certain
things, he contended, were "manifestly obscene." "Who is to
be the judge of that?" a delegate asked. Ingersoll answered,
"There are books nobody differs about. . . . Don't tie us to
this nonsense—to the idea that we have an interest in immoral
literature. . . ." Wakeman said that a grand jury should sit on

every case of alleged violation of the Comstock laws. "No," said Ingersoll, "when something is manifestly obscene, burn it up." Ingersoll's old friend, Parker Pillsbury, accused him of filibuster tactics. "I beg pardon if I have done anything so horrible as has been described by Mr. Pillsbury. . . . I wish to trample upon the rights of no one . . . . but I say this: I have the right to make a motion in this congress, I have the right to argue that motion . . ." Ingersoll's final words were: "I don't want the splendid prospects of this League put in jeopardy upon such an issue as this. I have no more to say. But if that resolution [for repeal] is passed, all I have to say is that, while I shall be for liberty everywhere, I cannot act with this organization, and I will not." A few minutes later Wakeman's resolutions were passed. Ingersoll got up, resigned as vice-president, and walked out. Several other delegates left with him. Two years later when the League met in St. Louis, Wakeman acknowledged that Ingersoll's defection was partly responsible for the League's failure in political action. "Ingersoll went right out," said Wakeman, "and was rebaptized into the Republican party, and has been the hewer of wood and the drawer of water for it ever since."[19]

HEWER OF WOOD
AND DRAWER OF WATER

B<small>Y</small> 1880 Republican leaders like Conkling, Blaine, and Simon Cameron were so irked with the good works of President Hayes that they resolved to return him to obscurity. He had not appointed their friends to office; he had cleaned out the New York Custom house; he had reformed the civil service; and he had routed most of the carpetbaggers from the South. Since it was usually old-line Republicans who were the victims of these changes, Hayes came to be regarded as a traitor to the

party. "Hayesism," they called it, and they pined for "Grant-
ism," the good old days of pork and pelf.

The best that Ingersoll could say of Hayes was that now that
his administration was coming to a close he showed signs of improvement. He had just vetoed several measures of the Democratic Congress which were designed to end the use of the military in the South. But this was hardly enough, Ingersoll thought,
to give him even the status of a dark horse at the coming convention. The man whom Ingersoll supported for the nomination was, of course, Blaine, a "competent man of affairs . . . .
and then he has acted in such a chivalric way ever since the
convention at Cincinnati, that those who opposed him most
bitterly, now have for him nothing but admiration."

Ingersoll went to the Republican convention not because
he wanted an office, he said, and not to nominate anybody, not
even Blaine, "but to beat Washburne and Sherman."[1] He had
not forgotten that Washburne had been lukewarm toward
Clark and himself in Illinois political contention. And he
strongly suspected John Sherman, who had become Hayes'
Secretary of the Treasury in 1877, of advising against his appointment to a political post. Ingersoll did not speak at the
convention. William J. Campbell of the Illinois delegation
reported, however, that at one point in the protracted balloting
Ingersoll told him, "I've give one hundred dollars a minute for
fifteen minutes on the floor right now." He thought that he could
break the deadlock among the three who were in the lead—
Grant, Blaine, and Sherman—in favor of Blaine. About midnight of the third day of the convention with wild demonstra-
tions breaking out for both Grant and Blaine, Ingersoll who
was among those on the platform could be seen ecstatically
waving a woman's red shawl.

On the 34th ballot Garfield, who had made a great impression with his speech for Sherman and who had gotten a vote
or two from time to time, unexpectedly received 17 votes. On
the next ballot, it was 50. Then the Blaine forces threw their
strength to him. Ingersoll wrote him a note urging him to ac-

cept the nomination if it came. It came, on the 36th ballot, with 399 votes.

Ingersoll was not too pleased with the choice of Garfield and Arthur. "I do not intend," he wrote his brother, John, "to tear any of my underclothing whatever happens."[2] Then he began to get pleas from Garfield and Blaine to come to the aid of the party. He had heard, however, that once Garfield had introduced in the House of Representatives a resolution endorsing Federal aid to religious education. He wrote to Garfield about it. The reply was satisfactory: "I not only never introduced such a resolution as that to which you refer—but in several public speeches I have praised the wisdom of our fathers for prohibiting Congress from legislating on the subject of religion —and leaving it to the voluntary action of the people."[3]

His doubts dispelled, Ingersoll did "tear his underclothing" for the Republicans. Again he stumped the country, from Illinois to Maine. As in 1876, so in 1880, huge audiences acclaimed him.

On the night of October 30, Ingersoll spoke in Brooklyn, at the Academy of Music. The man who introduced him was Henry Ward Beecher. What a gesture of Republican solidarity that a famous minister should introduce a famous infidel! Six thousand listeners were brought to a feverish pitch by Beecher's words: "I am not accustomed to preside at meetings like this; only the exigency of the times could induce me to do it. . . . I stand not as a minister, but as a man among men, pleading the cause of fellowship and equal rights. . . . The gentleman who will speak tonight is in no conventicle or church . . . . and I take the liberty of saying that I respect him as the man that for a full score and more of years has worked . . . for the cause of human rights. I consider it an honor to extend to him, as I do now, the warm, earnest, right hand of fellowship."[4] The palms of the two men met with a clasp that "was heard all over the house." The audience arose as one with tumultuous cheering and applause that subsided, after several minutes, only when Beecher indicated that he was not yet done. He went on, "I now introduce to you a man who—and I say it not flatteringly

—is the most brilliant speaker of the English tongue of all men on this globe. . . ." And now there was delirium; "The great building," said New York *Herald,* "trembled and vibrated."[5]

The building shook again when Ingersoll finished his speech and again when Beecher and he effusively clasped hands. Beecher proposed a vote of thanks to Ingersoll—thunderously affirmed—and Ingersoll proposed three cheers for Beecher, which were given thrice over.

Many saw a meaning other than political in the Beecher-Ingersoll camaraderie. Beecher, known for his doctrinal looseness—he had denounced the doctrine of eternal damnation—might be in sympathy with the infidel teachings of Ingersoll. The *Herald,* a week after the occasion, reported that much speculation had been voiced and that the question had been asked. "Is the keen logic and broad humanity of Ingersoll converting the brain and heart of Christendom?" Its own question was, "Did the hand that was stretched out to him [Ingersoll] on the stage of the Academy reach across the chasm which separates orthodoxy from infidelity?" In the effort to get answers to these questions, the *Herald* sent a reporter to interview Beecher and Ingersoll. Neither was aware that the other was being interviewed.

Two questions were put to Ingersoll: "What is your opinion of Mr. Beecher? What is his forte?" Two also to Beecher: "What is your opinion of Mr. Ingersoll? Is his influence upon the world good or otherwise?" Ingersoll replied that Beecher was the greatest man in any pulpit in the world, "greater and grander than any creed of any church," but "he holds to many things I most passionately deny." Beecher's forte was "a wonderfully poetic temperament; his brain is controlled by his heart. . . . Now and then he pulls for a moment the leafy curtain aside and is horrified to see the lizards, snakes, basilisks and abnormal monsters of the orthodox age, and he utters a great cry, the protest of a loving, throbbing heart. . . . Manhood is his forte. . . ." Beecher replied: "I do not think there should be any misconception as to my motive for indorsing Mr. Ingersoll. I never saw him before that night. . . . Yet I regard him as one of the greatest men of this age. I am an ordained clergyman and believe in revealed religion. I am, therefore, bound to regard all persons who do not believe in revealed religion as in error. . . . I admire Ingersoll because he is not afraid to speak what he honestly thinks. . . ."[6]

If some wondered whether Beecher was an unconfessed Ingersoll, others wondered that Garfield, a devout Disciple of Christ and erstwhile lay preacher, accepted Ingersoll's support. Little did they know the ardor with which Blaine and Garfield solicited his services. From Blaine: "You must come to Maine and dig us out—We need you—Everybody is crying aloud for you."[7] From Garfield: "Republicans of Middletown (Ohio) are very anxious that you should speak there before Nov. election"[8] and again, on October 16, "You are called for everywhere."[9] Ingersoll could meet only a small percentage of the requests that came to him from Maine to California. A reputation as an atheist made no difference on the stump.

None were more appreciative of Ingersoll's efforts than the Garfields themselves. After his speech in Wall Street, Lucretia Garfield wrote him, "Though your theology may not be able to give me much comfort your magnificent friendship does; and I thank you for every word you uttered."[10] James wrote, "I cannot say it as well as Mrs. Garfield has said it, but yet I must tell you that no man was ever so royally defended as I have been by you. Though I know, as you do, that the cause was worth much more than either of us, yet so far as I am personally concerned, I am inclined to care more about the friendships which this contest has developed than for the victory we have won."[11]

BLASPHEMY!

T HAT in 1880 the Republican leaders did not shy away from Ingersoll was not because of any let-up in his anti-religious lecturing. If in October his time was so taken up with political speeches that he could not squeeze in a lecture, up to that month he was frequently on the platform from Boston to Chicago with "The Liberty . . .", "The Gods," and a new lecture, "What Must We Do to be Saved." This lecture was particularly provocative in that he concentrated on the New Testament and attacked Catholicism, Episcopalianism, Methodism, and Prebyterianism. He said that he did not have time to consider the Baptists, the Quakers, the Campbellites, and the hundreds of other sects. Besides, he was inclined to be lenient with the Baptists and the Quakers, the first because they allowed in some little degree for liberty of thought, the second because he remembered George Fox, the founder, "that loving man," who for preaching the doctrine that God is love was pilloried, whipped, and flung in a dungeon.

Ingersoll examined the foundations of Christianity as found in the gospels of Matthew, Mark, Luke, and John. He allowed that Matthew, Mark and Luke presented fundamentally a decent, humane, reasonable God; he was certain that interpolations accounted for the inacceptable sentiments, like this one in Matthew—"And everyone that hath forsaken . . . sisters, or father, or mother, or wife, or children . . . for my name's sake, shall receive an hundred fold, and shall inherit everlasting life;" or like this one in Mark—"He that believeth and is baptized shall be saved; but he that believeth not shall be damned," which Ingersoll considered "the most infamous in the Bible." He pointed out that Matthew says not a word about belief and that Mark does not until the verse in question, which supposedly was uttered by Christ just before his ascension. The ascension was so momentous an event, argued Ingersoll, that it must fix in the minds of all those present the last words of Christ, especially such crucial words as those on the necessity of belief. But "Matthew did not hear it [the verse], or did not believe it, or forgot it;" Luke did not hear it, "maybe he forgot it;" and "John might not have been listening." The verse in Mark must be an interpolation.

The real trouble with Christianity begins, however, according to Ingersoll, with John. John was not written "until long after the others. John was mostly written by the church." There are two theological afterthoughts in John: that salvation depends upon belief in the Lord Jesus Christ and that it is necessary to eat the flesh and drink the blood of Christ. If it had not been for John, Christianity might have emerged as a religion of justice, kindness, and love. "Read Matthew, Mark, and Luke, and then read John, and you will agree with me that the first three gospels teach that if we are kind and forgiving to our fellows, God will be kind and forgiving to us. In John we are told that another man can be good for us, or bad for us, and that the only way to get to heaven is to believe something that we know is not so."

Ingersoll pitches into Catholicism, first, by having fun with its dogma, then by denouncing the church for bigotry and persecutions. With mock gravity he quotes canonical writings interlarding his own sallies, for instance: " 'The Father is uncreated, the Son uncreated, the Holy Ghost uncreated. The Father incomprehensible, the Son incomprehensible, the Holy Ghost incomprehensible'—And that is the reason we know so much about the thing."

As for the Episcopal Church, Ingersoll conceded that it was not without good works—"And some went so far as to say that people could play cards, and that God would overlook it, or would look the other way"—but it could not claim too much credit. It was less tyrannical and cruel than the Catholic Church because it had less power and fewer opportunities. Look at its treatment of the Irish, "a crime lasting for three hundred years. That church persecuted the Puritans of England and the Presbyterians of Scotland." The difference between the Episcopal creed and the Catholic was that the former contained a few more absurdities.

The best that Ingersoll could say of the Methodist Church was that it was relatively harmless. The preaching was noisy but most of its converts backslid. He wanted to say a good word for the founders, John Wesley and George Whitfield. "About a hundred and fifty years ago, two men . . . said, If everybody is going to hell, somebody ought to mention it. The Episcopal clergy said: Keep still; do not tear your gown. . . . But they believed their doctrine. And they said: If there is a hell, and a Niagara of souls pouring over an eternal prejudice of ignorance, somebody ought to say something. They were right; somebody ought, if such a thing is true. Wesley was a believer in the Bible. . . . God used to do miracles for him; used to put off a rain for several days to give his meeting a chance; used to cure his horse of lameness; used to cure Mrs. Wesley's headaches."

Ingersoll, as usual, reserved a special vial of wrath for the Presbyterians, whose creed was the worst in the world. Look at the founders, John Calvin and John Knox; they were "made for each other . . . fitted each other like the upper and lower jaws of a wild beast." As a result, "The Presbyterian god is the monster of monsters. . . . He will enjoy forever the shrieks of the lost—the wails of the damned. Hell is the festival of the Presbyterian god."

Toward the end of his lecture, anticipating the question, what do you propose, Ingersoll spoke of his own gospels, of Cheerfulness, of Good Nature, of Good Health, of Liberty, of Intelligence. The concluding words wrought strongly upon his hearers: "I had rather think of those I have loved, and lost, as having returned to earth, as having become a part of the elemental wealth of the world—I would rather think of them as unconscious dust, I would rather dream of them as gurgling in the streams, floating in the clouds, bursting in the foam of light upon the shores of worlds . . . than to have even the faintest fear that their naked souls have been clutched by an orthodox god. . . . I have made up my mind that if there is a God, he will be merciful to the merciful.

"Upon that rock I stand. —
"That he will not torture the forgiving. —
"Upon that rock I stand."

Ingersoll was now a commodity for ticket speculators, who plied their trade outside the auditoriums of New York, Boston, Philadelphia, and Chicago. And hawkers of his printed lec-

Robert G. Ingersoll, about 1883.

The observance of Sunday was routine for a public cultural institution like a museum but not for an "entertainment" like an Ingersoll lecture. It was bad enough to "blaspheme" for pay on weekdays; to do it on Sundays, and before capacity houses——!!

The Ingersoll-Gladstone theological encounter in
the *North American Review*, 1888, was a major
intellectual event.

THE TRUTH SEEKER

A JOURNAL OF FREETHOUGHT AND REFORM.

Entered at the Post-Office at New York, N. Y., as Second-class Matter.

15. No. 26. {PUBLISHED WEEKLY. | New York, Saturday, June 30. 1888. | 28 LAFAYETTE PL. | $3.00 per year.

THE RACE BETWEEN AMERICA'S INFIDEL ORATOR AND ENGLAND'S CHRISTIAN STATESMAN.

nd after all, it may be that "to ride an unbroken horse with the reins thrown upon his neck"—as you charge me with doing—give a greater variety of sensations, a keener delight,
better prospect of winning the race than to sit solemnly astride of a dead one in "a deep reverential calm," with the bridle firmly in your hand.—*Ingersoll*. *Reply to Gladstone.*

That inmates of public institutions should be enabled not only to have their own mode of worship but also to choose their own spiritual advisors was deduced from a bill before the New York State legislature.

THAT FREEDOM OF WORSHIP BILL.

A REALIZATION OF AN IDEAL.

tures did a thriving business. The night of May 23, outside Booth's Theater of New York, speculators and hawkers vied with a "half score of missionaries" (New York *Herald*) who distributed gratis New Testaments from an anonymous donor. At Philadelphia, May 25, the American Tract Society posted "polite young men" (Philadelphia *Press*) outside the Academy, who before and after the lecture distributed yellow eight-page tracts entitled *What Shall I Do to Be Saved,* which were reprints of an article in the *Christian Weekly* by Lyman Abbott. The only apparent effect of the tracts was that the streets "looked as though visited by a storm of yellow snow." In many cities men of the Y.M.C.A. badgered lines at the box office with admonitory cards and leaflets. In Chicago, September 19, in front of McVicker's Theater, they passed out cards bearing the question, "What must we do to be saved?" and the answer, "Believe on the Lord Jesus Christ, and thou shalt be saved." Some of the cards seemed to have an effect, according to the Chicago *Tribune,* "but the great bulk of them were contemptuously cast aside;" the house was "packed, and crammed, and jammed to overflowing."

The political campaign over, Ingersoll devoted a month to the preparation of two new lectures, "Some Reasons Why" and "Great Infidels." The first was essentially a restatement of "What Must We Do to Be Saved." The second dealt with the bigotry and tyranny of the church through the ages, with special attention to the heretics, philosophers, and scientists persecuted or defamed, infidels like Emperor Julian the Apostate, Giordano Bruno, Voltaire, Diderot, Hume, Spinoza, and Paine.

In December, 1880, Ingersoll delivered "What Must We Do to Be Saved" in Wilmington, Delaware. The ministers of the city raised a great outcry, preaching "twenty or thirty sermons," said Ingersoll, "not one of which, considered as a reply, was a success." Things came to a head the following February when it became known that Ingersoll was scheduled to deliver "Great Infidels" in Wilmington. This was more than Chief Justice Comegys, of the Supreme Court of Delaware, could stand. A staunch Presbyterian, he urged a grand jury under a law of

1740 to indict Ingersoll for blasphemy. He declared that Ingersoll's lectures were not only blasphemous but also tended to a breach of the peace, to riot and bloodshed. "And we shall in no wise be deterred from our duty by the sneers of the devotees of any other faith than that of the body of the people of this State or the deprecatory expressions of those who think the right of free speech will be infringed thereby."

Although the grand jury refrained from bringing in an indictment based on his lecture delivered in December, it reported as follows: "The audacity with which the notorious blasphemer, known as Robert G. Ingersoll, recently announced his purpose to lecture in this city on Infidelity, has no parallel in the habits of respectable vagabondism."[1] If he carried out his purpose, the jury warned, he would "be taught that in Delaware blasphemy is a crime, and as such will be punished by fine and imprisonment."

The press of the country gave the affair much attention. Most of the papers of the large cities protested and ridiculed the virtual ban on an Ingersoll lecture in Delaware. Support for the Delaware action came from the religious journals and from, as Ingersoll put it, a "few rural sheets." The *Evening News* of Chester, Pennsylvania, for instance, commented that the rebuke "from so high a source of authority will have a most excellent effect, and will check religious blasphemers from parading their immoral creeds before the people."

One of the most interviewed men of his time, Ingersoll was afforded plenty of space to express his views on Judge Comegys and Delaware. And he made the most of his opportunity. He said of the Judge, "After reading his charge [to the grand jury] it seemed to me as though he had died about the date of the law (1740), had risen from the dead, and gone right on where he left off;" and again, "I have no doubt that Judge Comegys is a good and sincere Christian. I believe that he, in his charge, gives an exact reflection of the Jewish Jehovah. . . . Every word he said was in exact accord with the spirit of orthodox Christianity. Against this man personally I have nothing to say. . . . I am forced simply to say, Judge Comegys is a Christian."[2]

Ingersoll cancelled his lecture for Wilmington. He realized that in the light of the law of 1740 the crime of blasphemy could be proved against him. No fine and imprisonment for him. He had had his say; the issues had been aired. The only effect of his imprisonment, said Ingersoll, would be that "the judge having become acquainted with me during the trial, would probably insist on spending most of his time in my cell."[3]

On March 29, under the auspices of the Central Young Men's Republican Club of Brooklyn, Ingersoll lectured at the Brooklyn Academy of Music on "The Liberty of Man, Woman and Child." It was the Lenten season. The Reverend Dr. Buckley of the Hansen Place Methodist Church in Brooklyn was incensed at the gall of the Young Republican group in sponsoring such a man at such a time. The following Sunday, April 3, in his sermon, "The Christian's Liberty *vs.* the Infidel's License," Buckley assailed Ingersoll for blasphemy compounded and denounced his sponsors.

Interviewed on Buckley's sermon by the Brooklyn *Eagle,* Ingersoll commented with great relish on two charges in particular: that he had shown "execrable taste" in lecturing during Lent and that he had maliciously lectured in Brooklyn, to interfere with the revivals which Henry Ward Beecher and De-Witt Talmage were holding. "Lent," said Ingersoll, "is just as good [for lecturing] as any other part of the year, and no part can be too good to do good. . . . If they think that there is some subtle relation between hunger and heaven, or that faith depends upon, or is strengthened by famine, or that veal, during Lent, is the enemy of virtue, or that beef feeds blasphemy, while fish feeds faith—of course, all this is nothing to me. They have a right to say that vice depends on victuals, sanctity on soup, religion on rice, and chastity on cheese, but they have no right to say that a lecture on liberty is an insult to them because they are hungry. . . ."[4]

As for the revivals of Beecher and Talmage, Ingersoll said he had not the slightest intention of interfering with them. They were not worth his attention: they were "not alive enough to be killed." But "surely one lecture could not destroy two revivals."

The fact that he had had a "great house" while Beecher and Talmage had had small houses indicated something bigger than the power of a single man, namely, that people were thinking for themselves, "they are getting tired of the old ideas."[5]

INGERSOLLISM AND ASSASSINATION

GARFIELD's victory in the election enhanced Ingersoll's standing not only with the victors but also with those who sought to share the spoils. He was besieged with the request of office seekers that he intercede for them with the President-elect. Not infrequently he complied. He was now in the intimate counsels of both Garfield and Blaine, and the White House was always open to him. Often in the evenings he would take the short walk from his home on Lafayette Square to the White House, there to chat with the President about all sorts of matters.

One day, shortly after Garfield's inauguration, a man named Charles Guiteau came to Ingersoll's law office at 1421 New York Avenue and asked to see him. Ingersoll's nephew, Burton, who was a clerk in the outer office, asked his uncle if he would see the man. Yes, send him in. Guiteau went in, sat down, and broached his business. He was from Chicago, he said, and he remembered that Ingersoll was from those parts and had cut quite a figure in Illinois politics. One Illinoisan ought to help another. Well, he hoped Ingersoll would try to help him. He wanted a consulate and would Ingersoll please write in his behalf to Secretary of State Blaine. Ingersoll said, "I cannot do so because I do not know you." With that, the man was dismissed. He made no particular impression: "He appeared like most other folks in search of a place or employment. . . . He talked about the same as other people." A few weeks later, Guiteau came to see Ingersoll again, this time to his house. He was let in—as who was not who knocked at the Ingersoll door. "Everyone Welcome" would have been an accurate inscription on the door, for no one of the large number of callers, friends or strangers, was ever turned away. Guiteau was not unaware of the well known Ingersoll hospitality and generosity. He said he was hard up and he wondered if Ingersoll would lend him twenty-five dollars.[1] Ordinarily a "soft touch," in this case Ingersoll refused. He had heard from Garfield himself that Guiteau had become a nuisance at the White House. This was in the days when just about anybody could get to the White House doors and if his mission seemed legitimate gain admittance. Guiteau who had campaigned a little for the Republicans managed to see the President two or three times, and, as Ingersoll put it, "The President was troubled by him—ordered him to keep away—told the servants not to admit him."[2]

When Guiteau was refused the loan, he wondered if it could be because of what he had said about Ingersoll. "I never knew that you ever said anything against me," said Ingersoll, "Good evening." Later Ingersoll concluded that Guiteau must have had in mind derogatory remarks he had made about Ingersoll in certain lectures he had given.

On Friday evening, July 1, Ingersoll was with the President from eight o'clock till ten. The next morning Garfield was to leave for Williamstown, Massachusetts, to be present at the Commencement of his alma mater, Williams College. Ingersoll had an appointment to see him again before he left but he overslept, and as he was hurrying to the White House, he met the President driving toward the Pennsylvania Railroad Station. They waved to each other and Ingersoll returned home. Fifteen minutes later as he was looking out a window upon Lafayette Square he saw a man running up to the house. He opened the front door to see what was going on and the man cried out, "The President has been shot!"[3]

Ingersoll went immediately to the railroad station, the scene of the crime. The President had been carried to a room upstairs and when Ingersoll was admitted, he found Garfield stretched on the floor, surrounded by doctors. Garfield recognized him and signalled that he should kneel down beside him. They talked briefly about what had happened and about Guiteau, who had been seized immediately. For the next three or four days, with Garfield hovering between life and death, Ingersoll received hourly bulletins from the White House. On July 5 he wrote, "We have been so stretched and strained on the rack of hope and fear that we are all worn out."[4]

Rumor had it that the deed was born in the hostility between the Conkling-Platt-Arthur forces and the Blaine-Garfield forces. Ingersoll was absolutely sure that the crime had no political significance: "All the charges that Conkling and Arthur are responsible are too absurd to be talked about." Although Guiteau had attributed his action to his desire to unite the Republican factions—"if the President was out of the way, everything would go better"—it was clear to Ingersoll that Guiteau was motivated by one thing only, revenge at not getting an office.[5]

Another rumor making the rounds in Washington was stated to Ingersoll by a reported for the Washington *Gazette*: "Are you aware that it had been attempted to show that some money loaned or given him by yourself was really what he purchased the pistol with?" Ingersoll replied that he had never lent Guiteau "a dollar in the world" but that even if he had he could hardly be held guilty for trying to kill the President. You could not hold Guiteau's tailor guilty because he made his clothes, even though without those clothes Guiteau would never have gone to the Pennsylvania Station. "Nothing can exceed the utter absurdity of what has been said upon this subject."

Equally absurd, commented Ingersoll, was the charge made by certain Washington and New York preachers—Sunderland, Newman, Power, et al.—that the teaching of a secular liberalism had shaped Guiteau's thinking and character to a woeful end. Did not these preachers know that Guiteau was a Christian, that he belonged to the Y.M.C.A., that he was a follower of Moody and Sankey, and that he had delivered lectures against infidelity?[6] It would seem that the logic of the preach-ears had boomeranged. Yet he, Ingersoll, would not go as far as to say that Christianity was responsible for the crime.

THEOLOGICAL POLEMICS

IN the summer of 1881, in response to a request from the *North American Review,* Ingersoll wrote an article for the August issue on the subject, "Is All of the Bible Inspired?" The *Review* having been roundly criticized for publishing too much matter of a skeptical tendency stipulated as a condition of publication that Ingersoll allow them to submit his piece to someone who would write a reply, both articles to appear in the same issue. This was satisfactory to Ingersoll, provided the *Review* would accept for later publication his rejoinder. Agreeing, the *Review* set out to find a worthy opponent. Several clergymen were asked but they declined. Then a scholarly and devout layman, Jeremiah S. Black, accepted, provided the title were changed to "The Christian Religion." He was willing to write a reply because the request, as he stated in the introduction to his paper, came to him "with the effect of a challenge, which I cannot decline without seeming to acknowledge that the religion of the civilized world is an absurd superstition, propagated by imposters, professed by hypocrites, and believed only by credulous dupes."

Black was a man to contend with. He had been an eminent judge on the Supreme Court Bench of Pennsylvania. He had been successively the Attorney General and the Secretary of State in President Buchanan's cabinet. Later an outspoken opponent of Republican Reconstruction policies, he was a supporter of Andrew Johnson and drafted Johnson's veto message on the Reconstruction Act of March, 1867. In the impeachment proceedings he was one of Johnson's counsel.

Black's reply to Ingersoll was in rather severe terms. "I am assuming no clerical function," he said.[1] "I am no preacher exhorting a sinner. . . . My duty is more analogous to that of the policeman who would silence a rude disturber of the congregation by telling him that his clamor is false and his conduct an offense against public decency." Admitting that Ingersoll "stands at the head of living infidels, 'by merit raised to that bad eminence,' " Black dwells on his opponent's defects as a lecturer. Ingersoll is "all imagination and no discretion," a man with "inordinate self-confidence" that makes him "at once ferocious and fearless," a one-time "practical politician" who in taking the stump against Christianity "has proved his capacity to 'split the ears of the groundlings' and make the unskillful laugh." But Black noted that Ingersoll's paper was in a style more suited to a serious theme. Therefore, it "was not wholly unworthy of grave contradiction." Black himself was not above salting the gravity of his contradiciton with *ad hominem* bits, as when he said it was preposterous that the man who should wax indignant over the bulls and goats sacrificed by the Jews three thousand years ago should be this "carnivorous American, full of beef and mutton."

Black defended the essentials of Christianity, arguing, for instance, that the authors of the gospels were men of "unimpeachable characters, plain-thinking, sober, unimaginative men," whose testimony might differ in expression and unimportant detail but who were as one with regard to the sublime reality of their experience. That they differed in this and that was proof positive that they did not act in concert. Black flatly denied—and here he ran counter to much orthodox doctrine—Ingersoll's assertions that "Christianity offers eternal salvation as the reward of belief alone" and that "The mere failure to believe is punishable in hell." As for the Atonement, Black held that it might seem " 'absurd, unjust, and immoral' " to a "rash and superficial man" but that to wise men the whole plan of salvation "could have been framed only in the councils of the Omniscient."

Ingersoll had a field day in a long rejoinder in the December *Review*. First he protested the personal detraction to which he had been subjected; "in the investigation of such a subject vituperation is singularly and vulgarly out of place." Then employing to the full his legal and rhetorical talents he went after Black's arguments.[2] How do we know that the writers of the gospels had " 'unimpeachable characters?' " And the real question is, who were the writers? It is absurd to say, as Black said, "the witnesses could not have been mistaken, because the nature of the facts precluded the possibility of any delusion about them." The nature of the supposed facts was *supernatural* —the Holy Ghost, the Sonship of Christ, conversations with angels, the resurrection, the ascension; how is it that human witnesses, finite minds, could not be mistaken about such matters? If the ascension, "a miracle great enough to surfeit wonder," happened, why did the witnesses, Luke and Mark, say so little about it, and Matthew and John, nothing. Again, "Luke testifies that Christ ascended on the very day of his resurrection. John deposes that eight days after the resurrection Christ appeared to the disciples and convinced Thomas. In the Acts we are told that Christ remained on earth for forty days after his resurrection. . . ."

As to the Atonement, what if, as Black stated, "the wisest and best of men" believe it? Does that make it true?" A Mohammedan, speaking in Constantinople, will say the same of the Koran. A Brahmin, in a Hindu Temple, will make the same remark, and so will the American Indian, when he endeavors to enforce something upon the young of his tribe." Again, why execrate Judas Iscariot for performing an act necessary to the plan of salvation? And how in the name of common sense can the sufferings of the noble and innocent Christ "satisfy justice for the sins of the guilty?" It is no answer to say, as Black said, " 'This raises a metaphysical question, which it is not necessary or possible for me to discuss here.' "

The length of the rejoinder irritated Black and he wrote to the *North American Review* alleging unfair treatment. He was invited to write another reply, but he declined. The *Review* then negotiated with Professor George P. Fisher, an authority on religion at Yale University, who agreed to answer provided

Ingersoll, whom he would not name in his reply, were not allowed another rejoinder. Ingersoll, according to the original conditions, was to have had the last say, but he readily accepted the change.

Fisher's reply appeared in the February, 1882, issue of the *Review*. Informing his readers that he would follow "a positive method of handling the subject," he refused to answer particular objections "one by one, because it's like the business of picking up pins." Besides, if he did essay such a detailed defense, it would seem apologetic and imply weakness. But he did want to point out that discrepancies of testimony can be found whenever two or more persons detail what they have witnessed; indeed, if discrepancies are absent, fraud may be present. The gospels differ in certain details because human beings wrote them and human beings translated them. Yet the testimony on "the essential facts in the life of Jesus," the crucifixion and the resurrection on the third day, is in agreement.

Fisher's reply lacked Ingersoll's agile reasoning and popular rhetoric but it was scholarly and often convincing. His erudition in the Old Testament and ancient Hebrew culture showed to advantage in demonstrating that Mosaic law was as humane and enlightened as the times would allow and that Judaic warfare, harsh and ruthless, was indispensable to self-preservation. The only basic doctrinal question that Fisher dealt with concerned the Atonement. What was so unreasonable, he asked, about the idea of vicarious suffering? If human beings voluntarily undergo privation and death for others and expiate the wrongs of others, was anything less to be expected of Christ in his infinite love of man and his infinite knowledge of God? The Atonement revealed Christ's oneship with man and his oneship with God.

Of all the fracases with the clergy that Ingersoll had during his career, the one that stands out for volume of words and acrimony was with the Reverend DeWitt Talmage of the Brooklyn Tabernacle. An inspirational preacher, he drew at the height of his success, in the eighteen-seventies and eighties, the largest regular church audiences in America. His sermons were published weekly in some thirty-five hundred religious and secular journals. He also was in the habit of delivering one lecture a week. A handsome man with strong, clearcut features and tall, erect carriage, he had a flair for histrionics. His language was picturesque, his delivery bizarre. In 1879, the Brooklyn Presbytery brought him up on a charge of "falsehood and conceit, and . . . using improper methods of preaching which tend to bring religion into contempt." Since his fundamental adherence to the Presbyterian faith could not be controverted, he was acquitted, although on some counts the vote was close.

In the early months of 1882, Talmage delivered six sermons on Ingersoll, which were also widely printed. Attempting to substantiate the literal truth of the Bible from the creation to the Ascension, he took up all the questions and objections that Ingersoll raised. And how he went after the infidel himself. Ingersoll wanted a public office but the parties would not have him; he had signed a petition for the circulation of obscene literature; he had stained the fair name of Queen Victoria; he had called his father a "fool," a "bigot," a "tyrant"; he was the champion blasphemer of America.

Ingersoll answered Talmage's six sermons with six "Interviews," "The Talmagian Catechism," and three lectures on "Talmagian Theology." The "Interviews," which he published in April, 1882, were based on the questions put to him by the reporters of many papers. "The Talmagian Catechism," in the same volume, had as a foreword the following statement of purpose: "As Mr. Talmage delivered the series of sermons referred to in these interviews, for the purpose of furnishing arguments for the young, so that they might not be misled by the sophistry of modern infidelity, I have thought it best to set forth, for use in Sunday schools, the pith and marrow of what he has been pleased to say, in the form of 'A Shorter Catechism.' "

But it was in his lectures on "Talmagian Theology," which he delivered from St. Louis to Boston, that Ingersoll was at his best. Capitalizing on Talmage's eccentricities of delivery and his imaginative, sometimes fantastic, rationalizations of orthodoxy and the Bible, he indulged in unrestrained lampoonery. "His audience," said the *New York Times* of his second, three-hour, lecture on Talmage, "was kept alternating between shouts of laughter and bursts of applause." "Oh," said Ingersoll, "*I have nothing to say about his reputation. . . . Some ministers think he has more gesticulation than grace. Some call him a pious pantaloon, a Christian clown, but such remarks, I think, are born of envy. He is the only Presbyterian minister in the United States who can draw an audience. . . . He believes in a literal resurrection of the dead, that we shall see countless bones flying through the air. . . . I am charged, too, with saying that the sun was not made till the fourth day, whereas, according to the Bible, vegetation began on the third day, before there was any light. But Mr. Talmage says there was light without the sun. They got light, he says, from the crystallization of rocks. A nice thing to raise a corn crop by! There may have been vol-canoes, he says. How'd you like to farm it, and depend on volcanic glare to raise a crop? That's what they call religious science. . . . I've misquoted the story of Jonah. . . . Talmage doesn't think Jonah was in the whale's belly—he said in his mouth. Well, judging from the Doctor's [Talmage] photograph, that explanation would be quite natural to him. He says he *might* have been in the whale's stomach, and avoided the action of the gastric juice by walking up and down. Imagine Jonah, sitting on a back tooth, leaning against the upper jaw, longingly looking through the open mouth for signs of land! But that's Scripture and you've got to believe it or be damned."

There was more of the same when he spoke in Chicago, on November 12, to over three thousand people who occupied even the standing room of McVicker's Theater. How they laughed as Ingersoll said: "But, says Talmage, God works gradually. No hurry about it! . . . Suppose we wanted now to break certain cannibals of eating missionaries—wanted to stop them from eating them raw? Of course we would not tell them, in the first place, it is wrong. That would not do. We would induce them to cook them. That would be the first step toward civilization. We would have them stew them. We would not say it is wrong to eat missionary but it is wrong to eat missionary raw. Then, after they began stewing them, we would put in a little mutton—not enough to excite suspicion but just a little, and so, day by day, we would put in a little more mutton and a little less missionary until, in about what the Bible calls 'the fullness of time,' we would have clear mutton and no missionary. That is God's way."

In 1882, Ingersoll was at the crest of his fame, or notoriety. And people in the highest places seemed to lend him sanction. At the memorial services at the Academy of Music, New York City, the evening of Decoration Day, May 30, Ingersoll was the speaker. As if such a man on so solemn an occasion were not enough to shock the orthodox, who should be seen sitting on the platform with him but men of the greatest national prominence: Ulysses S. Grant; Charles Scribner; August Belmont; George W. Curtis; Roscoe Conkling; Carl Schurz; Charles J. Folger, Secretary of the Treasury of the United States; Benjamin H. Brewster, Attorney General of the United States; and, to top it all, Chester A. Arthur, the President of the United States. "Twenty years ago it would not have been possible," protested the New York *Sun,* "It means, in our judgment, that there has been a general decline in religion; that infidelity is spreading in the community; . . . that there is scoffing now where reverence and adoration formerly prevailed."[3]

THE STAR-ROUTE TRIALS

Ingersoll's exertions as an infidel, in 1882, somehow left him enough time to be the chief counsel for the defense, the United States as plaintiff, in one of the celebrated trials in the annals of the American courtroom. During the Hayes administration, rumors abounded that fraud and corruption existed in that branch of the Post Office Department having to do with the "star" routes. An extensive network of these routes brought mail service to the parts of the country without railroad connections. The government entered into contracts with private parties to set up and maintain such routes. The contracts were starred to indicate special conditions of schedule and security under which the mails were to be carried.

President Hayes, reformer though he was, shied away from an investigation of the star-route business. But when Garfield came into office and Thomas L. James, formerly postmaster of New York City, became his postmaster-general, an investigation promptly got under way, which, said James, "shall be pushed fearlessly, regardless of whom it may strike."

It struck soon. Thomas W. Brady, second assistant postmaster-general, who had official control and direction of the star-route service resigned April 20, 1881. One of his clerks, J. L. French, was dismissed April 26; and a Mr. McGrew, Sixth Auditor of the Treasury, in charge of Post-Office accounts, resigned June 2. The Investigation continued under President Arthur, leading to an indictment that charged certain parties with conspiracy to defraud the government. The indictment named Brady; John W. Dorsey, John M. Peck, and John R. Miner, who bid for certain star-routes and obtained the contracts; Harvey Vaile, a sub-contractor, to whom the routes were transferred; Stephen W. Dorsey, former senator from Arkansas and brother of John, who was accused of directing the course of the contractors and of using his influence as a Senator; M. C. Rerdell, Stephen Dorsey's secretary, said to have been the supervising agent and manager for the combination in Washington; and W. H. Turner, a clerk in the contract office with control of the territorial routes under Brady.

It was charged that the combination by means of false petitions, false letters, and false affidavits connived to increase the contracted pay on one hundred and thirty-four routes from $143,169 to $622,208; on twenty-six of these routes from $65,216 to $530,318. The increases were alleged to be far in excess of the cost of actual improvements, if any, in the mail service, and of the revenue which the government received. A route in Dakota Territory, for instance, between Sioux Falls and Vermillion brought a yearly return of $240; the original consideration for the contractor was $398, which went up to $6133.50.

The indictment which the government, on March 4, 1882, laid before Judge Wylie in the Criminal Court of the District of Columbia was shortly withdrawn for amendment. It was presented again May 2. With reference to twenty-two specific contracts, it set forth thirty-six overt acts as evidence of a conspiracy to defraud the government.

The trial started June 1. Leading the counsel for the government, with Benjamin Brewster, the Attorney General of the United States, in close supervision, was District Attorney Corkhill. Although Ingersoll heading a battery of seven prominent attorneys was in general charge of the case for the defense, he also specifically represented the Dorsey brothers. In the course of the trial the government introduced masses of evidence on the alleged fraudulent character of various kinds of documents used in the conspiracy: (1) the petitions and letters requesting better mail schedules, (2) the affidavits of the contractors setting forth the men, stock, and equipment needed to implement the proposed schedules, (3) the orders issued by Brady authorizing increased pay to the contractors. The strategy of the defense was mainly (1) to restrict the admission of evidence as much as possible on the ground it did not support the overt acts specified in the indictment, (2) to show fatal discrepancies between whatever evidence was admitted and the overt acts as described.

On August 7 the defense rested and on August 9 the prosecution began summing up. The counsel for both sides presented thirteen closing addresses to the jury, Ingersoll giving the last speech for the defense September 5-6 and Brewster, for the government, September 6-7. Ingersoll's speech was considered a forensic masterpiece. Said the Washington *Post,* September 6, "A powerful and splendid argument was the address of Colonel Ingersoll to the star-route jury yesterday. It astonished even his admirers by its depth and comprehensiveness." The *Evening*

Critic, of Washington, declared, "The members of the bar without exception pronounce it a brilliant effort and one of the most masterly ever made to a jury."[1] And from the Washington *Capital,* "The most characteristic feature of the Star-route trial, which has been the central point of interest in our city for the past three months was the marvelously powerful speech of Colonel Robert G. Ingersoll." If there had been some who thought the great orator might lack depth as a lawyer, "they heard him," said the *Capital,* "and the doubt ceased."[2]

The day before Judge Wylie gave his charge to the jury he caused a sensation in the courtroom by announcing that during the last weeks of the trial several jurors had reported to him that parties representing both sides had approached them with bribes.[3] Wylie said he had urged the jurors to keep quiet, as he did not want to interrupt the trial. But now he would disclose the goings-on because "this thing has grown, and within the last twenty-four hours it seems that these wolves, which have been around this jury, have become fiercer, more determined." He cautioned the jurors to shun the evildoers and to take care not to let their judgment be distorted. Once the verdict was in, then they should make known to the proper authorities whatever information they had. As soon as Judge Wylie ended his commentary, the counsel for both sides jumped to their feet and demanded an investigation. They were told there would be time enough for that when the jury was released.

In his charge to the jury the following morning, September 8, Judge Wylie clearly and fairly set forth the conditions of guilt or innocence in a case of conspiracy to defraud the government. But it was evident that the tendency of the charge was unfavorable to the defense. He rejected the contention of defense counsel that the government had to prove every one of the overt acts in the indictment. There was only one count, conspiracy to defraud, and only one overt act had to be proved. "Surplusage in an indictment will not vitiate it." He also held that the government in trying to prove an overt act did not have to prove the exact means, as described in the indictment, of executing the act. Conspiracy was of such a secretive nature, the exact means so shrouded in darkness, that proof of means other than those described if it was germane to the given overt act must be considered valid. Another of Wylie's instructions that tended against the defense went as follows: "It is in your power to acquit every one of the defendants, except two, and find them guilty." It is easier to find two persons guilty than seven.

The jury went out at noon. At six o'clock they reported they had not agreed except as to one of the defendants. Late that night, still no agreement. Foreman William Dickson requested further instructions on two questions: (1) could evidence of two conspiracies be a basis for a verdict; (2) must the date of an overt act as proved agree with the date as set forth in the indictment. The Judge answered the first question in the negative, the second in the affirmative, but he reminded the jury that exactness of proof was necessary as to only one of the alleged overt acts. All the next day, Saturday, the jury remained in disagreement. Sunday they were allowed to go home. Monday at noon they reported no change. Late in the afternoon they reported agreement on some of the defendants, disagreement on others. Judge Wylie said he was ready to hear their verdict.

The verdict was not guilty as to Peck and Turner, guilty as to Miner and Rerdell, disagreement as to Brady, Vaile, and the Dorseys. Outside of Turner, Peck having died before he was arraigned, the verdict pleased no one. Brady and the Dorseys "looked glum,"[4] said the *Nation,* probably because they feared that in the event of a new trial the guilty, out of revenge and in hope of a pardon, would testify against them. The government immediately moved for a new trial, which the Court granted. The defense moved a new trial for Miner and Rerdell, which the Court took under advisement.

With the public at large, the verdict was also unpopular. "It has surprised the country," declared *Harper's Weekly;* "It convicts two of the least prominent conspirators, and fails to convict the chief of the conspiracy. But the great majority of the jury held them to be guilty, and that verdict is ratified by public opinion."[5] The *Nation* expressed a similar view.[6] Three weeks after the trial Judge Wylie ruled that the verdicts with regard to Miner and Rerdell were set aside because of the inconsistency of the verdicts in general and because of disclosures that Foreman Dickson, contrary to the Court's orders, had dragged into the deliberations of the jury the bribery attempts. A new trial was set for December 4.

If Ingersoll had any scruples about representing the Star-Route defendants, he at no time expressed them. He was concerned, however, about the possible effect his connection with the case would have upon his popularity as a lecturer. But he was reassured by the receptions accorded him on his tour following the trial. He wrote from Chicago, November 13, "I am having a great success. The Star-Route has helped, instead of hurt me."[7] In the interval between trials, September to December, Ingersoll frequently made comments affirming the innocence of his clients and censuring the government. The *Nation* inferred that Ingersoll and the defendants, who were also talking freely, were parties to a scheme to influence public opinion in advance of the second trial in order to get a well disposed jury. "We advise Colonel Robert Ingersoll," said the *Nation,* "that his conduct of the defense in the Star-Route cases is not helping him as an apostle of Agnosticism . . . If his theology has no department of political morality in it, it will certainly fail, no matter how amusing his sermons may be."

So the second trial opened in an atmosphere of suspicion and ill will. Two weeks elapsed before a jury was agreed upon. Wylie was again the judge. The counsel for both sides were the same except for two additions to the defense, one being Walter Davidge, considered the Dean of the Washington bar. The defendants, but for Turner, were the same. George Bliss, special counsel for the government, gave the opening address to the jury on December 19. Attorney Chandler spoke for the defense on December 20 and Ingersoll, December 21-22. The trial dragged on for six months.

Ingersoll had no time for anything else. On March 9, 1883, he wrote, "I have been working like the very devil and the end is not yet." By that time he was sure that no one would be found guilty and he had hopes that all would be acquitted. When the time came for the summing up speeches, the first to appear for the defense was Jeremiah Wilson, whose client was Brady. The defense was then entitled to four more speakers but it was decided that only one should speak—Ingersoll. "The defts and their lawyers paid me a great compliment. . . . They all came to me and asked me to close the case for all. The request was urgent and unanimous. So I closed the case."[8] And what a marathon his final address was. He talked six days, beginning May 10, "long enough," he said, "to kill all concerned. . . . I hope I shall never have another case like this."

The jury received the case the evening of June 12. According to the New York *Sun*, "Everyone expected the jury to disagree." The *Sun* reported that several days before the end of the trial Judge Wylie called up the counsel for the prosecution and said to them. "I do not think you are going to get a verdict out of that jury. I have watched it carefully, and I am certain that four of the best men on it are in doubt."[9]

At ten o'clock on the morning of June 14 the jury took their places in the box. The courtroom was packed. It was observed that "Colonel Ingersoll's face showed great self-control although he was evidently laboring under strong nervous excitement." Presently Judge Wylie in his slow, hesitant manner was saying to the jury, "Gentlemen, I have sent for you to learn— ahem—to learn if you have agreed—ahem—upon a verdict." The foreman arose and said, "We have agreed." Visibly startled, the judge paused, then said to the Clerk, "Receive the verdict." With all eyes upon him, the foreman said, "We find the defendants not guilty."

Bedlam ensued. The judge could do nothing. "The humblest person connected in the most remote degree with the defense was," said the *Sun*, "crazy with joy." Ingersoll wrote, "The scene in the court cannot be described. The people were simply insane with joy. I never saw such excitement before."[10] When Mrs. Stephen Dorsey went into hysterics and shouted, "Glory to God! Glory to God!" the irony of this tribute to an agnostic was lost on everyone, apparently even Ingersoll whose eyes filled with tears.

When Ingersoll came out of the Court House, a large crowd was waiting. "Three cheers for Colonel Ingersoll!" and "Speech! Speech!" they cried. Declining the speech, but joking and laughing in the full relish of his victory, he stood on the broad sun-lit steps of the Court House until a carriage bearing his family drew up. As he came down the steps, the crowd slowly made way for him while he ran a gauntlet of back-slapping and handshakes. As the Ingersolls drove down Pennsylvania Avenue, the news of the verdict having preceded them, many people from passing carriages and the sidewalks called out congratulations. He was obliged to raise his hat so often that finally he sat bareheaded and, like a conquering hero, waved his hands to the right and to the left.

"THE REAL TEMPLE IS HOME"

Paul Blouet ("Max O'Rell"), the French journalist and satirist, who stayed with the Ingersolls several days in 1883, wrote of his host that although he was impressed with his genius as a writer and orator, he was impressed above all with "the example he sets of all the domestic virtues. One must have the privilege of knowing him intimately, of penetrating into that sanctuary of conjugal happiness, his home, before one can form an idea of the respect that he must inspire even in those who abhor his doctrines. His house is the home of the purest joys; it holds four hearts that beat as one. . . ."[1] A similar testament came from George Jacob Holyoake, the English freethinker: "It was to me an equal privilege and pleasure to see and know and to share the life of your household. I have never known a home made so radiant by what I shall call the abandonment of Love—or 'abandon' without the 'ment.' I never saw more plainly how much life is more than words."[2] Ingersoll practised what he preached: "The real temple is home."

But there were people who believed that all was not well with the Ingersolls. The Reverend W. W. Landrum of the First Baptist Church of Atlanta, Georgia, announced the conversion of an Ingersoll daughter to Presbyterianism. He said, "Ingersoll hates Presbyterians and his beloved daughter was perhaps driven to this step by his blasphemy and intolerance." Maud took prompt issue with the minister, "I wish to say emphatically that there isn't a word of truth in this statement. Neither my sister nor myself is connected with any church in any way. Although our father has always wished for us to study and think for ourselves, we agree with him heartily in his religious belief."

Another rumor had it that Ingersoll's son was a drunkard and that more than once in the presence of guests he had to be carried away from the table. To which Ingersoll replied, "It is not true that intoxicating beverages are served at my table. It is not true that my son ever was drunk. It is not true that he had to be carried away from the table. Besides, I have no son." And there was also the daughter who got drunk and whose father swore at her. Ingersoll wrote to a Major J. K. Barry, of Chicago, "I wish to know whether you ever said that you were once at my house to dinner, and that during the dinner my daughters drank wine until they were under the table and that one of them had to be helped out of the room. Also that I swore at her for being so foolish as to drink so much?

"I wish to know if you have ever said the above or anything like it?"[3] The Major did not answer, and Ingersoll let the matter drop.

The daughters had had little formal schooling. Their school had been their home, their teachers their parents except for private instruction in German, French, and Italian, music and art. Ingersoll had little use for the schools. He objected to the religious slant in textbooks and instruction. He thought study of history was superficial and misleading, "for the most part a detailed account of things that never occurred." He objected to the reverence for the classical languages, the "dead languages." Teach the languages of the living, German, French, Italian. And do not shun the education of the hand. Train the students in some craft, some art, enable them to earn a living. And do not wield the birch, "The schoolhouse should not be a prison or the teachers turnkeys." Ingersoll's philosophy of education stressed that "children should be taught to think, to investigate, to rely upon the light of reason, of observation and experiment; should be taught to use all their senses. . . ."

Ingersoll's daughters were educated as he said children should be. Never hurried in their development, never forced to learn, they could read and write at the age of six. Reading matter was selected for them, but not assigned, according to the stage of their development and with an eye to a wide variety of subjects. Did they learn prayers as children, Eva was once asked. She replied, "We were never taught prayers as children, but when old enough to reason mother selected the prayers that are considered most beautiful and touching, and told us, as she always did in making selections of poetry and prose, to read them carefully and learn the ones that pleased us. None pleased me especially, and I didn't commit any of them to memory."[4] Well, did they read the Bible and other religious works? Yes, later, when they reached sixteen or seventeen. They even helped their father find material for his lectures. As Maud put it, "Father had read with us and together we have looked up references, localities, and proofs."[5] She also said that the more they came to know about Christianity the less they liked it.

When the Ingersolls moved to Washington, the girls took up music and art in earnest and studied German, French, and Italian. Both girls took piano and singing lessons. Eva was discovered to have a soprano voice of great potentiality and for a while she seriously considered a career on the concert and operatic stage. She studied later with the Italian master, Ferronte. Having like her father histrionic tendencies, she relished public performance. She liked to sing or act or read aloud from Burns, Shelley, Keats, and Whitman. Often she and her father, and others including guests from the stage, would act out scenes from Shakespeare of which she had memorized a large number. Maud, more reserved, though she might be induced to take part, preferred to be one of the audience. Maud was more a critic than an artist. Though both girls liked to hear their father speak, Maud was his assiduous attendant. She would go on a lecture tour with him and was often in the court room to hear him. In writing of the "two lovely daughters," Blouet caught their differences, referring to Eva as Venice and to Maud as Athens.

Ingersoll's family attended religiously to his physical welfare. In 1883 he weighed around 220 pounds. Worried about it at times, he took exercise, and he dieted but with the limited perseverance of a confirmed bon vivant. One day in April, 1883, a friend, Representative E. J. Sherman of Massachusetts, visited at his home, and among the topics of conversation were Ingersoll's weight and sedentary habits. Sherman earnestly recommended a long walk every day. Ingersoll wrote to Sherman:

> After you went away, the family commenced. No man ever received an equal amount of advice in an equal time.
>
> "You must walk, Colonel Sherman says that you are liable to fall dead for want of exercise. Do you *hear*? You must *Walk*!"
>
> "Yes," said Grandmother, "the apoplexy is lurking in your blood."
>
> "You are liable to be paralyzed," said my wife.
>
> "Or to die in your sleep," said Mrs. Farrell.
>
> "Or after you wake up," chimed in the baby.
>
> "You must walk," said Eva.
>
> "You ought to run," added Maud.
>
> "And never sit down again as long as you live," shouted Clint.
>
> So I started for Georgetown, and walked five miles before breakfast. And walked and walked and walked.
>
> Result:
>
> 1. Both my feet are covered with blisters.
> 2. The cords in my legs are as tight as the strings of a bass viol.
> 3. Great pain in the small of my back.

4. Sudden flashes of heat running up and down the spine.
5. Knees badly swollen.
6. Mind wandering.
7. Pulse about 120.
8. Temperature of the body 115 degrees.
9. Fur enough on my tongue to make a seal skin sacque.

I think I have walked enough.[6]

A couple of years later, after a month or so of "fasting," he triumphantly wrote Clint Farrell, " '211 lbs'—That is what the man said as I stepped off the scales today. '211 lbs' is what I said to the folks as we sat down to dinner. 'Don't fast any longer,' said Maud, 'you will be a living skeleton.' " But he resolved to go to 200 pounds. He did not make it because even as he set the objective he savored the feast he would have when the diet was over. The menu would be, as he described it:

1. Potatoes—fried not too hard
2. Green corn—lots of butter
3. Cantaloupes
4. Hot biscuits and butter
5. More potatoes
6. More green corn
7. Some cantaloupes
8. Glass of cream
9. A little fried chicken with potatoes
10. Corn fritters with chicken gravy
11. Another cantaloupe.

Amid such imagery Ingersoll compromised at 210 pounds.

Another hindrance to the success of his fasting was a large assortment of wines, champagnes, and cordials in his cellar. A favorite cordial was cherry bounce, a rather potent mixture of wild cherries, sugar, and Jamaica rum. After meals he would take a drink or two of whiskey because it was good for the digestion. "Whiskey is what you need," he once wrote his indisposed secretary, Newton Baker. "After each meal take a good swallow. One swallow will not make a summer but it will make you feel as though summer had come. . . ."

IN Washington the Ingersolls began having regular weekly "at homes." First on Sunday nights because friends got into the habit of calling then, the "at homes" soon shifted to Saturdays because the servants wanted Sundays off. The functions became a standard and popular feature of Washington social life. The guests, fifty or more in number, comprised, in the words of a correspondent for the Denver *Daily News,* "all the celebrities and wits in town:"[1] members of the cabinet and Supreme Court, foreign ministers, many congressmen, state governors, tycoons of finance and industry, lawyers, writers, actors, and musicians.

Arriving at the mansion on Lafayette Square about nine o'clock, the guests were ushered into a large hall boasting a marble floor, an immense mirror in a gilt frame on a marble base, and marble arches leading to the stairway, the dining room, and the parlors. They could not help noticing on the walls of the hall lithographic allegorical figures of superstition, justice, truth, liberty, and human love. They smiled when they saw at the entrance to the parlors that bust of Shakespeare, for on the head of the bust was the hat of their host set at a rakish angle. In the summer the hat was a white Panama, in other seasons it was a black derby or a topper. As the guests went into the first double parlors, they saw walls painted a light red and adorned with oriental tapestries. They walked on thick oriental rugs and sat in armchairs upholstered in red and purple velvet. In season, they saw a bright coal fire in the marble fireplace. On the mantel were boxes of choice Havana cigars.

The next parlor presented a similar décor. Above the fireplace was a portrait of Clark Ingersoll and next to the mantel a bust of Robert. On a small stand in the bow window was a cast, about three feet high, of the Venus de Milo. There was a Steinway Grand, and, as the evening would bear out, not for appearances only.

As other guests arrived and all were put at ease ("Everybody does what he wants to when he wants to, in this house," Ingersoll liked to say), some wandered across the hall into the spacious library. Here was a profusion of art objects—oil paintings, lithographs, engravings, framed photographs, busts, and statuettes. There were representations of family scenes, beautiful women, gladiators and athletes. On one wall hung a portrait of Beethoven. In prominence were busts of Voltaire, Newton, and Paine. And sure to attract attention was a collection of religious curios, everything from beads and icons to idols and totem poles. (Once a sharp-eyed reporter detected Ingersoll poking around and buying such things in a shop on Bleecker Street in New York and in a column note on his discovery posed the naive question, was Ingersoll becoming religious.) Lining the four walls, halfway from the floor to the ceiling, were shelves of books. On one of two center tables was a massive book in heavy morocco binding edged with gilt, the complete works of Shakespeare. Inscribed in gilt on the front cover were the words, "The Inspired Book" and on the title panel the words, "The Volume of the Brain." In the middle of the book, as in a family Bible, were blank pages for the family register. "My Bible," Ingersoll would say, and then pointing to a smaller volume, the poetry of Burns, on the other center table, "and my hymn-book."

Since the newspapers, of other cities as well as Washington, often carried accounts of these receptions, the general public was able to form impressions of an agnostic and his family at home. Some readers who knew that godlessness led to depravity could hardly believe that the mammoth punch bowl on the dining room table held nothing stronger than a claret and fruit concoction. Others could hardly believe that Ingersoll did not curse or beat his family in public, that he did not philander or practise free love. Yet the more they read about the Ingersolls the more they had to believe that this infidel family was happy, gracious, and cultured.

The two daughters, Eva and Maud, were now, in 1883, twenty and nineteen. At the receptions they moved among the guests with savoir-faire and charm. Their conversation revealed that they were versed in music, art, and literature and that, young as they were, they were interested in a variety of causes, child welfare, birth control, equality and suffrage for women, slum clearance, prison reform, and the improvement of the conditions of labor. They reflected their father's practical humanism:

> I have a creed for this, the only world of which I know anything:
> 1. Happiness is the only good.
> 2. The way to be happy is to make others so.
> 3. The place to be happy is here.
> 4. The time to be happy is now.
> 5. Help for the living.—Hope for the dead.

Eva struck most beholders as the prettier of the two. A correspondent for the St. Louis *Globe-Democrat* taken with her "mass of golden brown hair" called her "a most decided beauty, being of that fresh, dewy-eyed and virginal type that the English painters depict."[2] Of less poetic mold, Maud, a brunette, had her share of comeliness. She resembled her mother, the clear-cut, strong face, the quick smile, the flashing eyes, the smooth black hair. To set off the beauty of Eva, Ingersoll gave her on every occasion a bouquet of lilies-of-the-valley; to set off that of Maud and his wife he gave roses of deep crimson. Both the daughters knew how to dress to point up their particular virtues. At one reception, Eva was observed to be wearing "a medieval dress of puce-colored velvet and brocade, with quaint puffs at the elbows and a broad pompadour neck filled and outlined with creamy lace." Maud was wearing a dress of black brocade unadorned except for "a dainty white fichu drawn about her shoulders." Mrs. Ingersoll, no signs of grey in her hair, looked "strikingly handsome" wearing a be-trained polonaise of black silk velvet over a beaded satin skirt and an embroidered black lace fichu. She had a large diamond solitaire in each ear and she wore on her nuptial finger diamonds observed to be "immense."

Sooner or later in the course of an "at home," those who wished gathered around the Steinway to sing or to hear Eva, a soprano, and Maud, a contralto, sing while Mrs. Farrell accompanied, or to hear Mrs. Farrell, an accomplished pianist, play solo. After an hour or so of music, the guests were led into the spacious dining room to partake of the great quantities of sandwiches, cold meats, cakes, and ices that bedecked a long table. At one end of the table was the punch bowl, Ingersoll presiding. He dispensed the contents with gusto, with something of the air of a celebrant at a joyous human rite.

The receptions were especially gala on such occasions as the victory in the Star Route trials or the appearance of noted actors and musicians in Washington or the Ingersolls' wedding anniversaries. On February 13, 1883, the Ingersolls' twenty-first anniversary, five hundred guests attended. Extraordinary numbers also attended the festivities for the actor, John Mc-Cullough, the Austrian violinist, Edouard Remenyi, and the English freethinker, George Jacob Holyoake.

Because of his abounding good nature and lavish hospitality Ingersoll came to be known as "Royal Bob." Washington reporters with whom he was on the best of terms also called him "None Such."

"A POSITIVE GENIUS FOR LOSING MONEY"

IN 1879 Ingersoll became the attorney and an entrepreneur of The Coney National Spirit Aging Company, Limited, of Pittsburgh. As attorney for the new company he helped set the financial structure and secured the patents for the aging process. As entrepreneur he endeavored to impress prospective investors with the worth of the Coney process which was guaranteed to make freshly distilled whiskey taste in one month as if it were five or six years old. Once he tried to bamboozle the taste experts. He received from a fellow founder of the company a gift of a demijohn of whiskey which he assumed had been treated by the Coney process but which instead had undergone several years of natural aging. The mistake came about because no letter accompanied the gift and nothing on the bottle specified the contents. A letter about the whiskey came later, after Ingersoll had had several taste experts sample it. They had pronounced it "tolerable" but "slightly raw." Ingersoll then decided to capitalize on his own error. He asked the giver of the whiskey to send him a gallon which had been Coney treated. "I think now I have a joke on these gentlemen and will endeavor to cap the climax when the treated whiskey comes, by passing it off as absolutely twenty years old. . . ." It is not known whether the hoax worked. It is known that all attempts at the artificial aging of distilled spirits have been found wanting. In any case, the company went into a rapid decline.

While Ingersoll had a large annual income from his lectures and law practice, $150,000 to $200,000 a year, he was never able to get out of debt. He spent money lavishly for the comfort of his family and contributed generously to the support of relatives and charities. What was left, and more that he borrowed, he invested, in oil, mining, and railroad projects, in a woodenware and veneer company, in a cattle ranch.

In July, 1881, the Ivanhoe Mining Company, incorporated under the laws of Colorado, came into being, with Ingersoll as the chief sponsor. For three years he and his associates had fought to secure legal rights to a mining property in the mountains of northern New Mexico territory. They had contested the constitutionality of an act passed by Congress in January, 1880, retroactive to January 1, 1879, requiring the expenditure of $100 yearly on mining property to make a claim valid. The Ingersoll interests had registered a claim in 1878 but had done nothing on the property in 1879 and so their claim was automatically vacated. While the constitutional question was being aired, certain other parties staked and registered a claim, but Ingersoll representatives took forcible possession. The issue was brought to the Commissioner of the General Land Office of

the New Mexico Territory, who ruled against Ingersoll. The
rival claimants, however, relinquished their rights for a considerable sum of money. Then it was discovered that two other
parties, named "Harvest" and "Welfare," had registered a
claim. A series of dramatic negotiations followed, climaxed by
a hectic all-night drive to "Harvest" and "Welfare," who agreed
to accept for their claim $10,000 cash payable on the spot,
though they had earlier accepted an offer of $10,000, payable
in thirty days, and had made bond to turn over the property
when payment was made.

Because of Ingersoll's reputation and assurances, capital
quickly came to the Ivanhoe Mining Company, of which he
was elected president. An issue of five hundred first mortgage
bonds at a par value of $100 with seven percent annual interest
payable semi-annually found immediate takers. Stock at a par
of four dollars, minimum lot one hundred shares, was snapped
up. A condition of sale of bonds and stocks was that the taker
pledge himself not to sell below the par value.

Ingersoll's nephew, Burton, employed in his office, was enthusiastic over the Ivanhoe prospects. He persuaded his father
and his brother, in Wisconsin, to invest. On November 15,
1881, Burton wrote his brother, John, "You now have 535
shares and I 250. You are three times as rich as I." John still
had $500 which he was worried about. "Send the remainder of
your money and stop those old maid predictions." John replied,
"I am nearly crazy to think I have no more money to invest—
but $500." Then from Burton to John, "Sunday Uncle read
letter from Prof. Silliman at the mine. He has been assaying
some of the ore they have been throwing away all along, esteem-
ing it worthless. It assayed at $175 to the ton, $35 of which was
gold. This astounded even Uncle." On November 27, Burton
wrote that his Uncle was planning to form another corporation
to develop a mine, The Little Bear, on the same ledge with the
Ivanhoe, the stock to sell at one dollar a share. Meanwhile John
had lent Burton his $500, who was happy to relate that his
uncle was going to let him invest the money in the new mine.
But John ought to get into it too—was it impossible for him to

get hold of some more money? Then the boys' father decided that the time had come for caution. Although he had "very great confidence in Ivanhoe or somebody has been doing some very muscular lying," he was not so sure about the other mine.[1]

Bad luck hit the Ivanhoe mine early in 1882. Because of delays in finding a second-hand mill—a new one would cost $100,000—production had to be put off until summer. But the prospectus had set February as the latest time. Some investors took fright and sold, despite their pledge not to sell below par. Ivanhoe stock's became almost worthless. Burton's uncle gave him fifty shares and John one hundred saying that they might as well have them as cheaply as anyone else—for nothing. Burton regarded the gift as "a piece of rare good luck."[2] Ivanhoe would still bring riches.

Production at the mine actually started in the summer of 1883. But it was soon clear that the specimens of ore assayed at a high value were not typical. On December 21, 1883, the Ivanhoe Mine Company was sold to satisfy debtors.

Ingersoll was heartsick at the outcome. He proceeded to repay his relatives for their losses. To Clint Farrell he wrote, "If you want some money let me know. . . . I owe you anyway. It was never my intention that you should lose a cent in Ivanhoe. And I will not allow you to." He also refunded money to many women of small means. Thereafter when women asked him for advice on speculative prospects he discouraged them, particularly if he were backing an enterprise. Several years later, in 1889, when he became the president of another mining company he wrote to a Dr. C. D. Jenkins of Boston, "Long ago I made up my mind never to sell a share of stock of any kind to *a woman* . . . and while I think the Cholchis mine is good, and while I am willing to put some money in it myself, and am willing to sell to men, I do not want anything to do with women.

"So I have not signed the stock intended for the women. . . ."[3]

Ingersoll's involvement with the Palo Blanco Cattle Company of New Mexico originated with the Star Route trials and his client, Stephen Dorsey. Before the trials Dorsey owned a huge ranch close to Chico Springs, New Mexico. Comprising

24,000 acres near the Atchison, Topeka and Sante Fe railroad, it was about eighty miles long and sixty miles wide and included a water right controlling 4,500,000 acres. The livestock numbered about 45,000 cows and steers, 600 bulls, and 800 horses. There were seventy houses and barns. To meet the expenses of the Star Route trials, which did not include cash fees for Ingersoll because none were charged, Dorsey with his ranch holdings formed a stock company. One J. W. Bosler, of Pennsylvania, bought a two-thirds interest for $250,000. About the time the trials were over, Bosler died. The executors of his estate set an initial price of $700,000 on his holding but sold it for $475,000 to Ingersoll and John B. Alley, a retired millionaire shoe manufacturer from Boston. Alley in his own right put up $400,000 and Ingersoll, the balance, which he borrowed, that is, as Alley put it, "Ingersoll is being 'carried' by myself and some other friends."[4] Thus, with Dorsey who still had a one-third interest, there were three owners of the ranch.

In the fall of 1883, the three formed the Palo Blanco Cattle Company of New Mexico. Alley was the president and Ingersoll the secretary, with Dorsey remaining incognito. They decided to increase the capital stock to $2,000,000, shares to sell at $100 each. Thus Alley's holding came to 4,000 shares, Ingersoll's to 750, and Dorsey's to 1600. If the capitalization scheme worked out, they stood to make an easy, if honorable, million.

Enter troubles. A number of claimants to small plots or "floats" within the ranch boundaries asserted their rights. Some of the claims were valid, some fraudulent, but all had to be disposed of either by a cash payment or granting a property right or by legal measures to prove fraudulence. One of the fraudulent claims involved the very land upon which the main ranch buildings stood. Another set of complications lay in the indebtedness outstanding at the time the Palo Blanco Company was formed. It came to about $12,000, larger than expected. It proved a real stumbling block only because Ingersoll insisted on paying it off and did pay it off himself. Alley and Dorsey were unwilling to honor the debts; "nobody would do it but me." The task was not easy. He wrote to one creditor, "I would

"ROYAL BOB"
1890

Grandpa Ingersoll with Eva and Robert, 1898.

Ingersoll speaking in a tent at the funeral of Walt
Whitman, in Harleigh Cemetery, Camden, N.J.,
March 30, 1892.

The caption on this *Puck* cartoon quoted a Rev. Dr. R. S. MacArthur as saying, "There are going to be two big surprises in heaven. The first will be the number of people we expect to see there whom we shall not find. The second surprise will be the number of people we shall meet whom we did not expect would get there." Accordingly, here we see Bob Ingersoll face to face with his arch-foe the Reverend DeWitt Talmage, a famous Brooklyn preacher. Among the others who have made it are the "rich man," merchant prince John Wanamaker, and that impresario of corrupt politics, Boss Richard Croker, chief of Tammany Hall. Croker has the arm of the Rev. Dr. Charles Henry Parkhurst, the zealous reformer who tried to expose the Croker gang.

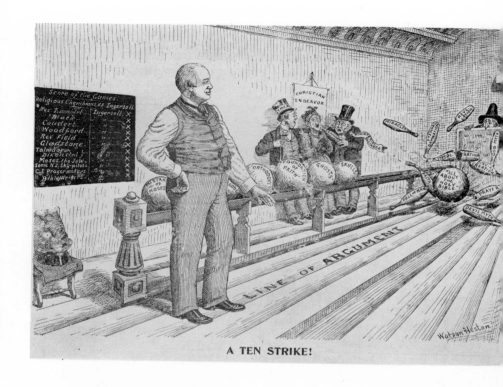

A TEN STRIKE!

The mighty agnostic overwhelms his opponents named on the blackboard. See what the invincible balls, Ingersoll's lectures, do to the vincible doctrinal pins. Note the distress of the three spectators. Observe the horror of the two ecclesiastical pin-setters. Nineteen years after Ingersoll's death, *The Truth Seeker* recalls the exploits of one of its heroes.

gladly step out and let somebody take my place, as I know nothing about the business. . . . I want you to take into consideration that this thing is simply a drag and a loss so far as I am concerned, and that I most sincerely wish that the Ranch was in heaven." This was the way Ingersoll felt in October, 1883. But he began to see that the ranch might be a heaven on earth.

Early in 1884 Ingersoll went on a lecture tour to the West and Southwest, a tour arranged to enable him and his wife and daughters who were with him on the tour to spend some time at the ranch. They were guests of Dorsey, who, in the exercise of his right, was occupying the ranch as his permanent residence. They arrived the last week of February and after spending ten days walking and riding they decided that here was the place they would stay every year, from June to November. But first a new ranch house would have to be built, large enough to accommodate the Dorseys and the Ingersolls. Architectural plans were drawn up for a log house that was to be ready for occupancy by July. It was not ready until October.

After another lecture tour that took the Ingersolls as far west as Portland, Oregon, they reached Springer, New Mexico, close to the ranch, on October 5. They were met at the railroad station by Dorsey's coachman, Crandall, who had been instructed, because a housewarming party had been arranged, to delay the arrival of his charges at the new house until nightfall. This was not easy. First, the Ingersolls were in Springer at six in the morning; second, they were eager to see the house; third, it would take only four hours to reach the house. But Crandall, an ingenious man, was equal to the task. He took the Ingersolls to a hotel and simply disappeared. After four hours of fretful waiting, Ingersoll went out to look for him. He found him. Crandall was profusely apologetic. The front seat of the carriage was being repaired! Depend on it, he would be at the hotel at eleven. Eleven came but no Crandall; twelve, and no Crandall. Twelve-thirty he appeared. Were the Ingersolls ready? Yes. Good, he would feed the horses and be right back. An hour and a half went by. Where was he? He must be drunk. Oh, there he is. "Are you ready?" he asked. "Good

God, Yes!" said Ingersoll. Well, they would leave as soon as
one of the carriage tires which was loose was reset. And Crandall was gone again. Finally, at four, he drove up before the
hotel and they were on their way.

As they neared the house, they realized why Crandall had
procrastinated. The premises and the long veranda were aflood
with the bright lights of gas lanterns and every window gleamed
from the gas lights within. As the Ingersolls alighted from the
carriage, the Dorseys, the ranch hands, and the servants
whooped it up.

What the Ingersolls saw inside pleased them no end: a large
dining room done in oak, a completely equipped kitchen, sleeping apartments furnished in cherry, bathrooms with hot and
cold water, a billiard room, a smoking room, and a library.
Nothing like it in all New Mexico.

So sure was Ingersoll that they were going to live in the
house a few months each year that he wrote to Clint Farrell
about a location for a house for the Farrells "right near us."
I beg of you to come. My reasons are, *1st,* the climate is per-
fection—mild, balmy, delicious. *2nd,* the country is a poem by
Shakespeare set to music by Wagner. *3rd,* Sue would get well
and grow fat. In a few days you would see hollyhocks on her
cheeks. *4th,* the same would happen to you and the baby."[5]
They should come at once and see for themselves. There was
plenty of room in the new house, which Ingersoll named Mau-
deva, and there were plenty of horses, saddles, and vehicles.
What a time they would all have. With the letter to Clint, Ingersoll enclosed a note to Sue, "You are so weak and thin—
and your cough is so persistent that I am afraid you are going
to lose your health. . . . Climate is something wonderful . . .
we walk and ride, read and talk, eat and sleep—look at the
shadows of the clouds upon the undulating plains. . . . Come—
Come, Come, Come—*Come! !*" But the Farrells, a little concerned about tagging along, did not come.

By the end of October, the undulating plains took on a tedious aspect. Ingersoll was gregarious. He missed the variety
and bustle of Washington. He missed the "at homes." He missed

the excitement and hubbub of audiences. And he missed the Farrells. "We are anxious to see you," he wrote to Clint, "but as Dorsey took so much pains to build and furnish the house, we must stay at least to the twentieth of November."

They left, however, on the twelfth. They left then because the New Mexico delegates to the national convention of cattlemen to open two days later in St. Louis gathered for a celebration on the twelfth, in Springer, and Ingersoll, appointed delegate at large by Governor Sheldon, was the guest of honor and the speaker. What a day it was for Springer. Ropes and wreaths of evergreen bedecked main street and town hall. A community orchestra and the Tenth Infantry Band from nearby Fort Union made the welkin ring. At a barbecue and a banquet great quantities of New Mexico beef went into the maws of the largest number of people ever to gather in Springer. It was "the grandest affair in the history of this city," reported the *Colfax County Stockman*. The affair also turned out to be Ingersoll's valedictory to the cattle business.

Within a year Ingersoll gave up his holdings in the Palo Blanco Cattle Company. The operating expenses of the company were high; the income low. Also Ingersoll had to meet the interest charges on his loans from Alley and "some other friends." To his great annoyance, he was also called upon to take care of the interest on several notes Dorsey had given. Ingersoll's losses amounted to about $20,000. This and his other business adventures prompted him to say, "I have a positive genious for losing money. Well, no matter. If it is better to give than to receive, I suppose it is better to lose than to find."[6]

"AFRAID OF FRIGHTENING
THE PREACHERS AWAY"

INGERSOLL, the erstwhile champion of the "Plumed Knight," stayed off the hustings in 1884 when Blaine was the Republican hopeful. He did not even attend the Convention, at Chicago, which nominated Blaine. If he had attended it, he would have supported either Walter Q. Gresham, onetime Postmaster General in Arthur's cabinet, or John M. Harlan, an associate justice of the United States Supreme Court.

Ingersoll had had high hopes, in October, 1883, that the Republican party would once again become the crusading instrument of human liberty. It was in October that the United States Supreme Court declared the Civil Rights Act, or the Equal Rights Act, passed in March, 1875, unconstitutional. This was an act which undertook to give Negroes equal rights in places of public business and resort within the states. The decision of the Supreme Court, Ingersoll had said, "says to the Republican party, 'Your mission is not yet ended. This is not a free country. Our flag does not protect the rights of a human being.' This decision is the tap of a drum. The old veterans will fall into line. This decision gives the issue for the next campaign and it may be that the Supreme Court has builded wiser than it knew."

On October 22, 1883, in Lincoln Hall, Washington, Ingersoll had been the main speaker at a large meeting held in protest of the decision. Frederick Douglass, the great Negro leader, whom Ingersoll had harbored one night at his home in Peoria, introduced him. In a two and a half hour speech, Ingersoll explained the historical and juridical aspects of civil rights legislation with stress on the relevance of the Thirteenth and Fourteenth amendments to the Civil Rights Act. His core contention was that the amendments empowered Congress to pass whatever legislation was needed to insure to all, in practice, the enjoyment of the rights, privileges, and immunities of free citizens. "The Supreme Court has failed to take into consideration the intention of the framers of these amendments. . . ."

One justice had dissented, John M. Harlan—"By the fortress of liberty one sentinel remains at his post." His opinion was not out at the time of Ingersoll's speech. Said the orator, "I anticipate a pleasure."

The opinion came out in November. To Ingersoll it left the

decision of the Supreme Court "without argument, without reason, and without excuse," and it placed Harlan in the front rank of constitutional lawyers. Moreover, the opinion furnished "a perfectly clear plank, without knot or wind-shake, for the next Republican platform." And because of the widespread favorable reaction to it, it made Harlan a likely prospect for the presidential nomination. He would be a tonic to the party and a drawer of votes—"his dissenting opinion has made every colored man his friend."

But the Republicans at their national convention ignored Harlan and the "perfectly clear plank." This was one reason that Ingersoll did not take part in the campaign.[1]

Another reason lay in the campaign strategy that the Republican managers decided to follow, particularly in regard to the State of New York. The state had a strong Irish Catholic vote which had always been Democratic. In 1884, however, the Republicans saw an opportunity to split that vote and they exploited it to the utmost. Grover Cleveland, the Democratic nominee, had had an exemplary public record as mayor of Buffalo and as governor of New York. But he was a bachelor and about all bachelors there must be something unsavory. So sleuthhounds followed various scents. They soon found what they were after. Cleveland was not only an unchaste bachelor, he was the father of a bastard.

Here was fine political fare to set before the Irish Catholics. The best of it was that Cleveland would not declare his innocence if innocent he were. Instead he told his dismayed followers "to tell the truth."

The Democrats sought desperately to find something similar against Blaine. They did unearth a few savory tidbits forty or so years old but nothing that could cause a good substantial stench. When Ingersoll read about the disclosures, he wrote, "The story about Cleveland is a settler. And the ones about Blaine are rather salty. Both the candidates are a little tainted with original sin and both seem to have suffered from the 'thorn in the flesh.' It is a nasty business and the principal issues in the campaign will be fornication and adultery. Great Country."[2]

It was not so much the gathering scurrility of the campaign that bothered Ingersoll as the calculated appeal to a religious group. Indeed it appeared that Blaine was making a try for all religious groups. He was saying in his speeches, "The State cannot get along without the church." The grand old party was going pious. Once when Ingersoll was asked why he did not participate in the campaign he replied, "I was afraid of frightening the preachers away."[3]

Came then October 29, the day that the Republican religious strategy boomeranged. Six hundred preachers paid Blaine a call at the Fifth Avenue Hotel in New York City. There was much talk about keeping that "self-confessed adulterer," that "moral leper," out of the White House. Blaine proclaimed that every measure of the Republican party challenged "the approbation of Christian ministers and the approval of God." The session was going along fine until the Reverend Dr. S. D. Burchard, of a prominent Presbyterian pulpit, had his say. Burchard, called "a Silurian or early Paleozoic bigot" by the New York *Sun,* announced that the assembled company could never support a party "whose antecedents had been Rum, Romanism, and Rebellion." The day might have been saved if Blaine had instantly repudiated the statement. When two days later he did issue a repudiation, it was too late. "Rum, Romanism, and Rebellion" was already one of the most effective, if last-minute, campaign slogans in the history of American politics. All over the country it sent the Democratic press into ecstasies of indignation. "Rum, Romanism, and Rebellion" was on placards outside Catholic churches. Ingersoll enjoyed the discomfiture of the Republicans. He might have done some good for them by scaring one of the preachers away but, he said, "I didn't know Burchard until it was too late."[4]

On November 5, the day after the election, as the returns alternately indicating victories for Cleveland and Blaine began to reach Ingersoll in New Mexico, he wrote, "We are all in the dark about the election. We have the news that Blaine and

Cleveland are both elected." The diehard Republican in him also said, "We hardly know whether to laugh or cry and are not quite sure which side we are on." When on November 8 he received the definite report that Cleveland was elected he wrote, "The position taken by the Republican party on the decision of the Supreme Court on the Civil Rights bill furnishes salve for this wound."[5] There were several other wounds salved. The Republican leaders had not treated him in a manner befitting his prominence in the party, "I think I shall enjoy seeing the Brewsters—and Arthurs, the Camerons—and Shermans, Blaines and Logans sitting on a back seat." Some of these leaders had condemned him for his role in the Star Route trials, "The atty for the defts in the Star Route Trial has his revenge."[6] And the appeal to the religious vote had failed, "The only persons for whom I am really sorry are the 600 preachers who called on Blaine and assured him of the support of Jehovah and Co.—I hate to have the old firm disappointed."[7]

LECTURES, HOME AND ABROAD

I N 1884-1885 Ingersoll was again on extensive lecture tours. Typical press reports on the size of his audiences were: "Largest ever in city," Denver; "Immense Audience," Kansas City; "Largest audience in the city since his last visit," St. Louis; "Largest audience ever assembled in the Boyd," Omaha; Dietz Opera House "crowded from pit to dome" Oakland, California; Central Music Hall "packed from pit to dome," Chicago.

Moreover, to the despair of his detractors, Ingersoll appealed to the "best people" as well as to atheists and such. In Cleveland the audience was composed not only of infidels but of "people of all sorts of religious creeds" including a number of local ministers.[1] In Brooklyn it was "a very well dressed,

intelligent looking audience . . . composed of business men,
lawyers, doctors, journalists, and other prominent men, the
most of them well-known church goers."[2] In Rockford, Illinois, "the audience were of the best class . . . with the usual
percentage of the fair portion of humanity."[3] Emancipation
was having its effect and the "usual percentage" meant a goodly
number. In Sacramento, California, "so many ladies" came
to hear Ingersoll and "seemed to admire him and to be in sympathy with his doctrine, or lack of doctrine" that the Sacramento *Daily Bee* concluded that the church was losing its "real
solid pillars."[4]

The outlook seemed equally serious in Brooklyn. The ministers of the "City of Churches," were much concerned with
the problem of Ingersollism. The Reverend Dr. Eddy advised
his brethren not to attempt to answer Ingersoll from the pulpit
lest the very answers breed doubts. The Reverends Dr. Hawk-
ins and Dr. Haynes recommended the same strategy. While
the Reverends Mr. Pullman and Dr. Van Dyke held that no
systematic defense was necessary, the Reverends Dr. Carpenter and Mr. Reed advised unremitting vigilance so that "thistle
and noxious weeds" could not get started. Ingersoll was pleased
at all this attention and prepared a reply, "The Brooklyn Divines," in which he advised the clerics to take note of the times:
the affairs of *this* world were displacing in the minds of men
the affairs of the next.[5]

One of the most vigilant warders of the nation's morals, the
Y.M.C.A., considered Ingersoll a major menace to the good
life. In the larger cities whenever Ingersoll was to lecture the
Y.M.C.A. turned out in force to distribute monitory materials
at the doors of the auditorium and, on the Sunday preceding
a lecture, outside the churches. On Sunday morning, February
22, 1885, for instance, the Y.M.C.A., "handed out at the doors
of Brooklyn churches 20,000 warnings, in circular form, to
the church attendants not to go to hear Colonel Robert G.
Ingersoll's demoralizing lecture in the evening."[6] Ingersoll had
fun with the Y.M.C.A. A ready jibe of his was to ask an audience why during a storm in Washington lightning should strike

a Y.M.C.A. hall but avoid his office in a building in the same block.

Another sign that Ingersoll was creating a stir was, in his count, the "hundreds of challenges" for platform debates that came to him. Isaac T. Dyer wanted to debate him on the existence of hell. He published his challenge in the *Quincy Herald*, Illinois, in December, 1884, and wrote Ingersoll about it. Dyer's stationery identified him as Patentee of the Engle and National Refrigerator. Ingersoll replied, "I came to the conclusion that being in the Refrigerating business, you did not want hell abolished but hoped to carry on business in the next world. Biassed as you must be by your business; prejudiced by your own interests; I think it hardly worth while to discuss the question of eternal fire with you. . . ."[7] In February, 1885, Siston McMillen, a retired lawyer in Oskaloosa, Iowa, and of local renown for therapeutic miracles, published a challenge in the New York *Tribune* and sent a copy to Ingersoll.[8] They would debate at some hall in Chicago "either or all" of the following propositions:

1. Christ was raised from the dead.
2. Delirium tremens is demoniac possession.
3. Insanity is demoniac possession whenever it assumes a violent or vicious form.
4. The sick can be healed and devils cast out in the name of Christ through faith in His name and promises.

The debate did not take place. Another challenge came from the Reverend Robert Nourse of Chicago, to whom Ingersoll wrote, ". . . you are hardly of sufficient importance to justify an acceptance."[9] When a Father Lambert who had published a tract against him issued a challenge, Ingersoll said he was not interested in "such little fellows" but "Let them bring on the pope or a cardinal and I will give him a whirl."

Now and then in an attempt to protect the people from an Ingersoll lecture the law was invoked. On May 24, 1884, he was scheduled to deliver "Which Way" in Philadelphia. It was bad enough to have the lecture at any time; it was intolerable to have it at a time when the Methodists were having their Annual Conference in the city. The Rev. Irwin H. Torrence, General Secretary of the Pennsylvania Bible Society, decided to do something about it. He consulted counsel who found what he wanted, a Pennsylvania statute on blasphemy. Passed March 31, 1860, the act read: "If any person shall willfully, premeditatedly and despitefully blaspheme or speak loosely and profanely of Almighty God, Christ Jesus, the Holy Spirit, or the Scriptures of Truth, such person on conviction thereof, shall be sentence to pay a fine not exceeding one hundred dollars, and undergo an imprisonment not exceeding three months, or either, at the discretion of the Court." "The law is with us," said the Reverend Torrence, "and Ingersoll has but to do what he had done before, to find himself in a cell."[10]

"What would you do," Ingersoll was asked, "if they should make an attempt to arrest you?" "Nothing," he replied, "except to defend myself in court."[11] Ingersoll did give the lecture as scheduled, and to a capacity house, but no one appeared to arrest him. Yet if anything he was more caustic than ever in his treatment of orthodoxies, particularly Catholicism. His concentration on Catholicism might have been the reason he escaped arrest. The Protestants would not mind. The Methodists would not mind. And the Reverend Torrence, who was in the audience to spot blasphemy, would not mind.

Ingersoll seldom lectured in Canada, but on his tour of the West Coast, in the late summer of 1884, he went across the border to deliver "Orthodoxy" in Victoria, British Columbia. Two days before the scheduled lecture, the fire commissioner refused a license to the lessor of the Theater Royal, where Ingersoll was to speak, because there were too few exits. The lessor promptly made the required changes and was granted the license a few hours before the lecture was to be given. But then certain parties complained to the commissioner that the theater still did not conform with the fire regulations. About a half hour before the lecture, the theater already two-thirds full, the police appeared and announced that the lecture would not be permitted because the theater had again been declared unsafe. A hurly-burly ensued but the police were adamant. They pointed out that the theater lacked one door. Thereupon several indignant would-be ticket buyers got hold of an axe and saw and cut out a door. The police bowed to the unmistakable fact that the letter of the regulation was observed. Ingersoll gave his lecture, without further incident. "I understand," he said later, "that those who opposed the lecture are now heartily ashamed of the course pursued."[12]

By 1885, Ingersoll was recognized abroad as a force of no mean consequence. His lectures, in a variety of authorized and unauthorized editions, at least three editions published in England, reached a large body of readers in the British Isles, where liberal and free thought societies abounded. The ground prepared by Darwin Spencer, and Huxley, these societies flourished under the leadership of such prominent freethinkers as George Jacob Holyoake, Charles Bradlaugh, George William Foote, Charles Watts, and Annie Besant.

Ingersoll had a heavy correspondence with Holyoake, whom he considered "the model man." In 1841, at the age of twenty-four, Holyoake was convicted of blasphemy in a public lecture and served six months in prison. Upon his release he established a journal, *Reasoner,* in support of his opinions for which he coined the term "secularism." In his later years he championed the co-operative movement, writing the *History of Co-operation in England* and *The Co-operative Movement of Today*. Ingersoll's acquaintance with Bradlaugh and Foote was through their published works. Both were often on the lecture platform in England and both wrote prolifically. Foote, with Holyoake, founded *The Secularist* and later he edited *The Liberal* and founded *The Freethinker*. Ingersoll followed with intense interest Bradlaugh's protracted struggles to gain a seat in the House of Commons. First elected in 1880 and repeatedly re-elected, Bradlaugh was denied a seat, under the Parliamentary Oath act, until January, 1886. He was excluded on the ground that the right, which he claimed, to affirm allegiance to Her Majesty in lieu of taking the parliamentary oath did not exist. Bradlaugh then offered to take the oath but in this he was rebuffed because of his atheistical opinions. In 1881 he attempted forcibly to enter the House but was ejected. In 1882, at the opening of the session, he marched up the House and with a Bible from his own pocket administered the oath to himself. This was adjudged an insult to God and Her Majesty. Interviewed on this "excitement in England" by the *London Secular Review,* Ingersoll denounced the oath as a "relic of barbarous theology, of the belief that a personal God interferes in the affairs of men." The oath "supplies the wolf with sheep's clothing . . . puts upon each witness a kind of theological gown."[13]

Annie Besant worked closely with Bradlaugh for many years. Only when she became an extreme Socialist and a disciple of Mme. Blavatsky, the theosophist, did they go their separate ways. Although Ingersoll knew a good deal about her, his only direct touch with her was a letter he wrote her in June, 1878, when she was denied the custody of her child. In 1867 she had married the Rev. Frank Besant. In 1873 she obtained a separation. Litigation resulted over the custody of their child and she, because she was an atheist, was declared an unfit mother. Ingersoll wrote her June 10, 1878, "A few moments ago I read an account of the proceedings in Court when your child was torn from your arms by a robed brute acting as an English judge. . . . There is no language strong enough to express my hatred of Sir George Jessel and my sympathy for you. . . ."

Ingersoll came to know Charles Watts well and had the highest regard for him. Watts campaigned for secularism in the United States as well as in England. He became an American citizen. His experience as a promoter of secularist organizations in England was put to good use in this country. Joining the American Secular Union, which took the place of the National Liberal League, he was elected vice-president in September, 1885. Ingersoll was elected president, an office which he was now willing to accept since the Union discarded the stand of the Liberal League that the laws regulating the circulation of obscene matter should be repealed.

In November, 1883, Ingersoll heard from Henry Musgrave Reade, secretary and bookseller of the Pendleton Club, Manchester, England, that his works were "the most popular Freethought works in the country, far more popular than Bradlaugh's or Besant's or Foote's at most our branches."[14] Reade noticed "from week to week" that these famous freethinkers often substituted the reading of an Ingersoll lecture for the delivery of one of their own, which was the more remarkable in that "they take the best [audiences]." Reade also stated: "As the book-seller of our Club I can say I scarcely sell any works but yours and that they are sold in all stationers' shops in Manchester." Himself freed from "fear and doubt" by Ingersoll's "What Must I Do to Be Saved," which he bought because he thought it was orthodox and would restore his peace of mind, Reade bought as many of the works of Ingersoll as he could find and "eagerly devoured them." He sent a copy of the *Religion of the Future* to "all the ministers in Dublin and they have been preaching about it ever since." An Edward O'Neill, of Dublin, wrote Ingersoll, "As a member of a small liberal society in Dublin, I beg to assure you of our deep sense of the splendid services you are rendering to humanity. We read your grand orations with delight and profit."

And from across the Pacific Ingersoll heard that the Japanese were reading him. A Dan Farrell, stationed at the U. S. Naval Depot at Nagasaki wrote him, in 1883, "The Japs like your works very much and have had their translation for some years back."

But for singular appreciation of Ingersoll, back to England. A district close to London populated almost entirely by freethinkers was named the Ingersoll District. And advertised for sale in London was "Ingersoll District Choice Cream Cheese." The cheese, by the way, at the Amsterdam Exhibition, in 1884, won the medal for first prize.

Part Four:
NEW YORK

"A SPLENDID BARGAIN"

IN April, 1885, Ingersoll wrote his brother John, "Most of the winter I have been in New York attending to law business during weekdays and lecturing on Sunday." Although Ingersoll preferred lecturing to law and considered Washington as good a center as any from which to go forth to proselytize, he was tendered too much lucrative litigation requiring his presence in New York not to have it forced upon him that Washington was becoming a mere headquarters for him and his home in Washington a home in absentia. His wife was not too happy with the trend of his activities. "Eva, I think, wants me to settle in New York."[1]

There was another, less practical, reason for moving to New York. The many cultural and artistic activities of the city beckoned to the Ingersolls. They could readily go to the Steinway, Chickering, and Carnegie halls, and to the new Metropolitan Opera House, where they could feast on the music of their favorite composers, Bach, Beethoven, Mozart, and Wagner— Beethoven and Wagner! who, to Ingersoll, "made the air of this world rich forever." They could go to the theaters—the Fifth Avenue, Booth's, Daly's, Wallack's—and see fine productions of Ingersoll's "Bible," Shakespeare, see Booth as Hamlet, Brutus, Macbeth, Lear, Richard III, Shylock, Othello, or Iago; Barrett in the same parts, and sometimes as Othello to Booth's Iago or as Cassius to his Brutus; Modjeska as Desdemona, Ophelia, Juliet. "If we only had," said Ingersoll, "some strolling preachers like . . . Booth and Barrett, or some cru-

sade sisters like Madam Ristori . . . or Madam Modjeska, how
fortunate the church would be."[2]

The decision made to move to New York, the Ingersolls
sold their house in Washington and the furniture with it to
A. B. McCreary, a California millionaire. House-hunting in
New York in October and November, 1885, they decided to
rent for one year a furnished mansion at 101 Fifth Avenue,
which, wrote Ingersoll to the Farrells, is in "one of the most
aristocratic localities in New York." The house, owned by the
literary historian and critic, Brander Matthews, was indeed
a mansion. Having three floors, not counting the basement
which contained office facilities and a billiard table, it was
richly appointed and decorated. All the walls were frescoed,
with those of the front parlor, middle parlor, and dining room
covered with tapestries and paintings. "The library is very
beautiful all inlaid and frescoed." In the front parlor, between
the windows, stood a life size statue of Delilah; in the middle
parlor was a Steinway Grand. The hall was entirely of marble.
The second and third floors each had upright pianos, "beautiful
beds—curtains to them," two bathrooms and two washrooms.
Ingersoll estimated that the house, without appointments, was
worth $150,000. "I got it at a splendid bargain."

"THE LAW AND THE PROFITS"

IN the practice of law Ingersoll was now avoiding criminal
cases because, as his wife said, they "wore on him so much."
He would be so sympathetic with his client and so anxious
about the verdict that he could not sleep or put his mind to
anything else. He had a theory about criminals to which he
frequently gave utterance. As every man thought as he had to
think and every man was as he had to be, so a criminal had
to be as he was. In a *Lay Sermon* to the Congress of the American Secular Union, at Chickering Hall, November 14, 1886,

Ingersoll declared: "Every crime is a necessary product. . . . If you want less crime, you must change the conditions. Poverty makes crime. Want, rags, crusts, failure, misfortune . . . sweatshops . . . tenements. . . ."

If criminal cases worried Ingersoll too much, he was also quite aware of the fat fees of railroads and telegraph companies. As he wrote after he opened law offices at 40 Wall Street, "Here I am among the bulls and the bears listening to the bellowing and the growling, ready to take the side that hands over the money first."[1]

From 1885-1889, much of Ingersoll's legal work had to do with his clients versus the rapacious Jay Gould. This ever ready monopolist, having obtained control of the Western Union and the Manhattan Railway Company, sought by all the means, fair and foul, of which his genius was capable to eliminate rival interests. In 1885, Western Union having forced out of business the American Rapid Telegraph Company proceeded with dispatch on the basis of an unconfirmed contract with the receivers of American Rapid to take over the property of the company. But in so doing Western Union, not for want of guile, made no distinction between the property of American Rapid and that of the Bankers' and Merchants' Telegraph Company. Western Union agents throughout the country had emerged from their stations at an identical hour to cut several thousand miles of wire and dismantle four hundred offices of American Rapid *and* Bankers' and Merchants'.

In July, 1885, Ingersoll, with three other outstanding attorneys including Roscoe Conkling, commenced suits against Western Union to recover property and damages in behalf of the receivers of Bankers' and Merchants'. Outstanding legal talent, Joseph Choate for one, also represented the other side. The suit to recover possession of property ended quickly in a ruling favorable to Bankers' and Merchants'; that for damages came to trial, after several delays, in May, 1886. This suit also ended favorably for Ingersoll's client, though the damages were scaled down.

One reason for the delays in the damage suit was Ingersoll's throat trouble. In April, 1885, he began to be bothered with hoarseness. He cancelled his lecture engagements for the year. "I shall attend strictly to the law and the profits and let the prophets alone." But even the vocality of the law was too much for him and he stayed at home for a while "enjoying the throat business." Meanwhile the United Telegraph Lines also retained him, in a case involving foreclosure proceedings against United by Western Union. The case was to come up for trial December 17, 1885, but again because of his throat Ingersoll had to ask for a postponement. The hearing was set for December 31, at Syracuse.

On the train to Syracuse, December 30, Ingersoll demonstrated the quickness of comprehension and the retentive memory which made him a formidable lawyer. Roscoe Conkling, associate counsel, took the same train. No sooner were they aboard than Conkling, who, on account of Ingersoll's ailment, was supposed to argue the case, said he was not ready. Ingersoll's secretary, I. Newton Baker, on the train with them, relates what was said and done:

> "I'm ashamed to confess it, Colonel, but I really haven't had time properly to examine the papers in this case and I don't feel prepared to argue it; you must do it, or we will have to move a postponement." "No, no, that won't do, it will damage our suit; let me see the papers." Mr. Conkling produced them. The Colonel examined them. Before reaching Syracuse he handed them back, saying: "Conkling, I will argue this case, although, as you know, my throat is bad to-day and I'll have to whisper my argument in the court's ear." "I'm extremely sorry, Colonel, to put this burden on you, but I see no other way. Do you think you understand the case with this brief inspection?" "Perfectly; as well as if I had studied it for weeks," and for the next few miles he laid it all out before his astonished auditor. "Is that the way you prepare your briefs, Colonel?" "Why not? If I can't catch on to a case by reading it, as soon as the Court does by hearing it, I'd make a nice judge or lawyer, wouldn't I?" "You're a strange man, Colonel, I can't fathom you."[2]

Ingersoll argued the case and won it.

The throat condition hung on and in July, 1886, Ingersoll was thinking of going to a specialist in Paris and another in London. But his physician, Dr. Thomas Robertson, advised him that specialists in New York or Philadelphia were just as good. He then had several operations to remove growths on the vocal cords. It must have been a blow to the spreaders of the rumor that God was silencing the infidel to hear that the growths were benign. "Now I am nearly well," wrote Ingersoll on February 4, 1887.[3]

Soon he was ready for action, again against Jay Gould and associates. The Gould-controlled Manhattan Railway Company was the majority stockholder in the New York Elevated Railroad and Gould to get rid of troublesome minor stockholders hit upon a scheme to issue in the name of New York Elevated $15,000,000 of 5% mortgage bonds for "improvements and betterments." Manhattan Railway would take the entire issue. Then when New York Elevated could not meet the interest charges, there would be nothing that Manhattan Railroad could do but foreclose. With Gould in this scheme were other titans of finance, J. P. Morgan, Samuel Sloan, Russell Sage, and Cyrus Field. A meeting of the stockholders of New York Elevated naturally resulted in an overwhelming approval of the issue. But Messrs. Quigley and Harkness, who owned 810 shares, refused to knuckle under, knowing full well that foreclosure would make their shares worthless. Retaining Ingersoll and a Robert H. Strahan, they brought suit to restrain New York Elevated from issuing bonds with a mortgage provision. And they won.

In January, 1888, Ingersoll again tusseled in the courts with Jay Gould and Western Union. This time Jay Gould tried to "corner" the transmission and reporting of Stock Exchange transactions. A competitor, the Commercial Telegraph Company, had started operations, in Exchange business, in 1883. Western Union then negotiated a contract with the Exchange by which it received exclusive transmission rights. The Exchange ordered Commercial Telegraph to discontinue its operations. In behalf of Commercial Telegraph Ingersoll succeeded first in obtaining a temporary injunction restraining the Stock Exchange from carrying out the order. Western Union and the Exchange sought to have the injunction vacated arguing that the Exchange was a private company and, as such, could make a private contract. Ingersoll contended that in this case common law ruled: a private company had to bow to the public good. He showed that a Western Union monopoly of transmission rights would mean that Jay Gould and his confederates could monopolize the Stock Exchange. They could easily keep each other well supplied with advance market information and could collude to influence market developments. On June 18, 1888, the court handed down a decision restraining the Stock Exchange from giving exclusive reporting rights to any agency whatsoever.

Although Ingersoll preferred not to engage in criminal law, he was more than willing to take the case of Charles B. Reynolds because it involved the alleged crime of blasphemy. In the summer of 1886 Reynolds, an ex-Methodist minister, appeared in Boonton, New Jersey, to hold a series of free thought meetings, in a tent. The churches of Boonton became uneasy and agitated against him. An ominous air hung over the town the day of the first meeting. That evening, just as Reynolds was well under way, a mob invaded the tent and assaulted him with rotten eggs and vegetables. They cut the guy ropes of the tent and slashed the canvas. The tent collapsed and in the melee Reynolds escaped, no more to be seen in Boonton, though the pamphlets he left behind came into the hands of many a reader.

On October 13, Reynolds appeared in Morristown, New Jersey, not to hold meetings but to distribute pamphlets. A Boonton delegation, hearing he was there, arrived on the scene and demanded his indictment for blasphemy. A grand jury, then in session, found under a statute from early Colonial days two indictments against him, blasphemy at Boonton and blasphemy at Morristown. Reynolds was put in jail, but Ingersoll, on his own initiative and soon after one of his throat operations, made a hurried trip to Morristown, on a raw and rainy day, and bailed him out. He donated his legal services.

The trial, postponed several times because of Ingersoll's throat trouble, began on May 19, 1887. During the six months' delay, the impending event was the chief interest of Morristown: "it monopolized attention at the stores, and became a fruitful subject of gossip in social and church circles."[4] When the day finally came, all Morristown turned out. By 9:30 A.M., the trial set for 11, the courtroom was packed and the building and grounds were overrun. At 11, Ingersoll appeared, and such was the interest in the famous lawyer that the defendant entering at the same time was unnoticed.

Ingersoll examined twenty prospective jurors on their church affiliation and their understanding of the word prejudice. "Presbyterians had a rather hard time with the examiner."[5] But the selection of the jury proceeded with dispatch and at 12:30 the prosecutor opened. Announcing that he would try only the indictment for blasphemy in Morristown, he summoned sixteen witnesses most of whom testified that Reynolds had given them a pamphlet. They need not have read it. If the State proved, under the Colonial statute, that the excerpts of the pamphlet specified in the indictment were blasphemous, the mere act of distribution was the crux of the case. Ingersoll tried to get "the Presbyterian witnesses to say that they had read the pamphlet" but none of them admitted it. Other than that, he attempted no cross-examination. Asked by Judge Francis Child if he had any witnesses to call, Ingersoll replied, "I do not know that I shall have any witnesses one way or the other," and then suggesting a recess, "Perhaps after dinner I may feel like making a few remarks." Said Judge Child, "There will be a great disappointment if you do not."[6]

Ingersoll had a hard case. Public sentiment was bitter against Reynolds. The Morristown pamphlet, a slight variation of the one Reynolds circulated in Boonton, was particularly obnoxious to the Methodists and Catholics because of a cartoon, based on the Boonton uproar, which adorned the front cover. It showed a tent in the background and pig pens in the foreground. Reynolds was carrying a basket from which he scattered pearls to the swine issuing from the "M.E. Hog Pen" and from the "Pig Sty of the Holy Virgin." A minister stood over the one pen with a bucket entitled "Methodist slop" and a priest over the other with "Catholic swill." Both menaced the scatterer of pearls with clubs. Over the head of the priest was a placard spelling "Boonton." The pamphlet contained other indecorous cuts and tasteless writing but in the main it was Ingersollian.

In his two and a half hour address to the jury, Ingersoll began by stressing the point that the case was one of the most important that could be presented to a jury: "It involves the freedom of speech, the intellectual liberty of every citizen of New Jersey." Tracing the growth of religious toleration, he showed that a dominant sect always branded differences of belief as heretic and blasphemous. Taking up the statute clause by clause, Ingersoll said that it would make John Calvin laugh in his grave, the man who for a difference of belief had Servetus burned at the stake—"It is written exactly as he would have written it."

Yes, Reynolds had the right to say what he had to say. What if he did say of Christ as a child, " 'God cried and screamed,' " why, said Ingersoll, "I have seen the time, when absent from home, that I would have given more to hear my children cry, than to have heard the finest orchestra that ever made the air burst into flower." What if Reynolds did say of Christ, " 'He was nursed at Mary's breast,' " Said Ingersoll, "No painting, no statue, no words can make a deeper and a tenderer impression upon the heart of man than this: The infinite God, a babe, nursed at the holy breast of woman." Was this, in the term of the statute, "Contumeliously reproaching" Jesus Christ? Reynolds must be acquitted. Show the world that New Jersey is not "a survival of the Dark Ages."

But Reynolds was convicted. The judge, however, was lenient, imposing a fine of twenty-five dollars and costs of fifty, which Ingersoll paid. If the verdict was adverse, the reaction to his speech was not. As he was leaving the courtroom just after he had spoken, "a throng pressed after him to offer congratulations." One old man said, "Colonel Ingersoll, I am a Presbyterian pastor, but I must say that was the noblest speech in defence of liberty I ever heard! Your hand, sir; your hand."[7]

Reading the speech later, Holyoake wrote Ingersoll, "Now I see why Reynolds was indicted. It was a conspiracy of the court in order that it might have the luxury of hearing a great speech from thee."[8]

THE HAYMARKET AFFAIR

LONG hours, miserable wages, and widespread unemployment brought in the 80's a rapid growth of labor unions and agitation for socialism and anarchism. Industrial strife broke out all over the country. In the summer of 1885 the Amalgamated Association of Iron and Steel Workers ordered a paralyzing strike in the Pittsburgh area. A strike closed the iron mills in Cleveland. Early in 1886, 20,000 men quit work in the coal mines of Pennsylvania, Maryland, West Virginia, and Ohio. Thousands went on strike in the textile and shoe industries of New England. The Knights of Labor—organized in 1869 and by 1886 grown to 1,000,000 strong—boycotted and struck steamship lines and railroads, wrecked equipment and attacked scabs, denounced child labor and the competitive goods of convict labor, incited violence against Chinese labor.

Although Ingersoll was aware of the plight of labor, he opposed boycotts and strikes. In this he was unrealistic. He himself said in "A Lay Sermon" to the Congress of the American Secular Union, at Chickering Hall in New York City, November 14, 1886: "Don't you know that if people could bottle the air, they would? Don't you know that there would be an American Air-bottling Association? And don't you know that they would allow thousands and millions to die for want of breath, if they could not pay for air?"[1]

Ingersoll knew of the pitiless exploitation of labor. He knew that telegraph operators working ten to fourteen hours every day of the year, including Sundays, averaged $46.50 a month; that miners got $23.00 a month and had to spend this at company stores and saloons; that for a like pittance street car drivers in New York City worked sixteen to eighteen hours a day. Ingersoll admitted that existing laws did little to help these workers. But the way to make things better was the ballot. The poor could use the ballot to change the laws. "The poor are in the majority in this country. If there is any law that oppresses them, it is their fault."² Very good, but what if the poor while using the ballot starved to death?

The poor, thought Ingersoll, had a wonderful chance in the mayoralty election of New York City in the fall of 1886. "I want them to show that they have the intelligence to act together, and sense enough to vote for a friend."³ That friend was Henry George, the independent candidate, whom Ingersoll supported but could not speak for because of his throat ailment. Advocating the "single tax," Henry George argued that the fundamental factor in the economy was land, the source of wealth. The trouble was that the rents from land, "unearned increments," went into the pockets of monopolists and stayed there. The remedy was to tax 100% the rent from land above a certain margin allowed the landlord to induce him to collect the rent and pay the tax. The government would use the revenues to alleviate the ills of the poor.

Was this socialistic? No, said Ingersoll, the fierce opponent of socialism, overlooking the confiscatory tendency of the single tax. No, private ownership of property still remained.

But the poor did not take full advantage of their chance and Henry George, though he ran a strong and frightening race, went down to defeat. Large property owners and the rich read the election returns with great relief. Abram S. Hewitt, the Tammany candidate, polled 90,000 votes; Henry George, 68,-000; and twenty-eight-year-old Theodore Roosevelt, the Republican choice, 60,000.

Of all the irruptions of industrial strife, the one that concerned Ingersoll the most was the Haymarket affair. On the night of May 4, 1886, in Chicago, several thousand disgruntled workers gathered at the Haymarket, an open place, to protest the actions of the Chicago police who in quelling riots the previous day at the McCormick reaper plant had fired upon the rioters, wounding and killing a number. This inflamed the revolutionary elements among socialists and anarchists. In Chicago the militantly anarchist *Arbeiter Zeitung,* edited by August Spies and Michael Schwab, trumpeted for action. Spies, Schwab, and others called the Haymarket meeting. The mayor of Chicago was at the meeting for a while but, nothing ominous occurring, he went home. But then, while one Sam Fielden was speaking, the police entered and ordered the meeting to disperse. Someone threw a bomb. Seven persons were killed and over sixty injured. Eight men, including Spies, Schwab, and Fielden, were indicted for murder.

The trial in July and August, 1886, took place in at atmosphere hardly conducive to impartiality, "in one of the strangest frenzies of fear," writes Brand Whitlock, "that ever distracted a whole community."[4] The press clamored for conviction. Fail to hang the men and society is doomed. The chief counsel for the defendants, William Black, sought Ingersoll as an associate, and sent an assistant, George Schilling, to New York to confer with him. As Schilling later reported, Ingersoll "fully realized that the entire machinery of justice was perverted to satisfy the implacable cry for blood." But he decided he had better not enter the case because " 'the tocsin has already been sounded by the press and pulpit that Anarchism is the logical fruit of Ingersollism, and that the doctrine of no God, no accountability to a Supreme Power, must inevitably lead to no government, no authority on earth.' " Clearly the foremost infidel in the country would jeopardize the accused. "Schilling," said Ingersoll, "you must get a lawyer of national reputation who is a pillar of the church and who can cover these men with his conservative life and character."[5]

Not entering the case, Ingersoll was nonetheless outspoken on the conduct of the trial. When he was asked, "Do you uphold the Anarchists?" he replied, "Certainly not. There is no place in this country for the Anarchist."[6] He had "not the slightest sympathy with the methods that have been pursued by Anarchists, or by Socialists, or by any other class that has resorted to force or intimidation."[7] But everybody was entitled to a fair trial and this the Anarchists did not get. The great excitement of the time was prejudicial: "It is hard to reason with a mob . . . whether acting in the name of the law or of simple brute force."[8]

Ingersoll agreed with Schilling that the factory foremen and superintendents who largely made up the jury would be susceptible to pressures from their millionaire employers. "Never," said Ingersoll, "get tried by the other fellow's hired man; if you do, you will get left every time. When I die and appear before the bar of Heaven for judgment, if God will come forward Himself and listen to my story, I'll stand a show. But if He will turn me over to one of His clerks, I'm gone."[9]

Ingersoll also objected to Judge Gary's instructions to the jury. It was erroneous for the judge to say that if men talked in a way tending to a crime they were responsible for the crime if it happened. Under such an instruction anyone on trial who had ever said a word against the forces of law and order, whether he knew of the Haymarket meeting or not, would have been convicted. Ingersoll held that the intention of the accused to commit the specific crime must be proved.[10]

Seven of the defendants were sentenced to death; one, Neebe, to imprisonment for fifteen years. On appeal, the Supreme Court of Illinois affirmed the convictions. As the day set for the execution, November 11, 1887, approached, Ingersoll was active in attempting to get a commutation or at least a stay of sentence. He and Governor Richard Oglesby had been friends ever since he served as attorney general in the governor's first term, 1865-1867. But having the greatest respect for his friend, Ingersoll still had the fear, as he wrote to George Schilling, that he might be "overawed by the general feeling—by the demand of the 'upper classes.' " And so he urged Schilling to "get some of the rich bankers, merchants, and capitalists" to write

Oglesby.[11] As for himself, "I shall write the best letter I can," but he asked that Schilling reveal nothing about it until Oglesby's decision was known. "I can do more good if nothing is said." If Oglesby refused to interfere, then Ingersoll wanted it known that he had done what he could to prevent the execution. His caution on his letter did not, however, extend to the signing of a public petition for a commutation, his signature being among the first. As it turned out, Governor Oglesby, on the recommendation of Judge Gary and the prosecuting attorney, commuted the sentences of Schwab and Fielden to life imprisonment but refused to interfere in the other five cases. One of the doomed, Lung, committed suicide; Spies, Parsons, Engel, and Fischer were hanged. "A great mistake was made," said Ingersoll.

Six years later, in June, Governor John Peter Altgeld took his political career in hand and threw it away—he pardoned the three anarchists who were still alive, Schwab, Fielden, and Neebe.

"THINK OF IT. 55"

On Ingersoll's birthday, August 11, 1888, he wrote his brother John, "Think of it. 55. That seems on the edge of the antique. In a little while ivy will be running up my legs. . . . The house is getting out of repair—shingles off *the roof*. . . ." Well, the shingles, his hair, had been off the roof for years. The only sign of disrepair was recurrent hoarseness. Otherwise the house was a going, productive concern. Ingersoll had a very profitable law business; he was again active in politics; and he took part in a theological polemic that aroused tremendous interest here and abroad because of the prominence of the participants.

In 1887, the editor of *The North American Review*, Allen

Thorndike, invited Ingersoll and the Rev. Dr. Henry M. Field, editor of the New York *Evangelist,* to contribute a series of papers on Christianity. Field began the series in the August issue with "An Open Letter to Robert G. Ingersoll"; Ingersoll replied in November; Field came back in December with "A Last Word" . . . ; and Ingersoll answered in January, 1888, with a "Letter to Dr. Field." Then across the sea The Right Honorable William E. Gladstone took note of the controversy and wrote for the May issue of the *Review* an article under the main title, "Colonel Ingersoll on Christianity," sub-titled "Some Remarks on his Reply to Dr. Field." In a letter to George Jacob Holyoake, Gladstone rated Ingersoll to be, in the words of Holyoake, "the one American adversary worthy of his steel."[1] Ingersoll's reply appeared in August. In September, the Cardinal Archbishop of Westminster, Henry Edward Manning, entered the fray with "Rome or Reason." Under the same title Ingersoll wrote a reply in two parts, one appearing in October, the other in November. With this reply, the controversy came to an end. Incidentally, the *Review* paid Ingersoll at a higher rate than the other three contributors. He received $25 a page; the "Grand Old Man" of England, $15.

Dr. Field conducted himself in a manner that Ingersoll was not used to in a clergyman. "I answer your letter," said Ingersoll, "because it is manly, candid and generous." Field said that he once spent an evening with the Ingersolls at their home in Washington and he came away with the impression that here was a "gentle and sweet-tempered" man. Then he read some of Ingersoll's lectures and was shocked; here was *"that other man,"* flippant, contemptuous, belligerent. Ingersoll should not be surprised if clergymen who knew only *that other man* should respond in unkindly terms. Field remembered that Ingersoll in his home had said to him, "Make the Sermon on the Mount your religion and there I am with you." So Ingersoll was not to be despaired of, he might yet feel the coming of "a new Presence."

Gladstone emphasized that he was interested in the essentials of Christianity, not in "some hole and corner of its vast organization." Conceding the possibility of "a wide range of local and partial error"—he could not, for instance, support Calvinism "all along the line"—he took Ingersoll to task for trying to confound the whole with a few of its lesser parts. Nor did he like Ingersoll's mode of attack. Though his opponent wrote "with a rare and enviable brilliance," Gladstone got "the impression of a battlefield where every man strikes at every man and all is noise, hurry, and confusion."

With all the profundity, and grandiloquence, of which he was capable, Gladstone attacked Ingersoll's "wide-sweeping proposition" that Darwin's discoveries, " 'carried to their legitimate conclusion, destroy the creeds and sacred Scriptures of mankind.' " Gladstone held that evolution and revelation were not incompatible. If the lineage of man goes back by minute stages to the primordial protoplasm, that does not mean that a Creator has not been at work. If man evolved from protoplasm via the reptile and the ape, this is progressive creation, progressive revelation of the mind and will of God. The marvellous order of the process—wherein "each preceding stage is a prophecy of the following, each succeeding one is a memorial of the past"—is a demonstration of divine plan. Gladstone advised Ingersoll to read John Fiske's *Man's Destiny;* there he would find Darwinism and theism admirable reconciled.

On another question, that of the problem of evil and injustice in the world, Gladstone readily admitted that much relating to divine government defied understanding. But the *much* should not be exaggerated. It was easy for Ingersoll to ask: "Why should an infinitely wise and powerful God destroy the good and preserve the vile? Why should He treat all alike here, and in another world make an infinite difference? Why . . .? Why . . .? Why . . .?" One would assume from Ingersoll's *why* habit that evil dominated the world. But this, to Gladstone, was untrue. As he viewed the affairs of men, the evidence that "a moral Governor" ruled the world was overwhelming. Furthermore, let Ingersoll consider that there is not a problem of human life which the teachings of Christ, if applied, cannot solve.

On "the favorite doctrine," as Gladstone termed it, of Ingersoll's "Reply" to Field, that a man thinks as he *inherently* has to, Gladstone declared that it was a doctrine that degraded human nature by destroying free choice and responsibility. One of his illustrations to show the power of the will had to do with the father who insists that his son charged with a crime is innocent. To which, in his reply, Ingersoll said: if the father is *"consciously* swayed by his love for his son, and for that reason says that his son is innocent, then he has not expressed his opinion. If he is unconsciously swayed and says that his son is innocent, then he has expressed his opinion. In both instances his opinion was independent of his will. . . ."

Ingersoll answered Gladstone's argument on the compatibility of evolution and creation as follows: first, of course a god may create by evolution but this is hardly the Mosaic version; second, if a god does so create and things become better, then the creator becomes better, but look around and what do you see, a world in which countless varieties of life, including man, live on each other, destroy each other, "everywhere claw and beak, hoof and tooth;" third, the attempt to reconcile Darwin and Genesis followed, significantly, the failure to refute Darwin. Since Gladstone had commented believingly on Adam and Eve, Ingersoll put this mocking question on Darwin-*cum*-Genesis: "Do you find in Darwin any theory that satisfactorily accounts for the 'inspired fact' that a Rib, commencing with Monogonic Propagation—falling into halves by a contraction in the middle—reaching after many ages of Evolution the Amphigonic stage, and then by the Survival of the Fittest, assisted by Natural Selection, moulded and modified by the Environment, became, at last, the mother of the human race?"

Walt Whitman read Gladstone's paper and said, "It won't do, Mr. Gladstone: you may try: you have the right to try— you try hard: but the Colonel carries too many guns for you on that line."[2] Whitman felt that Gladstone on theological questions was no match for Ingersoll either in scholarship or in agility of argument. Anticipating Ingersoll's reply, Whitman

pictured the fate of Gladstone (as recorded by Horace Traubel): " 'Oh, there will be a funny time of it!' Here he put his
two hands together scoop-wise. 'Bob will take him up in this
fashion, turn him over (all sides of him), look at him sweetly,
ever so sweetly, smile, then crunch him!'—to illustrate which
he worked his two hands together as if to crush their imaginative burden—'yes, crunch him, much as a cat would a mouse
till there's no life left to fool with.' "[3] At the same time, however, Whitman thought the controversy was "utterly super-
fluous." "I always feel that to one in the swim—in the swim
of modern science, democracy, freedom—the atonement, the
Mosaic records, are not worth the dignity of consideration, of
a reply."[4]

Thomas Huxley also thought that Gladstone was up against
his better. He wrote Ingersoll: "Gladstone's attack on you is
one of the best things he has written. I do not think there is
more than 50% more verbiage than necessary, nor any sentence with *more* than two meanings. If he goes on improving
at this rate he will be an English classic by the time he is
ninety."

The Chicago *Tribune,* however, was sure that Ingersoll was
overmatched. It was an "inspiring and noble spectacle" to the
Tribune that the venerable Gladstone had dropped the affairs
of state and the strifes of party to defend his faith. Here was
a formidable disputant who put the controversy on "broad
philosophical grounds" which Ingersoll could not answer "with
a laugh, or a sneer, or flash of wit."[5]

In a letter to Huxley, Ingersoll disposed of Gladstone as "a
kind of glorified London fog."

Cardinal Manning's contribution was in support of the infallibility of the Roman Catholic Church. All else, from atheism to Protestantism, was degree of error. Drawing the vest-
ments of his holy office about him, he trod the heights of
Catholicism not deigning to identify on the plains below those
heretics, Field, Ingersoll, and Gladstone. There was only one
true church, only one continuity of divine authority from St.
Peter to the last pope. Granted that from that church rebels

have sprung, Arius to Luther, look what happens, see the sects within sects—"Their multiplicity is proof of their human origin." While "the living unity and the luminous universality of the One Catholic and Roman Church" proves a divine origin.

Ingersoll's lengthy, two-part reply brought some satisfaction to Protestants, Jews, Mormons, etc., as well as to deists, agnostics, atheists, etc., for it was Catholicism that he dealt with mainly. Was it "worthwhile to try to convert the world to Catholicism? Are Catholics better than Protestants? Are they nearer honest, nearer just, more charitable? . . . Do the Catholic nations move in the van of progress? Would Ingersoll's non-Catholic readers object to his devoting several pages to the misdeeds of infallible popes? And more pages to the cruelties and tyrannies of the one true church? Nor would the churchly among the non-Catholics get too worried when he started in on the Catholic creed, though all creeds have mystic obscurities: this was the Catholic creed and this of course was patent nonsense.

Huxley said of Manning's paper, in a letter to Ingersoll: "I have not read Manning, and do not mean to. I have had many opportunities of taking his measure—and he is a parlous windbag—and nothing else, absolutely." Said Ingersoll in return: "the Cardinal seems as hard of heart as soft of head."[6]

WALSTON AND 400 FIFTH AVENUE

WITH the expiration of the lease at 101 Fifth Avenue, the Ingersolls rented in the fall of 1886 a house at 89 Fifth Avenue. Here they lived until 1888 when they rented a mansion at 400 Fifth Avenue. One of their problems in finding a suitable residence was the housing of the growing number of cats and dogs which the Ingersolls took to their bosom. A house with a yard was hard to find. Almost giving up on the yard, Ingersoll wrote of the pets, "They will probably have to have a room in the house, probably the front parlor." Happily, 400 Fifth Avenue had a yard.

In November, 1889, the Ingersoll household was enlarged with the addition of Walston Hill Brown to whom Eva was married on November 13. It was agreed before the marriage, with the glad compliance of all parties, that the Browns would live with the Ingersolls six months and the Ingersolls with the Browns six months. Neither Eva nor her parents could bear the thought of their separation. In fact, when the newlyweds left on their honeymoon they came back in two weeks. Eva was homesick. Even during the two weeks she sent telegrams home daily.

Since Walston Brown, a wealthy railroad builder, gave Eva as a wedding present an estate overlooking the Hudson River, at Dobbs Ferry, the pre-marriage agreement worked out so that every year the Ingersolls including the Farrells and Sue Sharkey were at "Walston," as the estate was called, from May to October. Walston Brown, like others with estates along the Hudson who tried to re-create the Rhine, had built a turreted and battlemented mansion. Situated atop the highest eminence of the forty-acre estate, Castle Walston commanded a far-reaching view of the Hudson and the ranges of hills on both sides. From his corner room on the second floor facing south and west, Ingersoll could see storied High Tor, Dunderberg, Storm King, Anthony's Nose, and Breakneck. On clear days he could see as far as the hills around West Point.

A spacious lawn surrounded the house. Beyond the lawn were gardens, woodland, and pasture. There were apples, pears, plums, peaches, and cherries; grapes, currants, raspberries, gooseberries, and strawberries; asparagus, sweet corn, peas, potatoes, and beans. Wisteria, honeysuckle, and morning glory gentled the granite of Castle Walston; ivy and trumpet creeper reached to the battlements. About half the estate was pasture, grazing the horses and the six to eight Jersey and Guernsey cows. There were four coach horses, a riding horse, a farm horse, and a pony for children. In the farmyard were ducks, turkeys, guinea hens, and hundreds of chickens. Livestock and poultry were housed in a style bespeaking the good life at Walston.

The vehicles and gear in the carriage house also bespoke the good life. There were formal Victorias and broughams, in deep blue; one and two seated runabouts, also in deep blue, but with bright red wheels; a wagonette with two long seats vis-a-vis; a couple of farm wagons; a sleigh and a cutter. The harnesses for formal occasions were inscribed in silver with the initials of Robert Green Ingersoll and Walston Hill Brown. There were harnesses with bells for the sleight and cutter.

Life inside Castle Walston was no less prepossessing. On the first floor were the music room, the billiard room, the parlor, the dining room, and the kitchen, all of ample dimension. The second and third floors had fourteen bedrooms and four bathrooms. All the rooms were lighted with gas, those on the first floor, except the kitchen, having large hanging chandeliers. In the hall opening into the parlor stood an imposing Bishop's chair, "Pope Bob" relished sitting in it. Close to it was Ingersoll's favorite statue, the Winged Victory of Samothrace. Tall book cases dominated one of the long walls, a granite fireplace the other. Ingersoll much admired the marble mantel, which Walston Brown designed.

The walls of the music room were papered in Chinese gold leaf with a Bird-of-Paradise motif. If the Steinway Grand took "center stage," not to be ignored were the music box and the bust of Wagner and the Queen Anne chairs. The billiard room was also done in Chinese gold leaf paper. Here Ingersoll could indulge himself in his favorite indoor pastime, billiards, and, as he often did, dictate a lecture at the same time, now and then saying a few words to the busts of Cicero and Demosthenes. On the gaming table he also enjoyed rummy, pinochle, backgammon, and chess, even, gregarious as he was, solitaire.

The dining room was the largest of the rooms. From the lofty ceiling hung the largest of the chandeliers. A massive Swiss sideboard guarded D'Vion and Baury china, cut glass tumblers, and a wide assortment of wine, champagne, and cordial glasses. Here Ingersoll spent some of his happiest hours. At meal time he took his customary seat at one end of the long table and while he partook of the pleasures of the palate he rejoiced in the nearness of those he loved.

Ingersoll liked to walk or ride about the grounds of Walston, or do a bit, a little bit, of gardening, or relax in a chair or a sofa on the vine-covered veranda. On good terms with the birds of Walston, which was a veritable open aviary, he had a special fondness for the robins, who were more reflective than the wrens, the scarlet tanagers, the thrushes, and the orioles. He also was friendly with several crows. He seldom was without the company of at least two or three of the dogs and cats that lived in luxury and harmony at Walston. Of one dog he wrote, "Rust is being petted to death. He is now the owner of a surrey, a horse and coachman and several servants. He is the richest dog in the world."

If Ingersoll could have spent more time at Walston during the six months of residence there, he would have been perfectly content. Except for Sundays and holidays and three or four weeks in midsummer, he was at his law office every morning at nine-thirty. That meant he had to get up at six. The routine of these days wearied him at times. "I am getting a little tired of the everlasting work," he wrote to John, "I am up at six— eat breakfast a little after seven—leave for the city at eight— get to the office at 9:30—leave for home 4:30—eat dinner at six, and this is called life." This letter was written on October 8, 1889, as the first of the six-month stays at Walston was coming to a close. Ingersoll was not unhappy that in a week he would not have to commute daily on the New York Central trains. And 400 Fifth Avenue was a pleasant home to come back to. A stately four-story brownstone, it had all the latest conveniences and luxuries.

"The Sunday evening receptions at Colonel Robert G. Ingersoll's are becoming quite 'events of the season' ", wrote the society reporter for the New York *Daily Graphic,* February 12, 1887. The guests illustrated Ingersoll's many-sided life.

To name a few, there were men of industry and finance like Andrew Carnegie and John Mackay of the Postal Telegraph Cable Co.; politicians and statesmen like Chauncey Depew, Walter Q. Gresham, General William T. Sherman, Thomas Bracket Reed (Speaker of the House), Charles W. Fairbanks (later Vice-president); reformers like Elizabeth Cady Stanton and Henry George; freethinkers like Charles Watts, Samuel Putnam, J. P. Mendum, George MacDonald, and John Lovejoy Elliott. There were writers, Elbert Hubbard, Horace Traubel, Edgar Fawcett, Ella Wheeler Wilcox; painters and sculptors, Edwin Howland Blashfield, John W. Alexander, George Grey Barnard, Frank B. Carpenter, and Gutzon Borglum.

But among all the callings that Ingersoll's guests represented, music and theater stood out. From the theater, and again to name a few, there were the players Minnie Maddern Fiske, Julia Marlowe, Mary Anderson, Mr. and Mrs. John Drew, Maurice Barrymore, Joseph Jefferson, Stuart Robson, Lawrence Barrett, and Edwin Booth; the playwrights Augustus Thomas and Steele Mackaye and the playwright-actor William Gillette. From the concert and operatic stage there were Anton Seidl, the conductor; Remenyi, the violinist; Italo Campanini, the Italian tenor; Sofia Scalchi, the Italian contralto, who sang duets with Eva Ingersoll; Lilli Lehmann, the German soprano; and Marcella Sembrich, the Austrian coloratura soprano.

Some of the guests were intimates and dropped in whenever they felt like it. Andrew Carnegie was one. Carnegie was for Ingersoll the prototype of American industrial genius; Ingersoll was for Carnegie the most eloquent figure in the realm of thought. By no means the agnostic that Ingersoll was, Carnegie was certainly a species of infidel, a deist, and was appreciative of Ingersoll's utterances. When Ingersoll sent him, in 1886, a specially bound volume of selections from his lectures, Carnegie replied, "That superb volume is not too fine for the really fine things it contains. . . . I am glad a selection of your pearls has been made—long have I quoted them. They are real, not imitation, and will give you an enduring place in the Republic of Letters."[1]

The two men had a common love, Robert Burns. Whenever they got together, out would come the "Hymn-book," and they would take turns reciting the songs. On one of his trips to Scotland, in 1891, Carnegie sent his friend two bottles of whiskey, which put Ingersoll in mind of an evening when he and Carnegie, aided with "bottled bliss," had read and talked Burns for hours. In thanking Carnegie, Ingersoll wrote, "I have not touched it. Both bottles are as they are. You must be present when they are opened and we four must have an evening—I mean Burns, Carnegie, the whiskey and myself."[2]

Another of Ingersoll's intimates was the effervescent Remenyi, whom Ingersoll called the "Shakespeare of the violin" or "my grand fiddler." Remenyi, not to be outdone, returned the compliment with "Jupiter" or "B.B.B." ("Big Boss Bob!") or "my grand man." Ingersoll first came to know Remenyi in the spring of 1880 at one of his concert appearances in Washington. The following August, Remenyi spent three days with the Ingersolls while they were vacationing at Cape Ann, Massachusetts. "And for three days," wrote Ingersoll, he "delighted and entranced the fortunate idlers of the beach. He played nearly all the time, night and day, seemingly carried away with his own music." In the years following, until his death in 1898, he was a virtual habitué in the Ingersoll home. Often invited to Walston, he stayed there, to the pleasure of everybody, for weeks at a time. "Tell the B.B.B. (Big Boss Bob) Jupiter," he wrote to Mrs. Ingersoll in June, 1892, "that I will live during my stay *everyday 100 days,* although I am not from the Emerald Isle. . . . Mind your ears, because on my arrival until my farewell I will sound the trumpet on my violin all the while. . . ." Which is exactly what he did, even getting up at 5:30 in the morning to play melodious alarms at the door of Jupiter's bedroom, alarms which lingered in Jupiter's ears as he commuted to the city.

Also close to Ingersoll were Julia Marlowe, Minnie Maddern Fiske, Stuart Robson, Lawrence Barrett, and Edwin Booth.

In 1888, Ingersoll was retained as counsel for the Actors' Order of Friendship, the Edwin Forrest Lodge of New York, and the Shakespeare Lodge of Philadelphia for the purpose of securing legislation to protect American actors, particularly the passage of an amendment that would apply to foreign actors the Federal law of 1885 which prohibited the importation of contract alien labor. The amendment was to apply to supporting companies, not to stars. Ingersoll regarded as the "sheerest cant" the argument of certain theater managers that the amendment would hinder the growth of dramatic art in America. "Their object is to make money." Foreign actors were cheaper. But they were not better. "I know of no English actor," said Ingersoll, "who can for a moment be compared with Joseph Jefferson, or with Edwin Booth, or with Lawrence Barrett, or with Denman Thompson. . . . John Gilbert, Mary Anderson, Mrs. Drew, Julia Marlowe."[3]

In the earliest days of Julia Marlowe's career Ingersoll saw her as "one who is destined to stand first in her profession." In January, 1888, when she was twenty-one and on tour with "The Tempest" in which she played Olivia, Ingersoll wrote to the Chicago dramatic critic, Murat Halstead, "In a few days Miss Marlowe, a young actress, will appear in your city. She has had but little experience—a month or two, and yet in my opinion she is one of the greatest artists on the American stage. . . . I want you to see her. Do not leave her to the negligence of some one who does not know."[4]

In the summer of 1888, while the Ingersolls were vacationing at Far Rockaway, New York, Julia stayed with them for a time and worked on the Shakespearian roles of Desdemona, Juliet, Ophelia, and Portia, though she had no commitment for the approaching season. Ingersoll came home from the office early and he and his daughters read with her, discussed interpretations, and assured her of her greatness. When she was on the road the following February and March, Ingersoll wrote to various influential persons in the cities where she was to appear, as to W. H. Calkins of Indianapolis: "Miss Julia Marlowe is going to be in your town I think on the 8th or 9th of March. I want you to go and see her play. It may be that you will say you are going to Washington to see the inauguration—but if you have sense enough to remain at home, go to the theater and see the best actor on the stage."[5] In November, 1890, Julia became critically ill. As her attorney, Ingersoll served notice on her manager, P. J. Falk, that the contract between the two was at an end. He alleged that Falk had hired to support Julia a company that was "notoriously incompetent," that the booking of her tour had been so poorly handled that it required "excessive haggling continually," and that in consequence the health of his client had broken down.[6] Falk did not contest the action. Her next manager was no less a person than Lawrence Barrett.

Minnie Maddern Fiske was another whom Ingersoll "discovered" and befriended. "In my humblest days in the theatre," she wrote, "I was never in a place too lowly for Ingersoll to seek me out."[7] She, and also Julia Marlowe, gave the Ingersolls a box seat for their "first nights." The day after Mrs. Fiske opened in an adaptation of *Tess of the D'Urbervilles,* Ingersoll wrote her husband, Harrison Grey Fiske: "We were all overpowered last night. Mrs. Fiske was marvelous. Her acting was perfect. . . . She was far greater than the play." Ingersoll found the last scene "vague, indistinct, and unsatisfactory" and suggested some concluding lines for Mrs. Fiske to think over, lines that would point up the tragic end of Tess.[8]

Ingersoll's friendship with Stuart Robson began in 1887. The team of Robson and William Crane was the rage of New York. Ingersoll could not get enough of them. At a dinner for Robson and Crane, at Delmonico's, November 23, 1887, he spoke of the power of the stage for good and of its ministers, the actors. "No man ever went to the theater and heard Robson and Crane, who did not go home better-natured, and treat his family that night a little better. . . ."[9] Robson reciprocated Ingersoll's esteem and affection.

"Have you forgotten," he wrote to Ingersoll, "that you promised me your picture with a 'sentiment' and your signature inscribed thereon?" He also wanted Ingersoll to send him a photographic copy of his medallion portrait of Voltaire. And he invited him to spend some time at Cohasset, Massachusetts, where he and his wife, and Booth and Barrett were summering. This was in 1887. Ingersoll had not as yet met Booth, and Robson wrote that they would all like to entertain Ingersoll and that Booth had said he " 'would rather meet you than any man in America.' " Ingersoll could not go to Cohasset, but he met Booth in the fall. From then on, the two were bound in a friendship that lasted until Booth's death in 1893.

In January, 1889, Booth and Barrett sponsored Ingersoll for membership in the Players' Club, which Booth had founded. Neither Booth nor Barrett could formally nominate Ingersoll, since both were members of the board of directors, which acted on nominations. The board met quarterly. The name of an applicant for membership, together with the names of two sponsor members, had to be posted for fourteen days before action could be taken. Ingersoll's name was duly posted before the January meeting but was withdrawn on the suggestion of Booth and Barrett because they could not be at the meeting. But Ingersoll heard that he had been blackballed. He wrote to Barrett, who was in Boston, about it, and Barrett replied, "Will you kindly tell me where you got the story. . . . I know it is false but the source of the story is worth knowing. . . . Booth and myself are very much exercised about this contemptible report."[10] In another letter Barrett said, "The cruel lie was the invention of disappointed critics who are disbarred by our constitution." He went on to say, "It was deemed advisable by Edwin and myself to postpone your nomination until we could both be present at the election." The reason was that since Ingersoll was not in the theater there might be some question under the constitution as to his eligibility. Booth and Barrett wanted to be on hand when his name came up. They would take the position that his good works for the theater and its personnel constituted a qualification for membership far beyond the requirements of the constitution.

But Ingersoll, despite the entreaties of Barrett and Booth,[11] declined to allow his name to be submitted again. Except for some lingering embarrassment on the part of Barrett and Booth, the cordial relations of the three remained unimpaired.

Both of the actors consulted Ingersoll whenever they needed a lawyer. In 1889, Barrett wanted to go to Europe but he owed money to certain theatrical interests in England, which had been threatening him with legal action, and he was afraid that if he went to England they would arrest him for debt. "What is the worst those rascals could do to me," he wrote to Ingersoll, "that I may frame my plans accordingly?"[12] Ingersoll advised him to go on a German boat and not to stop off at Southampton but to go straight to Bremen. If he wanted to risk it, he could visit England last. Barrett took the advice and all went well.

MARK TWAIN AND WALT WHITMAN

INGERSOLL and Mark Twain first met at the banquet of the Army of the Tennessee given for Grant, November 13, 1879, at the Palmer House in Chicago. Both were among the many speakers at the occasion. Ingersoll responded to the twelfth toast, "The Volunteer Soldiers of the Union Army, whose Valor and Patriotism saved to the world a Government of the People, by the People, and for the People." When the festivities ended, about five in the morning, Mark Twain retired to his room and wrote his wife, "I've just come to my room, Livy darling, I guess this was the memorable night of my life. By George, I never was so stirred since I was born. I heard four speeches which I can never forget . . . one by that splendid old soul Colonel Bob Ingersoll—Oh, it was just the supreme combination of English words that was ever put together since the world began. My soul, how handsome he looked as he stood on that table, in the midst of those five hundred shouting men, and poured the molten silver from his lips. Lord, what an organ is human speech when it is played by a master."[1] A few days later Twain wrote William Dean Howells, ". . . Bob Ingersoll's music will sing through my memory always as the divinest that ever enchanted my ears . . . to see . . . that vast house rise to its feet. . . . That's the only test . . . none but the master can make them get up on their feet."

Twain wrote Ingersoll, December 9, from Hartford, Connecticut, asking for a "perfect copy of your peerless Chicago speech. . . . I'm to read the speech to a young girl's club here, Saturday—but that's not the main thing. I want a perfect copy for my private scrap-book." The copy arrived an hour too late but "it was all right anyway, for I found that my memory had been able to correct all the errors. . . . I told them to remember that it was doubtful if its superior existed in our language."[2] Ingersoll sent with the speech his collected works. Said Mark Twain, "I am devouring them—they have found a hungry place, and they content and satisfy it to a miracle." But he missed the voice and presence of Ingersoll, "I wish I could hear you *speak* these splendid chapters."

During the ensuing years, their correspondence kept up. Twain followed with great enjoyment the Ingersoll-Black controversy on "The Christian Religion" in *The North American Review*. He wrote, "I have been well entertained by your theological article in the magazine, and Judge Black's ludicrous 'reply' to it. Still more delicious, perhaps, than anything in Black's juvenile performance, have been the grave (and I suppose sincere) laudations of it in the newspapers. These ought to make a body laugh, but they make me want to cry for it is so plain that to get men's praise or blame depends not upon whether one treats a religious topic well or ill, but merely upon which side of it he is."

Ingersoll's friendship with Walt Whitman sprang up during the last years of the "good gray poet." Partially paralyzed, Whitman hardly ever left his home in Camden, New Jersey. *Leaves of Grass* was Ingersoll's favorite American work,

which he first read in the middle 60's. Not until 1890, however, did he meet the author face to face, though previous to
that they had exchanged letters.

Ingersoll was Whitman's kind of man. Looking at a portrait of Ingersoll in the home of Thomas Harned, April 15,
1888, Whitman remarked, "That is a grand brow: and the
face—look at the face (see the mouth): it is the head, the face,
the poise of a noble human being. America don't know today
how proud she ought to be of Ingersoll."[3] On May 7, after
Horace Traubel, Whitman's Boswell, read Whitman a letter
which Ingersoll had written to the friends of Leonard Whitney,
deceased, a Unitarian preacher who had been the chaplain
of Ingersoll's regiment during the Civil War, Whitman said,
"How graphic, touching, powerful that is! What a substantial,
rounded fellow the Colonel certainly proves to be! He is in a
way a chosen man . . . Ingersoll is a prophet—he, too, is
called."[4] Not sure whether he quite accepted a sentence in the
letter, which read, " 'Generous men are not indigenous to this
world,' " Whitman said, "Why not to this world as well as to
any other? The Colonel himself is indigenous." And at another
time Whitman remarked, "Ingersoll stands for perfect poise,
nonchalance, equability; he is nonconventional: runs on like
a stream: is sweet, fluid—as they say in the Bible, like precious
ointment."[5]

Much as the two men admired each other, it was not without
a recognition of their differences. "I know quite well why and
where I must disagree with him," said Whitman. "The Colonel
and I are not directly at issue even about God and immortality:
I do not say yes where he says no: I say yes where he says nothing."[6] Ingersoll could not accept Whitman's pantheistic yes;
though when it came right down to it, he too preached a brand
of pantheism. While Whitman sensed that the universe was in-
stinct with beneficent divinity, Ingersoll found "that in all matter, in some way, there is what we call force; that one of the
forms of force is intelligence." But it was not an intelligence
that he could call either divine or good. "The weakest part of

Whitman," said Ingersoll, "was his God belief—that in some way all is good."[7]

Although Whitman saw Ingersoll as "a fiery blast for the new virtues," he also saw him as one who stopped short of the real thing. Reading Ingersoll's lecture, "The Gods," Whitman said, "Of course Bob does not go far enough: he gets rid of the old thing—does it without a quaver—ends it forever. But God? God? Well, there are other divinities: they are not of the hell and damnation sort: they are not of the legs and arms sort—the personal sort: they yet remain, more firmly on their thrones, in the race, than ever: they continue their supremacy. Bob does not intellectually account for them . . ." He did not account for them, according to Whitman, because he could not and he could not because whether he realized it or not he was fundamentally a believer in some sort of divinity. Indeed, this was, said Whitman, "one part of his noble protest." As close to God as the saint is the passionate infidel. But if Ingersoll did realize the divinity in him, could he, Whitman asked himself, "over and over again," do his work? But no matter, Ingersoll had done his work "his divinely appointed job." "O, the dear wonderful man! He was sent by high heaven to save the race and he has done it." He has liberated man from defunct systems, from "criminal institutions."

Whitman and Ingersoll did not see eye to eye in another realm, political ideas. Whitman, in 1888, leaned "just a trifle, a mere trifle" toward the Republican nominee, Benjamin Harrison, but he indicated that he would change his mind if the party made "their protectionism too malignant."[8] He could not understand how Ingersoll, the fervent believer in democracy, could be so chauvinistic in his support of the protective tariff. "I like Ingersoll, sure enough, but his logic in this matter is queer, to say the least. What will America do? Is she for the great mass of men?—the race, the whole globe? No man is a democrat, a true democrat, who forgets that he is interested in the welfare of the race. Who asks only, what is best for America? Instead of, what is best for men—the whole of man?" It might be said in palliation of Ingersoll's aggressive protection-ism that he also supported unrestricted immigration.

"I don't envy Rhys (Ernest) his big breakfasts and dinners and all that—I only envy him his call at Colonel Bob's!"[9] Such was Whitman's reaction to a letter he received from Rhys, dated May 21, 1888, in which Rhys stated that he had been a guest at the Ingersoll's. "I am told," said Whitman, "those nights at Bob's are halcyon nights. Next to being lucky enough to be there yourself is being lucky enough to hear about them from others who have been there. I don't believe the conventional literary class take any part in the Colonel's gatherings but all the unusual fellows seem to turn up there one time or another." But the ailing poet could not get to the gatherings. It was not until May 31, 1890, that he actually met Ingersoll, at a dinner in his honor, on his seventy-first birthday, at Reisser's Restaurant in Philadelphia. Ingersoll, who sat across from Whitman, was the main speaker. Afterward, while reporters took notes, Whitman pro and Ingersoll con had a spirited discussion on immortality. Listening to Ingersoll confirmed Whitman's high estimate of him. The *Camden Post* carried Whitman's words of praise—"a wonderful tribute," said Ingersoll.[10] "Some time," he wrote Whitman, "I will pay, as far as may be in my power, a fitting tribute to your character and genius."[11]

That time came the following October. On the twenty-first, Ingersoll delivered a benefit lecture, *Liberty and Literature,* for and on Whitman. The lecture was given at Horticultural Hall, in Philadelphia. Traubel who helped with the arrangements had tried to obtain the Academy of Music but the board said *no,* that it was the policy to keep out infidels. Despite widespread protests, the board would not relent. "I care nothing about the action of the directors of the Academy of Music . . . ," Ingersoll wrote Traubel September 2, "however, do not allow yourself to be annoyed, or worried. It will come out right enough. I have been through the same mill a great many times."[12] The main thing was to make the occasion a financial success; every dollar was to go to Whitman. "Considerable money will have to be advanced in advertising," Ingersoll said to Traubel, "and this I am perfectly willing to do myself." The lecture was a great financial success, with over three thousand persons in attendance.

Although Ingersoll extolled *Leaves of Grass,* he said that by no means did the whole of the work appeal to him. "In each [Shakespeare, *Leaves of Grass*] there are many things that I neither approve nor believe—but in all books you will find a mingling of wisdom and foolishness, of prophecies and mistakes—in other words, among the excellencies there will be defects."[13] But even in his defects, which were excesses of his virtues, Whitman was great. If some of his lines seem to sanction the sins of the flesh, that was Whitman denying the depravity of man, glorifying the human body, insisting, as Ingersoll put it, "that men and women should be proudly natural." If there was "a touch of chaos" in *Leaves of Grass,* that was Whitman, the destroyer of old forms, the exuberant creator of new.

As if to console the invalided Whitman whom death was stalking, Ingersoll recreated the witcheries of "Out of the Cradle Endlessly Rocking" and "When Lilacs Last in the Dooryard Bloom'd." He said in summing up Whitman as a poet, "above all, he is the poet of Love and Death."

Ingersoll was unable to be present with the many friends of Whitman who gathered at his Camden home, May 31, 1891, to celebrate his seventy-second birthday. He had scheduled a lecture tour to the Midwest. Expressing his regrets to Traubel, he wrote, "Give my love to Whitman. I think of him all the time as of one sitting on the shore, looking hopefully out on the sea, while the sun goes down." In December Whitman contracted pneumonia. On the twenty-first Traubel wrote Ingersoll, "I write this at W's home—on his own paper. He sleeps sweetly— but is feeble, feeble. . . .

"I am afraid our dear friend has but a few days more of leave, here, with us, on Mother Earth. Have you the least word to send? It would be a sweet consolation in the midst of things that do not propitiate or console. . . .

"I think the letter Walt wrote you was his last to anyone."

Ingersoll responded with telegrams. "Walt," Traubel wrote, "was profoundly moved and realized the love and consideration out of which you spoke." On the twenty-ninth Ingersoll wrote Whitman, "I am glad that you have lived long enough to know that 'Leaves of Grass' will live forever. . . . This is enough —and this is a radiance that even the darkness of death cannot extinguish." And then Ingersoll said, in utter sincerity for it was his utmost hope: "May be the end of the journey is the best of all, and may be the end of this is the beginning of another, and maybe the beginning of that is better than the ending of this."

Whitman overcame the pneumonia but not its debilitating effects. He lingered on, in pain and virtual helplessness, and on March 24 Ingersoll sent his last letter to Whitman, "I was pained to hear that you are suffering more and more, but was glad to know that your brave spirit has never been bowed— and that in all your agony your heart keeps sweet and strong.

"I think of you a thousand times a day—and of the great good you have done the world. . . .

"Again I thank you for your courage, and again I lovingly say farewell—and yet I hope to see you soon."

He saw Whitman soon, on March 30, but it was Whitman dead in a casket in the bare parlor of the Mickle Street cottage in Camden. Ingersoll was in Canada when word of Whitman's death, March 26, reached him. Having promised to speak at Whitman's funeral, Ingersoll arrived at the cottage just as the last of thousands were filing past the casket.

At three o'clock the funeral cortege reached Harleigh Cemetery. Three thousand people crowded the little dell where Whitman's tomb was set. Around a small tent they gathered, close packed, to hear the tributes of the speakers. "There was intense silence when (the last speaker) Colonel Ingersoll arose, and in those glowing periods for which he is world famous, scattered flowers of speech over the ashes of his friend.

"When the great orator had spoken—and his words dwelt on the ears like rich music—there was nothing left to do but to consign Walt Whitman to his tomb, and this was done without parade or ceremony."[14]

These were the final words of Ingersoll's speech: "He has lived, he has died, and death is less terrible than it was before. Thousands and millions will walk down into the 'dark valley of the shadow' holding Walt Whitman by the hand. Long after we are dead the brave words he has spoken will sound like trumpets to the dying.

"And so I lay this little wreath upon this great man's tomb. I loved him living, and I love him still."[15]

". . . I SHALL BE 58"

I N 1891, his throat ailment gone, Ingersoll again undertook an extensive schedule of lectures. In April and May he lectured almost every day on a tour from the Atlantic seaboard to the Midwest. He had a new lecture, "Shakespeare," which was non-controversial, unless some wished to contest his repudiation of Baconian authorship. "Shakespeare" was the product of a devotee. It showed emotional rapport, imaginative insight, and scholarship. It was full of specific matter on the life and times of Shakespeare, on the question of Baconian authorship, on the sources of plays, scenes, lines, and characters. With much example it set forth Shakespeare's gifts: his imagery, his wizardy with words, his fecundity in the creation of character, his powers of observation, his mastery of dramatic structure.

Some had conjectured that Ingersoll drew large audiences for his lectures because he was a sensation monger, that if he ever got off the subject of religion on which it required only brazenness to be startling he would come a cropper. The fact is that though "Shakespeare" was not one of his most popular lectures, it was still good "box office."

Ingersoll was now giving little time to the law. Associates in the firm of Ingersoll and McCune handled most of the business. But he took a case if there was something special to recommend it, as, for instance, the Davis Will case, the something special being a fee of $100,000 if he won.

In the Davis Will case Ingersoll was counsel for several heirs who sued to break the will of Andrew J. Davis on the ground of forgery. The will left the bulk of five million dollars, in liquid assets, accumulated from Montana mines, to a brother, John A. Davis, and but token bequests to other brothers and sisters. The trial commenced in Butte, Montana, the last week of July, 1891.

Butte in mid-summer was hardly the spot for a man accustomed to Walston and the watering places of the East. "It is the most frightful place I was ever in," wrote Ingersoll. A pall of smoke and dust hung over an inferno, "I am as homesick as a polar bear at the equator. Two hundred and fifty tons of sulphur are burned in the air every day."[1] If a man were a drinker or a gambler, Butte had compensations, "saloons by the hundred, licensed gambling saloons on every street." It did have one compensation for Ingersoll, "lots of intelligent, splendid people, good socially, hospitable and refined." These people made much of the famous man and his wife and daughter, Maud, who, happily, were with him. Maud was in the courtroom every day of the trial, which lasted six weeks.

The trial as it dragged on taxed Ingersoll's patience. Many witnesses were called but few were reliable. "Day by day," said Ingersoll, "I lose confidence in human testimony. Ignorance, prejudice, malice, perjury, forgetfulness, stupidity, cunning and even honesty all combine to hide or distort the truth."[2] Toward the end of the trial Ingersoll said, "We have had an awful time fighting the judge . . ."[3]

On September 4, Ingersoll gave his summation. In a preceding speech, opposing counsel, Senator Sanders, warned the jury to be wary of Ingersoll whose eloquence transcended the best that Ancient Greece could boast. He also said, quoting the Bible, " 'My son, if sinners entice thee consent thou not.' " Ingersoll began by "waiving congratulations, reminiscences and animadversions." He parried Sanders' Biblical quotation with a reference to the same source. "Don't be afraid of me because I am a sinner. I admit that I am. I am not like the other gentleman who thanked God 'that he was not as other men.' " Then he plunged into the maze of detail concerning the genuineness of the contested will.[4]

Courtroom and corridors were packed the day Ingersoll spoke. He did not disappoint. The *Anaconda Standard,* of Butte, wrote of his "matchless eloquence."

Without notes, except for documents and letters, Ingersoll spoke in language that was direct and graphic. Early in his speech, opposing counsel, skeptical that a man could remember accurately all the detail, interrupted him with questions. His answers left no doubt that his memory was reliable. And when meddled with, he was also quick with a quip. So they let him alone for most of his speech. The jury and the audience had a good time. Repeatedly Ingersoll made them laugh and Judge McHatton had to rap for order.[5]

The verdict was seven to five for Ingersoll, which, however, was one short of the legal requirements in Montana. "I am going to beat in the end sure," wrote Ingersoll to his brother. But the case dragged on with appeals and postponements, his clients refusing to pay the $100,000 until the will was broken. He collected only expenses. When, after his death in 1899, his wife tried to collect the fee, the clients contended that since he had not actually broken the will he was not entitled to payment. She brought suit, which finally reached the United States Supreme Court. A decision covering a compromise settlement was rendered in her favor in 1909.

On August 1, 1891, Ingersoll wrote John, "August is here again and on the 11th I shall be 58. The years are flying fast. . . . I wish I was rich. I am beginning to want money. So far, I have never been able to get out of debt." But he was making $175,000 a year. Much went for the abundant life, much for charities, but not so much as to keep him in debt. It was business ventures again, everyone of which came to naught—the Spokane Smelting Company, the Universal Box Factory, the

Casa Grande Improvement Company, the Colonial Mining Company. Then there was the Standard Veneer Company, dedicated to the making of dishes, about which Ingersoll wrote to General R. A. Alger: "And I sincerely hope that you will conclude to 'cast a little bread on the waters' with the rest of us."[6] If the bread was cast, it was on the wrong waters. There was also what Ingersoll referred to as "the Meat Co.," the ups and downs of which caused him to say, "We dine on hope and sup on sorrow."

On December 19, 1891, the New York *Evening Telegram* published Ingersoll's "A Christmas Sermon" and started a controversy that raged for two months and reached by January 9, according to the *Telegram,* "almost national dimensions." "A Christmas Sermon" was short but it was strong stuff for any Christian stomach. Ingersoll maintained that Christmas was originally a Pagan festival celebrating the triumph of the Sun-God over the powers of Darkness. Christianity adopted the festival, and corrupted it. "Christianity did not come with tidings of great joy, but with a message of eternal grief. It came with the threat of everlasting torture on its lips. . . .

"It taught some good things—the beauty of love and kindness in man. But as a torch-bearer, as a bringer of joy, it has been a failure. It has given infinite consequences to the acts of finite beings, crushing the soul with a responsibility too great for mortals to bear. It has filled the future with fear and flame, and made God the keeper of an eternal penitentiary, destined to be the home of nearly all the sons of men. Not satisfied with that, it has deprived God of the pardoning power."

A deluge of letters hit the *Evening Telegram,* some of which, the paper said, were of a "gushing or sentimental character" and some of "so scurrilous a nature that they are not fit to be seen by the public eye." The furore became formidable when on December 24 the Rev. Dr. J. M. Buckley, called by the *Telegram* "the most warlike soldier in the Methodist Church militant," published in the *Christian Advocate,* of which he was editor, a reply entitled "Lies That Are Monstrous." Buckley appealed to the public to boycott the *Telegram* for having printed Ingersoll's "gigantic falsehoods." Far from daunted by Buckley's appeal, the *Telegram* solicited and published a reply from Ingersoll, in which he verified the "gigantic falsehoods." He cited the New Testament to show that Christianity did hold to original sin and eternal punishment. These were not "tidings of great joy." As to his charge in the "Sermon" that Christianity "deprived God of the pardoning power," Ingersoll reasoned, "The Methodist Church and every orthodox church teaches that this life is a period of probation; that there is no chance given for reformation after death; that God gives no opportunity to repent in another world." Was this a tiding of great joy?

The next clerics to enter the fray, in space assigned them by the *Telegram*, were the Reverends James M. King and Thomas Dixon, Jr.; the first, Methodist, the second, Baptist. King denounced the *Telegram* for printing the "Sermon," a "prostitution of the powers of the respectable daily press, and a violation of the sacred rights of the clean families."[7] who patronized the paper. The *Telegram* should have prevented this "poison from dropping into the cup of their Christian family joys." After all, Ingersoll was "an infidel 'for revenue only.' " Thomas Dixon, Jr., was a more kindly critic. He thought that Buckley and others misjudged Ingersoll and took him too seriously. "The Colonel," he said, "is not a scientist, he is an orator. He is not a historian; but a poet. . . . He is a sentimentalist, first and last. His argument is always *ad hominem*. He is a superb demagogue. He is intensely human." Dixon saw that Ingersoll had "his uses . . . divine uses." He had awakened "slumbering orthodoxy" and had done "much to rid the world of the superstitions, lies, shams, humbugs, traditions and pretences that used to pass current as orthodox truth. . . ." "If God should choose Balaam's ass to speak a divine message, I do not see," said Dixon, "why He could not utilize the Colonel. Give him rope."[8]

The *Telegram*, publishing Ingersoll's reply to King and Dixon,[9] asserted in regard to Buckley's appeal for a boycott, "This paper cannot be bullied." The paper also noted that its circulation was "leaping upward."

Ingersoll rejected King's charge that he had issued "blasphemous utterances concerning Christmas." "How is it possible to blaspheme a day?" Is disagreement over the significance of a day blasphemous? Blasphemy was deliberate distortion of the truth or a desertion of the truth when it was unpopular. He had said what he considered the truth. This was not blasphemy. Moreover, he, unlike King, had couched his thoughts on Christmas in "becoming language." To King's thrust that he was "an infidel 'for revenue only,' " Ingersoll riposted, "Is he willing to admit that we have drifted so far from orthodox religion that the way to make money is to denounce Christianity? I can hardly believe, for joy, that liberty of thought has advanced so far."

Ingersoll was pleased to find in Dixon's letter acknowledgment of his services to enlightened thought, he hoped to expose many more superstitions and lies. But he was not altogether pleased with Dixon's comparing him to Balaam's ass. However, Dixon should read the story again, for the point of it is that the ass "was much superior to the prophet of God."

On January 6 the *Telegram* reported that it was "overwhelmed with letters commending its course" and that its circulation was "mounting day by day." The newsdealers were increasing their orders and the newsboys were struggling to get the earliest copies. "The great controversy," said the *Telegram*, "formed the leading topic of conversation in the homes of the people." All in all, it was "a grand boon for the paper."

At first, however, only a few of the letters to the *Telegram* were from the clergy, unless it was members of the clergy who wrote in under the pseudonyms of Advancement, Lumen, Liberty, Cattinello, and the like. Cattinello, for instance, rejoiced that Ingersoll was permitted to write himself an ass. Quoting Job, he rejoiced that the wish of Job had been realized—" 'Oh, that mine enemy would write a book.' " The *Telegram* deplored the dearth of clerical response and cried out, on January 9, "Where are the Luthers of to-day?"

The goad worked and the clergy of all faiths responded with letters, articles, and sermons. Some treated Ingersoll with forbearance and kindliness and even admitted a bit of truth in his "Christmas Sermon." The Reverend Peter M'Queen of the Dutch Reformed Church admitted that Christian orthodoxy had been preoccupied with the endless consequences of sin and that it had led to religious persecutions and wars, but this was all in the past: "The Colonel is evidently tackling an orthodoxy that is non est, and a form of thought which was rampant in the days of Philip I, but had gone out of use long before the regime of Grover Cleveland or Benjamin Harrison."[10] Another minister, Madison C. Peters, in a letter January 12, said that he regarded Dr. Buckley's plea to boycott the paper as "unmanly and un-American." The issues raised by Ingersoll were worth considering; Peters would give the following Sunday night the first of a series of sermons on the subject.

If a few of the ministers accorded Ingersoll respect and the right to have his say, most condemned him. "Wait," cried the Reverend J. Benson Hamilton of a Methodist Episcopal Church in Brooklyn, "wait until the icy fingers feel for the heart strings of the boaster . . . a few years at the most. . . ." When death comes close to an infidel "He sneaks and cringes like a whipped cur, and trembles and whines and howls." Said Ingersoll in a reply to Hamilton and others, "The spirit of Mr. Hamilton is not altogether admirable."[11]

LECTURING—"A BAD BUSINESS"

I N December, 1893, Ingersoll wrote to his brother John, "I think I shall put in the whole of January and Feby. in the same way—It is a bad business and I get tired enough but one must live."

Lecturing was not a bad business economically. But it was bad in that Ingersoll had to travel so much and undergo the assorted trials of hotel rooms, restaurant meals, and trains. Bad, just being away from home. If his wife or Maud or Clint Farrell could accompany him, which one or more often did, that was making the best of a bad thing. But it was not the same as being at Walston or 400 Fifth Avenue with all his loved ones about him, including, by 1894, two grandchildren, Robert and Eva.

In the early spring of 1894, for the first time in his lecturing career, Ingersoll ventured into the South, that is, as far south as Tennessee, on a tour that took him to several of the "border" states. The one-time lusty Republican waver of the "bloody flag" was surprised at the hearty receptions in Chattanooga, Memphis, Nashville, and Knoxville.[1] He found, as he said, "a great many warm friends" in Tennessee. Many had served under him in the Eleventh Illinois Cavalry. His wife was with him. And so, everything considered, the perfect weather and the beautiful country, "peach trees all in blossom and many of the trees clothed in green," it was ideal, as tours go. Still, as Ingersoll wrote the "Dear Girls" back home, "We hate to be away . . . we send love and kisses to you and the dear little babes. Do not let the things forget us. . . . We shall soon be with you, and then we shall forget the days of separation."[2] They returned home the first week of April.

A few days at home and Ingersoll was off again, this time alone, on a two weeks' tour of upstate New York. He lectured every day, came home again for a few days and then did two weeks in New England. The times were hard, in the wake of the Panic of '93, "as hard," wrote Ingersoll, "as the heart of John Calvin."[3] His lecture revenues were down a little, but he was weathering the depression as well as could be expected. He was certainly doing better lecturing than in the law which brought him little or no business, "all men living in perfect peace."

As he planned the extensive tours for the coming fall and winter months he was a bit worried: "I cannot tell how I will succeed. The times are so wretched." But almost without exception he had packed houses. His itinerary in October and November included Pittsburgh, Cleveland, Cincinnati, Chicago, Milwaukee, and some thirty other cities along this route.

Ingersoll had three new lectures for the season, "Abraham Lincoln," "Voltaire," and "About the Holy Bible." The first two, though eulogies, were free of the vaporings that often mark the genre. Full of specific matter they delineated figures who were human and credible. "About the Holy Bible" was new in title only; it set forth the ideas of "Some Mistakes of Moses," "Some Reasons Why," and "What Must We Do To Be Saved."

Ingersoll tried to find out which of his lectures people preferred. He would have ballots, each containing the titles of eight to ten lectures, distributed in advance in the locality in which he was to appear. Thus two months before he spoke in Indianapolis, March 28, 1895, his agent distributed six hundred ballots among forty business establishments in the city. In indicating preference, one could check as many titles as he wished. The tally of four hundred and thirteen ballots returned was as follows:

"About the Holy Bible," 270
"The Liberty of Man, Woman and Child," 190
"What Must We Do to be Saved," 162
"Foundations of Faith," 138
"Shakespeare," 65
"The Gods," 55
"Abraham Lincoln," 49
"Myth and Miracle," 47
"Voltaire," 9

Ballots were also distributed in nearby towns with similar results. The preference for the lectures on religion was plain.

An experience Ingersoll had in Atlanta, Georgia, also indicated that people preferred him on religion. On December 22, 1894, the *Journal of Atlanta,* anticipating Ingersoll's appearance in that city, February 13, printed a synopsis of "About the Holy Bible" and also the replies of several ministers who had received from the *Journal* copies of the lecture. The replies would have delighted the most pessimistic advance agent. Said Dr. Walker Lewis: "Can it be true that there are men in this City who, for the money to be gotten out of this man's coming, are willing to inoculate Atlanta with the virus that he brings.

They have even greater right, morally, to import smallpox or diphtheria to help trade." Said the Reverend R. G. Bigham: "He is a second-hand dealer in blasphemy whom no man can assimilate without pollution." And from Dr. W. B. Hawthorne: "What would become of this nation if the vilest of all living lepers should get it to accept his code of ethics?" The audience that greeted Ingersoll on February 13, was, according to the *Journal,* "an exceptionally light one for a man of Colonel Ingersoll's reputation." Not because he delivered "About the Holy Bible." Said the *Journal,* "There is very little doubt that the lecturer would have had a much larger audience had he chosen one of his religious themes." Ingersoll had decided to give "Shakespeare."

The tour during the first months of 1895, which took Ingersoll as far west as Minneapolis and Des Moines and as far south as New Orleans and St. Augustine, was proof aplenty that his power had not diminished. There were people in Lima, Ohio, who were so afraid of him that they organized several counter-attractions in order to deplete his audience the night of January 5. "The ladies of all the reading clubs in the city gave a fine literary and musical programme at the Elk's Hall," said the Cincinnati *Inquirer,* to keep the ladies away from Ingersoll and, if possible, the men. Several churches held "entertainments." Governor Ira P. Chase of Indiana delivered an address at the Church of the Disciples. But all was in vain: at the Ingersoll lecture "standing room was at par."

Ingersoll's engagement in Hoboken, New Jersey, February 24, caused a hubbub that attracted nationwide attention. That hundred-year-old New Jersey statute on blasphemy—the one which Ingersoll battled in the defense of Charles Reynolds in Morristown, in 1887—was again resurrected. A group of Hoboken Ministers were aggrieved that Ingersoll was to speak on the Bible. They knew he would utter blasphemy, and on Sunday at that. Led by the Reverend H. T. Beatty, of the First Presbyterian Church, they prevailed upon Mayor Fagan, on Saturday night, to order the closing of Jacob's Opera House, where Ingersoll was to appear.[4]

Ingersoll heard of the order late Saturday night, when he was in bed. His manager, C. A. Davis, brought him the news. Immediately he arose and with his manager got in touch with one Mr. Clarke, the manager of the Opera House, and the three went over to consult Edward Russ, a local lawyer. They scrutinized the blasphemy statute but could find no loophole. Sunday morning Davis and Clarke appealed to Mayor Fagan to rescind his order. He refused. Then they petitioned Chancellor McGill of Jersey City to issue an injunction in restraint of the closure order. He refused to act. Then they appealed to the Mayor again who now said that the Opera House would be closed not because of the blasphemy statute but because the house had a license for weekdays only. He admitted that if a minister had scheduled the house for a Sunday it would not be closed. He made a concession, however, and referred the appellants to City Attorney James F. Minturn for a ruling.

Minturn, who had written several articles on civil rights, ruled that to deny the house to Ingersoll would be to impair the right to freedom of speech. He cited Section 4 of the Constitution of New Jersey, which read: "Every person may freely speak, write and publish his sentiments on all subjects, being responsible for the abuse of that right. No law shall be passed to restrain or abridge the liberty of speech or of the press." Minturn also ruled that whether Ingersoll could be charged with abuse of the right of freedom of speech would depend on what he actually said. He could not be charged with blasphemy before he spoke. As a result of the ruling the Mayor gave in, though he still might have held to the technicality of the weekday license.

In his lecture that Sunday night Ingersoll deftly, and to the vast amusement of his capacity audience, evaded the letter of the blasphemy statute. He had to be deft for he knew that among his hearers were Reverends Beatty and other clergy, Detectives Nelson and Gallagher, Chief of Police Donovan, and a Judge Douglass, all there to detect blasphemy. But what could they do; he studiously introduced blasphemous material in an impishly ironic style, thus:

Mind you, I don't say that the Scriptures are not inspired. On the contrary, I admit that they were—in New Jersey, That's in accordance with the statutes, and I'm not foolish enough to fight any statute. You see, if the Legislature of New Jersey says a thing, that ends it with me. . . . This is what infidels say, I am simply repeating it to you. . . .

Or again: "I don't know, I don't know. If it were not for the Jersey blasphemy statute I might know. As it is, I don't. The Hoboken parsons know. Ask them. They can tell you all about it." He caustically dealt with ministers in general, even terming them "sanctified swine," but he said: "Of course I don't refer to the clergymen of Hoboken, because I don't know them"—at this point, it was observed, he paused a long time—and brought down the house. Going on, he said:

Most ministers believe that they are called to their profession, and I've got it in my mind that it's because they haven't got the physical constitution to be wicked. You can't blame 'em for their views. They get 'em in sectarian colleges and sectarian colleges are what might be called the storm centers of ignorance. They [the ministers] come out like the lands on the upper Potomac, as described by John Rogers—

here Ingersoll again paused and pointedly looked at three ministers sitting together, then concluded the sentence—" 'almost worthless by nature and—rendered wholly so by cultivation.' " Pandemonium now broke out; it was observed that even Rev. Beatty and the detectives laughed. With the restoration of order Ingersoll went on to say: "I do not see why these clergymen should wish to throw me in the penitentiary when they know what I shall have to endure in the next world. That ought to satisfy them I should think." While Ingersoll was lecturing and particularly when he finished, many of his hearers expected his arrest. In substance, if not in letter, he had surely violated the blasphemy statute. But the arm of the law, palsied perhaps from laughter, did not reach out to seize him.

The Hoboken affair made the press all over the country and drew widespread comment from the clergy. The Chicago *Times*

interviewed several ministers of the city; all but two were criti-
cal of the behavior of their colleagues in Hoboken. The two,
Bishop Charles E. Cheney, rector of Christ Reformed Episcopal
Church, and the Reverend Dr. Andrew J. Canfield, pastor of St.
Paul's, held that Ingersoll should have been barred from speaking. But the Rev. Dr. Carlos Mortyn, of the Sixth Presbyterian
Church, said: "I would shoulder a musket to put down an in-
surrection against free thought and free speech." And the Rev.
Jenkin Lloyd Jones, of All Souls Church, declared that this
affair "shows that Ingersoll has a work to do, a work not finished." In New York, Lyman Abbott, as might have been expected from a minister of his liberality, said. "I do not believe
in invoking the law to quell freedom of speech." Not to have
been expected was the comment of Ingersoll's fervent funda-
mentalist foe, DeWitt Talmage: "Religious matters should be
freely and fully discussed." Surprising too was the stand taken
by another oft-heard foe, the Rev. Dr. A. C. Dixon, of the Han-
son Place Baptist Church, Brooklyn, whom, in 1893, Ingersoll
had sued for libel. Said Dixon: "Let the devil speak."

INGERSOLL CONVERTED!

INGERSOLL was the object of much conversion energy. In October, 1895, an aged woman appeared nightly in front of his
residence at 400 Fifth Avenue and left tracts at the door and
knelt in prayer. Another woman sent him each week Bible lessons clipped from her country paper. One of the clippings he
particularly cherished; with scriptural quotations it adjured the
reader to come to Christ and doomed him if he did not, but it
also carried, a space below the last line of the lesson, a two-line
advertisement which the woman had overlooked and which
read: "Drink Bill's Brand of Rock and Rye, warranted pure;
only 50¢ a pint." Ingersoll wrote the woman and rebuked her

for leading him to drink. A man in New York City wrote him: "Only one thing seems lacking to make the links in the chain of your manhood perfect—and that is Faith in God. . . . Col. Ingersoll, I would be very glad to meet you, with your wife and daughters, and together kneel and ask God's blessing on each of you."[1] And from Portland, Maine: "I will pray for you next Lord's day morning at nine o'clock A.M., Maine time. And I hope the Holy Spirit will touch your heart to pray at that same hour wherever you may be."[2] The Reverend Dr. McCabe of the Board of Home Missions of the Methodist Episcopal Church sent a hortatory letter and leaflet every month. In one letter he pointed out that during the thirty years that Ingersoll had lectured the Methodist Church had gained 1,800,000 communicants and the church property had increased in value from $29,000,000 to more than $160,000,000, a gain of $12,000 daily for thirty years." "Colonel," said McCabe, "we have beaten you! Colonel, you had better join the Methodist Church! Saul of Tarsus persecuted the Church and he came in. You had better come in." Dwight Moody was also endeavoring to convert Ingersoll, whom he, too, compared with the apostle: "I am praying for his conversion. Why shouldn't he be converted? He is a better man than Saul of Tarsus. He would not have stood by and seen Stephen stoned as Saul of Tarsus did."[3]

A mass attempt at Ingersoll's conversion took place in November, 1895. On Wednesday, November 20, he lectured in Cleveland on "The Foundations of Faith." Three thousand people braved inclement weather to hear him. This would not do. Something had to be done to quiet the man. The youth of Cleveland took the initiative. On Monday, November 25, the Christian Endeavor Union at a meeting in Old Stone Church passed a resolution which provided that every member of the Union should pray for Ingersoll's conversion, on Thanksgiving Day, at high noon. The Epworth League of the Methodist Church, and the Salvation Army resolved to do the same. The Army held religious services in the forenoon of Thanksgiving Day and as high noon neared, "Joe the Turk," resplendent in a new outfit, arose and offered the following prayer: "I believe it.

I believe it, O Lord. We have an arch-enemy who is travelling over the country. He is working against Thee. He is working against us, O Lord. He is endeavoring to injure the cause, O Lord. We have all faith in Thee. We believe that Thou canst do this thing. Make a friend—a co-worker of him. Thou art all-powerful, and holdest everything in thy hands. Answer this, our prayer." At this point the entire audience, almost in a frenzy, arose and shouted "Amen" and "Bless the Lord" and continued to do so for half an hour.[4]

Three thousand Christian Endeavorers and several hundred Epworth Leaguers prayed at the appointed hours. A correspondent for the Philadelphia *Record* speculated that some of the members may have proved derelict, for a football game was in progress and exactly at twelve o'clock the local team made a touchdown. That Ingersoll just then was in the minds of any Endeavorers who were at the game was too much to expect.

The efforts of the Christian Youth of Cleveland spurred their brethren in other cities and in Canada. The New York *Sun,* of November 29, reported: "All Canadian Endeavorers have been requested to unite on December 1 (Sunday) at 2 P.M., in prayers to God for the conversion of Col. Robert Ingersoll."

On the night of the following January 11, in Kalamazoo, Michigan, Ingersoll gave all his would-be converters cause for joy. During the day he had visited the People's Church in the city, of which Miss Caroline J. Bartlett was the pastor. The Church, non-sectarian and creedless, had as its "Bond of Union," in Miss Bartlett's words, "the cause of pure and practical religion in the community." Equipped with reception rooms, study room, libraries, a dining room, a kitchen, and a gymnasium, the Church was an active community center. Included among its many activities were philanthropies, athletic contests, study clubs, a kindergarten, and a Frederick Douglass Club for young colored people. Subsisting entirely on voluntary contributions, the Church was a solvent concern. Ingersoll was impressed with it and took time midway in his lecture on "Lincoln" to say so. He said of the Church: "It is the grandest thing in your state, if not in the whole United States." And then he said, and this caused a countrywide stir, "If there were a similar church near my home, I would join it, if its members would permit me." When asked after the lecture if he said this in earnest, Ingersoll allegedly replied that he was very much in earnest.

A special dispatch that night, from Kalamazoo, reported that prominent members of the People's Church were convinced that Ingersoll had seen the light, that he would join the church and stop delivering agnostic lectures—"They say they see in his words the answer to the thousands of prayers sent up by the Christian Endeavor members all over the country." The press of the land carried the news under headlines like these: "Is Bob Saved?," Cleveland *Plain Dealer;* " 'Bob' Weakens," New York *Recorder;* "Is Ingersoll Converted?," New York *Sun;* "Ingersoll as a Convert," St. Louis *Globe-Democrat.* The New York *Journal* telegraphed Miss Bartlett and Ingersoll for confirmation of his remarks on the People's Church. She replied that what Ingersoll was reported to have said was substantially what he did say. He replied: "The object of this church is to make people better, kinder and nearer, just by developing the brain and civilizing the heart. . . . I like that Church."

With all this publicity, Miss Bartlett and her church became widely known. She received hundreds of letters, many with donations. Some raised the question, was she as godless as Ingersoll? To which she replied, "I believe in God and immortality and prayer." She wrote to E. M. McDonald, editor of *The Truth Seeker,* who was disturbed by the report of Ingersoll's apostasy to free thought; "I do not endorse Colonel Ingersoll's theological views, nor he mine."[5]

For the mass prayers that supposedly had brought about his conversion, Ingersoll was grateful because they showed that "the Christians were getting civilized." Time was that Christians would have burned him, "Now they pray for me." As far as he knew, the prayers neither harmed him, nor helped him. Anyhow the prayers probably fell short, he said, "for lack of postage." Of the Christian Endeavorers and their effort he remarked: "I feel much as the pretty girl did towards the young man who squeezed her hand, 'It pleased him,' she said, 'and it didn't hurt me.' "

THE CAMPAIGN OF '96

INGERSOLL did not participate in the campaign of 1892. "My God! What a choice we have," he had written of the rival candidates, Grover Cleveland and Benjamin Harrison; "It is terrible to choose one when we hate both. Think of marrying the girl you hate the least."[1] It was different in 1896. Ingersoll knew William McKinley well and could say of him, "He is a very good man and will give us a good administration."[2]

Ingersoll had had enough of the Democratic administration —"Cleveland has been a failure—a pudding-headed failure."[3] The panic of '93 and the hard times that followed were to be attributed to the low tariff and the cheap money of the Democratic party. Ingersoll overlooked the fact that it was Cleveland who against the strong opposition of Silverites had secured in 1893 the repeal of the Sherman Silver Purchase Act that had allowed the government to issue Treasury notes in payment for the annual purchase of 54,000,000 ounces of silver.

Nor did Ingersoll like Cleveland's foreign policy. Cleveland had opposed the annexation of the Hawaiian Islands and had repudiated the action of John Leavitt Stevens, minister to the Islands, in establishing a protectorate there after a revolution against the royal government. In a letter to the New York *Journal,* November 19, 1893, Ingersoll stated: "I believe that he [Stevens] acted with discretion and within the law.

"I am utterly opposed to the policy of Mr. Cleveland, because it is unconstitutional and un-American.

"It is not for him to destroy provisional governments, or restore kings or queens to their throne. . . ."[4]

Ingersoll also condemned Cleveland's intervention in the dispute between Great Britain and Venezuela over the boundary line between Venezuela and British Guiana. The Monroe Doctrine did not, he contended, apply, and to threaten to use force as Cleveland did was criminal. Who wanted to go to war "about a few square miles of malarial territory in Venezuela?"[5] Besides, and this cut Ingersoll close, Cleveland's tactics caused a sharp decline in the stock market.[6]

As for William Jennings Bryan, the Democratic hopeful in 1896, "He talks but he does not think."[7]

Ingersoll made his first speech of the campaign in Chicago, October 8. He spoke in a huge tent, at Sacramento Avenue and Lake Street, to twelve thousand people who found seats, eight thousand who stood, and three thousand who were outside. "The mass of people inside the tent was so great," according to the Chicago *Tribune,* "that a pin would have started a panic." Gasoline lamps on the tent poles capered and a large sounding board at the rear of the platform swayed. When Ingersoll tried to speak, a half hour late, he was drowned out by an ovation. Members of the crowd climbed on chairs and yelled for peace and quiet. A riot seemed sure. A call went out for an extra force of police. Then as if from collective exhaustion the commotion ceased, just seconds before the police appeared.

In this, and his other speeches of the campaign, Ingersoll as usual was fervent for protectionism. He also dealt with the issue of the right of the government by injunction and force to quell interferences with interstate commerce. The widespread strike of railway workers against the Pullman Palace Car Company had paralyzed train services, and the strikers with violence had defied a Federal injunction forbidding interference with the mails. The Democratic platform condemned the blanket injunction and the decision of the United States Supreme Court, May, 1895, sustaining it. "It is the duty of the President," said Ingersoll, "to lay the mailed hand of the Republic upon the mob"[8]—which actually Cleveland had done, by despatching troops to Chicago, in July, 1894. "The law," said Ingersoll, "is the supreme will of the supreme people, and we must obey it or go back to savagery and black night. I stand by the courts."

But it was the issue of the free coinage of silver at 16:1 that Ingersoll attended to most. This was the issue that united Democrats, silverite Republicans, and Populists. It was an issue that threatened to rend the country: West against East, debtor against creditor, worker against employer, poor man against rich. Bryan was the deliverer of the oppressed—"You shall not press down upon the brow of labor this crown of thorns—you shall not crucify mankind upon a cross of gold." While McKinley campaigned from his front porch in Canton, Ohio, Bryan travelled eighteen thousand miles and delivered over six hundred speeches in twenty-nine states.

Ingersoll, the champion of gold, charged Bryan with not knowing his economics. "Gold was not given value by being made a legal tender, but being valuable, it was made a legal tender. . . . Take a twenty dollar gold piece, hammer it out of shape, mar the Goddess of Liberty, pound out the United States of America and batter the eagle, and after you get it pounded, how much is it worth? It is worth exactly twenty dollars. Is it legal tender? No. Has its value been changed? No. Take a silver dollar. It is a legal tender; now pound it into a cube, and how much is it worth? A little less than fifty cents. What gives it the value of a dollar? The fact that it is a legal tender? No; but the promise of the Government to keep it on an equality with gold . . ."

Ingersoll also charged that Bryan was immoral in offering the temptation of a 16 to 1 dollar: "Mr. Bryan tells the farmers who are in debt that they want cheap money. What for? To pay their debts. And he thinks that is a compliment to the tillers of the soil. The statement is an insult to the farmers, and the farmers of Maine and Vermont [who had already voted Republican] have answered him.

"Suppose a man has borrowed a thousand bushels of wheat of his neighbor, of sixty pounds to the bushel, and then Congress should pass a law making thirty pounds of wheat a bushel. Would that farmer pay his debt with five hundred bushels and consider himself an honest man?"

Ingersoll accused Bryan of talking out of both sides of his

mouth at once. Bryan tried to satisfy debtors and creditors. To the one class he said, as Ingersoll quoted him, " 'Vote for cheap money to pay your debts' "; to the other, "We will . . . make it as good as gold." That Congress could make fifty cents' worth of silver worth one dollar was to Ingersoll an absurd proposition: "You cannot fix values by law any more than you can make cooler summers by shortening thermometers." But if Congress could, he was opposed to the scheme "on account of its extravagance: "What is the use of wasting all that silver? If Congress can make fifty cents' worth of silver worth a dollar by law, why can it not make one cents' worth of silver worth a dollar by law? . . . . The supply even of silver is limited—the supply of law is inexhaustible. Do not waste silver, use more law."

Ingersoll made seven speeches in Illinois, at Galena, Galesburg, Bloomington, Paris, Peoria, and another, October 26, at Chicago. He spoke at Peoria October 16. "Hereafter, all crowds in Peoria will be gauged by the wonderful Ingersoll meeting last night." Eight thousand people crammed the Tabernacle "and more than that many went away, unable to gain admittance." The great orator had come home and the town gave him a hero's welcome. Thousands waited around the Tabernacle to catch a glimpse of him. At a little before eight, escorted by Spencer's band playing "Marching Through Georgia" and the Union Veteran Club, Ingersoll hove in sight. Cheers rent the air and people pressed around him. For a while it seemed that he might not get in the Tabernacle. Then the Union Western Club, using a flying wedge formation, forced a passage for him. Into the Tabernacle and through the center aisle they went while the audience stood in ovation. Now he was on the platform, his bald head and cherubic face visible to all. For ten minutes "Our Bob" bowed acknowledgments to proud Peorians. He was one of their own. Even the religious cheered.[9]

A sidelight of the campaign exposed for Ingersoll a flaw in the thinking of many freethinkers. Zealous Populists, they wondered how Ingersoll could be so unorthodox on God and so orthodox on Mammon. Was he all for gold because he had received gold? They freely expressed their puzzlement, even making charges. The American Secular Union, of which they were members, was to hold a congress in Chicago in November. The Executive Committee, who did not suspect Ingersoll, invited him to speak. He declined. He wrote to his friend, Samuel Putnam, who sent him the invitation, "There seems to be a great deal of feeling among people who call themselves freethinkers as to the position I have taken on the money question and many of them seem to think that I am, for the sake of money, expressing views that I do not honestly entertain. . . . Under these circumstances I hardly think I would be welcome in Chicago. It seems to me that I had better stay away. . . . I have great feeling about this matter. It is bitter to find that you cannot depend on your friends.

"Please consider this as strictly confidential as I do not wish to add fuel to the flame."[10]

Putnam entreated Ingersoll to forget the foolish suspicions and reckless statements of some of their colleagues assuring him that the overwhelming majority knew better. But Ingersoll was adamant, "I do not care to meet the men who entertain these views and make these charges. I do not care to associate with them. . . ." He was hurt and he said so, "I know that there is no sudden cure."[11]

Ingersoll considered the election of McKinley to be the most fateful Republican victory since 1860 and 1864; the country had been saved "from repudiation and dishonor."

"Every drop of my blood is glad."[12]

A HARD WAY OF TAKING IT EASY

ON November 16, 1896, as he was lecturing at Janesville, Wisconsin, Ingersoll suddenly felt faint. Telling his audience to wait a few minutes, he left the platform. He came back and finished the lecture. Feeling fairly good the next morning, he decided, against the advice of his wife who was with him, to go on with the tour, which from Janesville would take him back East. He lectured a few more times, until he reached Chicago. Having had another spell of faintness and noticing that he could not talk as easily as he used to, he consulted Dr. Frank Billings of the Medical School of Northwestern University. He was ordered to take a complete rest for at least two months. He had had a slight cerebral hemorrhage.

Ingersoll with his wife returned immediately to New York. He went to see his old friend Dr. Thomas S. Robertson, who found in addition to the stroke evidence of angina pectoris. Until after his death, Ingersoll's family never knew that he had the heart condition so well did Robertson heed his caution not to drop a hint of it to them. But they knew of the stroke, this was alarming enough. Add the strict diet that this notable epicure religiously followed and they must have known that he was alarmed himself. Gone were hot biscuits and pies and cakes, potatoes and corn fritters with chicken gravy, and beef and mutton and pork. When he started the diet he weighed 235 pounds; six months later he weighed 175, and his waist was ten inches smaller. But it was no fun: "I stick to my diet—suffer like a martyr—hungry all the time—stomach as empty as a broken bank."[1] He was also taking nitro-glycerine and strychnine tablets.

Ingersoll sent some of these tablets to his brother John, who was similarly afflicted. His brother was a physician, but now Ingersoll was the doctor, his brother the patient. "Take one after each meal, he prescribed, on December 1, 1897, "Try this for a week and I believe it, or rather they, will help you" and in another letter, December 16, "I take three tablets [strychnine] a day and have for more than a year. Take them right along and I will send you more. You can take two of the nitro-glycerine tablets instead of one. The ones I take are just three times as strong as those I sent you and I take three a day." When John, then 74, who had been active for temperance, wrote that he was going to try a little whiskey, Robert replied, "I am glad. . . . It will do you good. You need a stimulant. Take it right *after* eating. Be sure and get good whiskey.[2] A friend of mine used to say: " 'There is no bad whiskey, but some is better.' Get the better—the best . . . I enclose $10 to get the whiskey." Andrew Carnegie sent Robert "two bottles of spiritual consolation."

Ingersoll did not need whiskey for his spirit. The closer he came to the valley of the shadow, the less his gloom at the prospect of death. The man whom death had haunted and cast down came now to accept it, even to welcome it, as a "fact in nature." True, in his sixtieth year and even later, there were hints of the old torment: "And yet, what a tragedy each life is or will be," as Robert wrote John, May 24, 1893, and again, July 18, on the death of John's wife, "What a riddle it all is. Life and Death, who can tell us what they are? And what is all this for—this living—this suffering—this labor and hope and love—this gold and poverty and after all, this death." Yet particularly after he was stricken in 1896, his thoughts of the close of life were in the vein of a letter he wrote July 11, 1899, to a Mr. Holladay: "For my part I am satisfied—content—knowing that I am compelled to submit—and that the world moves on without the slightest reference to me—or mine.

"To enjoy to-day—without regret for the loss of yesterday —or fear for to-morrow: this is the real philosophy . . ."

The two-month rest period prescribed for Ingersoll enabled him with a clear conscience to stay at home and enjoy his family. Early in 1896 the Ingersolls together with the Walston Browns, the Farrells, Mrs. Parker, and Sue Sharkey, moved to 220 Madison Avenue. The house at 400 Fifth Avenue, large as it was, did not have enough room when the Browns' children, Eva and Robin, passed their infancy. Nor was there enough playing space outside.

At 220 Madison Avenue a unique feature was the fully-equipped theater on the roof that would seat two hundred. Here at a "Sunday night" at the Ingersolls, an occasional entertainment was put on, the participants drawn from the family and the guests many of whom were professionals. On one such occasion the Ingersoll daughters staged a three-act comedy, *A Lesson in Love,* in which the Farrells' daughter, Eva, and Florence Lauterbach, daughter of one of Ingersoll's legal associates, "scored hits." During the intermissions the conductor Anton Seidl did Wagner selections on the Steinway Grand. After Seidl played at another "at home," Ingersoll wrote him, "You made the evening perfect. . . . We knew that the Master was present."

Ingersoll rejoiced in his grandchildren and was extraordinarily solicitous of their welfare. Seldom, for fear of infection, until Eva and Robin were beyond the toddling stage, were visitors permitted to see them, to say nothing of touch them. When the doctor came to look them over, Ingersoll made sure that he first washed his hands. As the children grew a little older, rarely did they get out on the street or play with other children. That did not mean that they were kept in a state of confinement. In the house they could run and play pretty much as they pleased and, at 220 Madison, they had a yard. They could eat when they wanted to, sleep when they wanted to, and make as much noise as they wanted to. They capered at will with their cooperative grandfather—unless he did not feel good and sometimes even then—pummeling his bald head, bending his spectacles, punching his ample stomach, jumping about in his lap, and hanging on his legs when he walked. Sometimes he took them to the Ringling Brothers Circus at Madison Square Garden. He could not tell who enjoyed it more, they or he.

By the middle of January, 1897, Ingersoll took to the platform again. He was well, at least he assured his family he was. But he was going to take it easy, that is, as he wrote to John, "I shall not lecture to exceed three times a week this winter," a curtailment but still a rather hard way of taking it easy. From this time on, when he went on a tour his wife accompanied him. From Litchfield, Illinois, on April 8, Ingersoll wrote to his daughters, "Mother is busy making my shirts smaller at the neck." They had a leisurely time on this trip which took them as far as St. Louis. Clint Farrell was with them too. It seemed to Ingersoll, with the light schedule of lectures, that they "just slept and rode and talked—took medicine and smoked."

There was one thing that the doctors had not denied Ingersoll—his beloved cigars. Or maybe they had, and he was recalcitrant, for he said of tobacco in thanking Major Orlando Smith, President of the American Press Association, for the gift of a box of cigars, "The doctors may say that it shortens life. But the longer life is without it, the worse it is."[3]

That Ingersoll had been a sick man was noticeable to some of his hearers in 1897. When he spoke in Chicago, March 8, he seemed to have "visibly aged since his last visit. . . . His features have lost some of their plumpness and his frame some of its appearance of vigor."[4] In Kansas City, Missouri, April 12, he looked "worn and weak and utterly tired out."[5] Six days later, however, in Louisville, Kentucky, he appeared, to an interviewer, younger than he was: "his fine, thoughtful face beamed with strength."[6]

Whatever the apparent state of his health, there was no dimunition in the size and the response of his audiences. In Chicago he packed Columbia Theater. The same reporter who noticed that he had "visibly aged" also noticed in the audience an uncommonly large number of women, "well-dressed women," who in full view of everybody, "would throw their heads back, clap their hands, and laugh." At Hartford, Connecticut, March 21, he "taxed the capacity of Parson's Theatre to its fullest extent."[7] On March 28, he spoke in New York City, to a "great audience that packed auditorium, galleries and boxes of the Star Theatre," At Kansas City, "Coates House was filled from foundations to rafter beams,"[8] despite the valiant efforts of the Salvation Army, who deployed their forces on various streets to pray and sing and shout "for the salvation of the city's irreligious visitor."

Ingersoll had a new lecture, "Truth," which was an exposition, brought down to the present, of the struggle between science and humanism on one side and theology and authoritarianism on the other. Later in the year around Thanksgiving, he gave essentially the same lecture but with the appropriate new title, "A Thanksgiving Sermon," and with emphasis on his gratitude to the thinkers, artists, and doers of the ages who had civilized mankind.

In January, 1898, Ingersoll with his wife and Clint Farrell commenced a six-week tour that encompassed most of the South. About the midpoint of the tour, February 1, they were in New Orleans. From New Orleans Ingersoll wrote his brother, "The people here have treated me splendidly—all friendly and all enthusiastic;"[9] and, February 11, from Denison, Texas, to his daughters, "Everywhere the people treat us with enthusiastic kindness."

But there were the many folk to whom Ingersoll was the devil incarnate. There was, for instance, "the great uproar" in Fayetteville, Arkansas, before his lecture there the night of February 13. "The ministers and the dear Christians were horrified that I was to lecture in their holy town, and that the lecture was to be on Sunday added to their horror."[10] They put pressure on the Fayetteville authorities to ban the lecture. They succeeded only in having the Sunday sale of tickets barred and in having the lecture put off one hour, from eight o'clock to nine. But at least they could have their regular eight o'clock services without the dread thought that even as they were in worship a popular lecturer in a nearby hall was desecrating their faith. Nor did they run the risk of direct competition with him. Moreover, if any of their members had yielded to temptation and bought tickets for the lecture, warning sermons in the evening, as well as in the morning, might yet save such errant souls, at least enable them to withstand Ingersollism if not to stay away from Ingersoll. "Well," wrote Ingersoll the next day, "I lectured and all who heard me became my friends. This morning the town was on my side."[11]

The letters that Ingersoll wrote on this trip suggested that he had recovered from his illness. "We are both in perfect health," he wrote from Hot Springs, Arkansas, February 16. "I sleep the best kind and my voice never was better." Warned by the seeming April of February in Arkansas, he and his wife felt young again: "Mother . . . looks as she feels." But they were counting the days before they would be home again: "We think and talk about you most of the time." Little Eva and Robin, his grandchildren, had scrawled letters to them: "Mother carries them around in her hands and reads them every few minutes." There would be no more long trips that season, "only short ones," and then they would all have "a good long summer together" which would "pay for all the separation and trouble."[12]

They did have a long summer together and Ingersoll did not undertake an extended tour until the following January. That tour took him, and his wife and Clint, to the Midwest. His lecture in Kansas City drew from the Reverend J. E. Roberts of the Church of This World a letter that went as follows: "Everybody is talking about your lecture. You have filled this town with your praise. Hundreds of people have talked with me about your great achievement. The common expression is 'the giant's strength is not abated nor his eyes dimmed.' "[13] Returning home the second week of February, Ingersoll was back in the Midwest the first week of March. A month later he was back East again but by no means to rest from his labors. During the last part of April and in May he covered New York and New England. In short, his lecture schedule was as strenuous as ever.

He had two more lectures in his repertoire, "Superstition" and "The Devil." The clamor with which the ministers greeted "Superstition" had led to "The Devil," a rejoinder and further irritant. In particular the ministers objected to "Superstition" because it contained a most uncomfortable proposition, that Christianity was founded on the Devil. In fact, said Ingersoll, "the success of the Devil in the Garden of Eden made the coming of Christ a necessity, laid the foundation for the Atonement, crucified the Savior and gave us the Trinity."[14]

In reply some of the ministers avowed their belief in the scriptural Devil; others simply denied his existence; and still others held that the Devil was not a being of evil but a personification thereof. "When I read these answers," said Ingersoll in *The Devil,* "I thought of this line from Heine: 'Christ rode on an ass, but now asses ride on Christ.' "[15]

Some the ministers charged that Ingersoll was attacking an obsolete theology, a man of straw. This was hardly substantiated, said Ingersoll, by recent well-known happenings. The man of straw had suspended for heresy the Reverend Charles A. Briggs because in his inaugural address as Professor of Biblical Theology in the Union Theological Seminary he had said that reason as well as Bible and Church was a source of religious experience and that all three sources were fallible. The man of straw had pitched the Reverend David Swing out of the pulpit because he considered the Bible not as a factual record but as a poem. The man of straw had ordained that the creed of the Presbyterian Church must remain unchanged.[16] Ingersoll could have mentioned that the Presbyterian General Assembly had affirmed by unanimous vote that the Bible was "the very word of God and consequently without error."

He could have mentioned the furore in religious circles over the lectures and writings of Lyman Abbott. Here was a Congregational minister of great repute who declared that traditionalism had obscured with doctrinal trappings the essential Christianity, that the concept of the Trinity was mediaeval and unsatisfactory, that much of the Bible was folklore, and that Christ did not rise from the dead. Now and then disparagingly paired with Ingersoll, Abbott often charged him with attacking a straw man. But he himself, in the voluble criticism that his ideas aroused, had reason to know that the straw man was very much alive and formidable.

On June 2, before the Free Religious Association at the Hollis Street Theater, Boston, Ingersoll spoke on the topic, "What is Religion?," his last public address. As if in anticipation that the time for summing up had come, he reviewed the main tenets of his agnosticism and *his religion.* On the problem of evil, Ingersoll asked: "Did an infinite God create the children of men . . . the intellectually inferior . . . the deformed and the helpless . . . the criminal, the idiotic, the insane . . .?

Is an infinite God . . . responsible for all the wars . . . the centuries of slavery . . . for religious persecution . . . for cyclones, earthquakes, pestilence and famine?"[17]

On the emergence of individual and corporate conscience Ingersoll denied that this was evidence of divinity working. He insisted that standards of conduct evolved naturally from the needs and wants of men. Men judge themselves and others by the varying standards of the societies in which they live.

"Has man," Ingersoll asked, "obtained any help from heaven? Can we affect the nature and qualities of substance by prayer? Can we hasten or delay the tides by worship? Can we change winds by sacrifice? Will kneelings give us wealth? . . . Is there any evidence for a *yes* to these question?"

Ingersoll summed up his own religion: "to do all useful things, to reach with thought and deed the ideal in your brain . . . to look with trained and steady eyes for facts . . . to increase knowledge, to take burdens from the weak . . . to defend the right."

"I AM BETTER NOW"

ON Thursday night, July 20, after dinner, the Ingersolls, the Browns, the Farrells, and Mrs. Parker gathered, as was their wont, in the billiard room at Walston. It was, as usual, a merry group, with everyone freely talking. Ingersoll and Walston Brown, exchanging the badinage of two friendly competitors, played billiards until about ten o'clock. Then Ingersoll, with Clint Farrell, strolled to the veranda, where he sat for a while, as he would almost every night, in an old white rocking-chair. He lighted a cigar and contentedly contemplated the stars. At about ten-thirty he said to Clint that he was going to retire and returning to the game room he bade everyone goodnight. He went upstairs to his bedroom, his wife accompanying him, and soon he was asleep. He awakened about one in the morning with pains in his upper abdomen and said to his wife, who was awake, that it must be indigestion. After that, he slept but little. At 9 A.M., however, he came down to breakfast. "I hear," Clint said to him, "that you had a bad night." And he replied, "Well, not so bad."

After breakfast, Ingersoll telephoned Dr. A. Alexander Smith, at Greenwich, Connecticut, and made an appointment to see him the next morning. Meanwhile, Dr. Smith advised, he was to take nitro-glycerine tablets at fifteen minute intervals until the pains subsided. After telephoning, Ingersoll walked out to his rocking-chair on the veranda, where, with his family around him, he sat reading and talking until about half past ten. He now said that he would go upstairs and lie down but that he would be back soon to beat Walston at billiards. "How do you feel, Papa?" his wife asked. "Oh, much better," he said.

Mrs. Ingersoll went upstairs with her husband and stayed with him while he slept for an hour. When he got up and went to a chair and sat down to put on his shoes, she said, "Do not dress, Papa, until after luncheon—I will eat upstairs with you."

"Oh, no, I do not want to trouble you," he replied, "I don't want anybody to wait on me yet."

Mrs. Farrell and Sue Sharkey were in the room at the time and Mrs. Farrell exclaimed, "How absurd, after the hundreds of times you have eaten upstairs with her!" Ingersoll laughed as Mrs. Farrell turned to leave and then his wife said, "Why, Papa, your tongue is coated, I must give you some medicine."

He smiled and said, "I am better now." Then his head rolled back, his jaw fell, his eyes glazed.

"He has fainted!" cried Mrs. Ingersoll to Sue Sharkey. "The Colonel is dying!" Sue cried as she ran out of the room to get help.

Everyone rushed to the room. Surely he had only fainted. Someone let a little brandy trickle down his throat, another gave him a hot foot-bath, others took off his clothing and gave him a hot mustard bath. Within minutes a neighboring physician, J. H. Salisbury, whom Clint had called for, arrived.

"The Colonel is dead," said Dr. Salisbury. A few minutes later Dr. C. P. Judson and Dr. Joseph Hasbrouck came. While the relatives beseeched their dear one for just one more look, one more word, the three doctors tried oxygen and artificial respiration. To no avail. The cause of death was angina pectoris.

On Tuesday, July 25, at four o'clock, the obsequies, private and simple, were held in Ingersoll's bedroom. His body covered with linen cloth lay upon a bier banked with flowers. A single red rose was upon his chest. The room was darkened except for a shaft of light from a shaded window that emblazoned a wreath beside his head and face. In addition to the family, some forty friends were present. Instead of speeches, there were readings from Ingersoll's works. Professor John Clark Ridpath read "The Declaration of the Free," an eighteen-stanza poem concluding the lecture, "The Devil"; Major Orlando Jay Smith read "The Creed of Science," from the lecture "The Foundations of Faith"; and Dr. John Lovejoy Elliott read "A Tribute to Ebon C. Ingersoll."

On July 27, the body of Ingersoll was cremated. The ashes in a bronze urn remained at Walston until after the death of Mrs. Ingersoll in 1923. One surface of the ovoid urn was inscribed with "Robert G. Ingersoll," the obverse with:

> *L'Urne garde*
> *La Poussiere*
> *Le Coeur*
> *Le Souvenir.*

Now the ashes of Mr. and Mrs. Ingersoll lie under a granite monument in Arlington National Cemetery.

THE POSTHUMOUS MAN

THE public response to the death of Ingersoll was an impressive testimonial of his great prominence and influence. Letters and telegrams poured in. There were countless sermons on him. The press of the country featured him, carrying, in addition to obituaries, accounts of his last day, anecdotes, editorials, and excerpts from his works. In several cities memorial meetings took place. A number of Ingersoll clubs formed and a number of infants, as before his death, so after, came to bear his name.

In Peoria, where Ingersoll lived from 1857-1877, thousands gathered on July 23, at a memorial meeting in the Tabernacle. Many of Ingersoll's old friends reminisced of him there and spoke his praises. A resolution read in part: ". . . he was greater than a saint, greater than a mere hero—he was a thoroughly honest man."[1] The Peoria Monument Association was formed, which later in an invitation to the public to subscribe to an Ingersoll monument stated: "The late Colonel Robert G. Ingersoll was a conspicuous figure in the history of the present century. Of . . . indomitable perseverance, and fearlessness, . . . he was at once the gentlest, most affectionable, lovable and the strongest character of his day." At a meeting in Peoria, July 26, Ingersoll's Eleventh Illinois Cavalry Regiment memorialized him as follows: ". . . We knew him as the general public did not. . . . We had the honor to obey, as we could, his calm but resolute commands at Shiloh, at Corinth, and at Lexington, knowing as we did, that he would never command a man to go where he would not dare to lead the way.

"Hence we recognize only a small circle around his recent heaven and home who could know more of his manliness and worth than we do. And to such we say: . . . try to be as brave as he was, and try to remember,—in the midst of a grief which his greatest wish for life would have been to help you to bear—that he had no fear of death or anything beyond."[2]

On August 6, a capacity house attended a memorial meeting in Studebaker Hall, Chicago. Among the many speakers was Clarence Darrow. In concluding his tribute he said: "Robert G. Ingersoll was a great man, a wonderful intellect, a great soul of matchless courage, one of the great men of the earth—and yet we have no right to bow down to his memory simply because he was great. . . . Great orators, great lawyers, often use their gifts for a most unholy cause. . . . We meet to pay a tribute of love and respect to Robert G. Ingersoll . . . because he used his matchless powers for the good of man."[3]

Also on August 6, thousands attended a memorial meeting in Denver. Governor Charles S. Thomas of Colorado was the principal speaker. He said, in part: "The character of Ingersoll was as nearly perfect as it is possible for the character of mortal man to be. . . . He had the earnestness of a Luther, the genius for humor and wit and satire of a Voltaire, a wide amplitude of imagination, and a greatness of heart and brain that placed him upon an equal footing with the greatest thinkers of antiquity. . . . He stands at the close of his career, the first great reformer of the age."[4]

Among the many personal messages that came to the family were those of Andrew Carnegie, Horace Traubel, and Mark Twain. Carnegie, from his Skibo Castle in New Brunswick, Canada, wrote Mrs. Ingersoll, "Truly, I feel as if one touching my side had been stricken, so close he seemed to have stood."[5] Traubel wrote to Clint Farrell, "Let us not compare mournful notes. He towered above annihilation. He escaped extinguishment."[6] Mark Twain wrote Eva Farrell, Ingersoll's niece, "Except for my daughter's, I have not grieved for any death as I have grieved for his. His was a great and beautiful spirit, he was a man—all man, from his crown to his footsoles. My reverence for him was deep and genuine. . . ."[7]

Amid all this acclaim, however, canards began to circulate. Ingersoll had committed suicide. He had recanted. An evangelist in Jamestown, Kansas, voiced the ghoulish rumor that after death the body of Ingersoll was left unattended until the odor of decomposition reached the nostrils of passers-by on the street. The authorities then compelled the relatives to bury him.

There were many who relished the thought that Ingersoll was a suicide—that would prove that infidelity ends in unbearable despair. Also, in Ingersoll's case, suicide would be an especially suitable desert. Had he not often declared that suicide was no sin, no crime, and that in certain situations—incurable cancer, for instance—it was justifiable? Among the many who savored the suicide rumor was the Y.M.C.A. Even four years after Ingersoll's death a lecturer for that organization went about the country saying that too late Ingersoll had seen the error of his ways and that in desperation over the evil he had wrought he took poison. Officially, and for publication, Dr. Joseph Hasbrouck wrote to Mrs. Walston Hill Brown, December 3, 1903: "In reference to the cruel and unwarranted attack made on your Father's memory, charging suicide, by a lecturer for the Young Men's Christian Association at Cincinnati and other places, I bear witness that it has no foundation in fact or suspicion.

"I was called to see Col. Ingersoll at the fatal attack of Angina Pectoris, from which affection he had suffered for two years, about, prior to his death and there is no doubt but that he died of said disease."

The recantation rumor was equally tenacious. In April, 1903, a minister in Lynn, Massachusetts, reported to his congregation that just before Ingersoll died he stated to his family that he was ceasing his lectures against Christianity. The minister said that Ingersoll's daughter, Maud, had circulated the report. A Mrs. Morill, who lived in Lynn, wrote to Maud, April 16, for confirmation. Maud replied April 29: "Mr. Norman's statement is utterly without truth. I never said that my father intended giving up lecturing against the Christian religion, and I would not have had him do so. At the time of his death—in fact, the very morning of his death—he was working on a new lecture on Jesus Christ to be delivered the next winter and in which he intended saying that Christ was a myth."

The rumors of recantation and suicide persisting, Mrs. Sue Farrell filed an affidavit in New York County on March 17, 1906, which set forth the facts of Ingersoll's physical decline from the day of the cerebral hemorrhage, November 16, 1896, to the day of death. Detailing what he said and did the morning before he died, the affidavit concludes: "It is said that he recanted. This is a cruel and malicious falsehood, without the slightest foundation in fact. His convictions remained absolutely unchanged. He died as he had lived—an agnostic."

But Ingersoll had been too much a force in the public mind, too much a thorn in orthodox flesh, to be an unsullied memory, or simply a forgotten man. In 1920 a man, employed in the office of the Secretary of Labor of the United States, wrote to Mrs. Ingersoll, "I constantly encounter in various forms the slander of Mr. Ingersoll's recantation on his deathbed, and as it is sometimes repeated by worthy people who are simply misled, I should like very much to have a succinct denial." Mrs. Ingersoll replied with a succinct denial. Then the man wrote for more details and said, "I shall be greatly obliged if you will include a statement that you and your daughters have always been in full accord with your husband's views on religion." It is not known if Mrs. Ingersoll answered this letter— she probably did answer it, for she and her daughters and grandchildren and the Farrells labored unremittingly to let the world know that Ingersoll was an agnostic to the end and that they shared his views.

In the December, 1911, issue of *Current Literature,* an unsigned article bore the title, "Ingersoll Still Troubling The World." The article said that he "continues to be violently attacked, even as he himself violently attacked others." The enemies of Ingersollism attested to its durability as well as its friends. *America,* a Roman Catholic weekly, quoted in the article in *Current Literature,* said: "By destroying their belief in Christianity, Ingersoll did thousands of his fellow citizens an irreparable wrong and seriously imperiled his country's future, for a nation of unbelievers can never be a great or an enduring nation." Of the power of Ingersoll the most ardent of his disciples could not have said more, though they would have challenged the dire effects. In 1925 the May issue of the *Catholic World* carried a lecture on Ingersoll which the Editor, the Reverend James M. Gillis, had delivered. The lecture was one of a series by Gillis that included Voltaire, Edward Gibbon, and Thomas Paine—good enough company for any iconoclast. Gillis attacked Ingersoll as a vulgar and scurrilous panderer to people who knew no better and lamented the current state of general intelligence and culture that was still tributary to such a man. "His fame, good or evil, persists as a tradition to the young; as a memory to those of middle age. He is the nearest approach we Americans have had to Voltaire. And he is evidently of interest to vast numbers of his countrymen." This was 1925 and a severe critic talking.

A less bitter cleric, the Reverend J. T. Sunderland, author of a noted book on the higher criticism, *The Origin and Character of the Bible,* wrote in the *Arena,* March, 1909, that while Ingersoll "pained the hearts not only of the ignorant and the narrow, but of many of the most intelligent and broad-minded men and women" his influence for good, as well as for evil, persisted. He had set "a sort of fashion . . . for irreverent and flippant dealings with the most sacred things of religion and life." But he had also set "tens of thousands to thinking for themselves on religious subjects;" he had "pricked the bubbles of many ecclesiastical and theological shams, hypocrisies, pretenses, make-believes;" he was in part responsible for the "new awakening of thought and inquiry which is making its appearance." This new awakening involved the testing of theological premises, a re-examination of the Bible, and the refining of conceptions of God.

Ingersoll's influence was diverse, not confined to the theological realm. Robert M. La Follette, the Wisconsin pioneer of social legislation, congressman and governor of his state, and founder of a political dynasty, said: "Ingersoll had a tremendous influence upon me, as indeed he had upon many young men of that time." Not that Ingersoll changed his beliefs, said La Follette, but that he liberated his mind. "Freedom was what he preached: he wanted the shackles off everywhere. He wanted men to think boldly about all things: he demanded intellectual and moral courage. He wanted men to follow wherever truth might lead them. He was a rare, bold, heroic figure."[8] La Follette included Ingersoll among the moulders of his social conscience.

Ingersoll exercised a like influence upon the Socialist crusader and four-time Socialist party candidate for the presidency of the United States, Eugene Debs, who, like La Follette, played a prominent role on the American scene well into the twentieth century—La Follette died in 1925, Debs in 1926. Debs idolized Ingersoll, though they were far apart in political ideas. He wrote Clint Farrell, March 13, 1889: "My wife, mother, father, four sisters, and my brother, and four brothers-in-law, all the children, in fact the entire relationship without a dissenting voice, are profound admirers (that poorly expresses it) of Colonel Ingersoll. . . ." When it is said that Debs and Ingersoll were far apart in political ideas, the emphasis is on the means of government, not the objective. On the objective no two men could be more alike—the improvement of the lot of man in the here and now. That they differed in means, and how they differed, is indicated by what Ingersoll wrote Debs in April, 1897: "I read the paper giving an account of your new Republic. I know that you desire to make your fellow creatures happy—I am perfectly sure of that. But the great question is—Can you control people who cannot, or will not control themselves? There is still another—Will men, who will not work for themselves, willingly work for others? Another still—Will the superior man voluntarily stand on a level with the inferior?" These were bedrock questions, enough to estrange a Damon and Pythias. But twenty-one years later Debs wrote Mrs. Walston Hill Brown, "I was the friend of your immortal grandfather and I loved him truly. . . . The name of Ingersoll is revered in our home, worshipped by us all, and the date of birth . . . is holy in our calendar."[9]

Clarence Darrow was another twentieth-century figure upon whom Ingersoll left his mark. Their views on religion and freedom of thought were essentially the same. Read Darrow on Fundamentalism and you read Ingersoll. Who knows, even without an Ingersoll, Darrow might have been the same man. Yet there are indications that Ingersoll was an influence on Darrow. At hearing Ingersoll, said Darrow, "with everyone in the audience I was entranced." He said that he and many others tried to ape Ingersoll's style of speaking—"every sentence was rhythmical"—and he thought he "succeeded fairly well, at that time" but he finally realized that he "could not be Ingersoll . . . ," that the best he could do was to be himself. A few, said Darrow, did master Ingersoll's "form of expression, but they lacked what Ingersoll never lacked, and that was something worth saying."[10] That "something worth saying" was not in politics, as Darrow saw it. On August 26, 1900, in Chicago, at a memorial meeting in honor of Ingersoll, Darrow, one of the speakers, declared: "Ingersoll believed in liberty so far as the church was concerned, but on political questions he was seemingly color blind. The older and more venerable a political superstition, the more he would cling to it." These statements caused one man who "shook with indignation," to arise and cry: "That is an outrage upon Ingersoll, and I must protest against it." There were "cheers and hisses, and cries of 'That's right' and 'Make him stop' " that went on until the chairman restored order.[11]

Darrow's heckler was right. Granted that Ingersoll was zealous for high protective tariffs and gold-backed money, that he was a war horse of the Grand Old Party, yet he also championed woman suffrage, equal rights for Negroes, unrestricted immigration, the division of land by law "so that no person would be allowed to own more land than he uses," Henry George for mayor of New York City, and the Haymarket Anarchists. Ingersoll's stand on these lively "hot" political questions hardly proves Darrow's charge that "the older and more venerable a political superstition, the more he would cling to it."

When order was restored in the hall, Darrow went on to say: "Ingersoll wanted honest opinions. He never would object to an honest opinion of himself. . . . I pay homage to Robert G. Ingersoll. . . . His acts mark him as one of the bravest, grandest champions of human liberty the world has ever seen."

Darrow's reflections on Ingersoll's style of speaking and those who tried to ape it raise the question, could one study to speak like Ingersoll and avoid thinking like him? It might mean some wrestling with the devil, but the answer is yes. It was said of William E. Borah, the forensic giant in the Senate from the state of Idaho, that "It was not the philosophies of Ingersoll that appealed to young Borah, but the style of expression."[12]

Albert J. Beveridge, the Progressive Senator from Indiana, also made a distinction between Ingersoll as an orator and a thinker: "At any rate, considered exclusively from the point of view of oratory as an art and without reference to his opinions, Ingersoll was one of the four greatest artists."[13] The other three were Daniel Webster, Wendell Phillips, and Patrick Henry. Beveridge was twenty when he first heard Ingersoll. He had been used to unkempt, violent stump speakers, when along came a man with an entirely different brand of oratory. This man was "perfectly attired." He spoke in the "most natural manner . . . as if he were conversing with each of us personally. . . . He stood still, made no gestures for a long time, and when they came at last, they were seemingly so spontaneous and unstudied that we scarcely noticed them. . . ." Here was "a real orator, a master of the art."

Hamlin Garland, realistic writer of farm and frontier, was another who felt the power of Ingersoll. Though he gained renown for something other than oratory, still he lectured often and well. For a while he was an instructor in the Boston School of Oratory. To Garland, Booth was "our greatest actor," Ingersoll was "our greatest orator."[14] How did Ingersoll do it? "He bantered us, challenged us, electrified us," writes Garland. "At times his eloquence held us silent as images and then some witty turn, some humorous phrase, brought roars of applause. At times we cheered almost every sentence, like delegates at a political convention. At other moments we rose in our seats and yelled. There was something hypnotic in his rhythm as well as in his phrasing. . . . His power over his auditors was absolute."

Chauncey Depew, one-time President of the New York Central railway and Senator from the state of New York, regarded Ingersoll as "one of the greatest orators of his generation, and I might say of ours." Depew did not share Ingersoll's ideas on religion, but he was, as he put it, "an intense admirer of him."[15] Andrew D. White, President of Cornell University and Minister to Germany and Russia, wrote of Ingersoll in 1917: "From the day when we were embarked on the Steamer Maine together years ago, I have known him to be one of the foremost men of genius of his time."[16] Luther Burbank, famous naturalist, wrote in 1921: "His life and work have been an inspiration to the whole earth. . . ."[17]

But let us leave the testimony of the famous for that of ordinary folk. In 1929 the relatives and friends of Ingersoll formed the Ingersoll League to establish a memorial. Much correspondence resulted, with comments like these:

¶ From a man in Billings, Montana, "His works are in my law library and I constantly refer to them."

¶ From Alamosa, Colorado, "None . . . gives the constant thrill and refreshment that Ingersoll's writings do. . . ."

¶ From Greenwich, Connecticut, "I was a great admirer of your father and always attended his lectures whenever I had the opportunity."

¶ From Oakland, California, "Two of the greatest crusaders that ever lived." (Ingersoll and Paine)

¶ From Charlotte, North Carolina, "And I've always felt grateful to him for setting me straight on the pathway of independent thinking concerning both the here and hereafter, and I shall reverence his memory while life lasts."

¶ From Emmett, Idaho, "In my judgment he was the greatest liberating and uplifting force in American history."

¶ From Allston, Massachusetts, "I simply worship the memory of the greatest mind this world has produced."

There were also comments like these:

¶ From Los Angeles, California, "I can think of nothing which would interest me less than in any way honoring the memory of your father. . . . He did his best to tear down the faith and comfort of humble souls who were too simple minded to see through his sophistries, and while it is true he combatted many unworthy mis-called Christian doctrines, he did it in the spirit of scorn and malice."

¶ From Rowe, Massachusetts, "When the name of Ingersoll

has been blotted out of the memory of this world the things of the Spirit will still be ruling the hearts and lives of men."

¶ "When I was young I remember him, and the awful menace he was to our country. . . ."

¶ "Instead of erecting a monument over the beast, the very soil that has been fouled by his hideous carcass should undergo some process of disinfection."

The evidence of Ingersoll's great impact upon his time and of his enduring influence could be multiplied. He was too big to be bounded by the date of his death. In an address delivered as late as January 27, 1929, the Reverend John H. Dietrich, of the First Unitarian Society of Minneapolis, declared: "And so Ingersoll is looked upon today as the most outstanding opponent of orthodox religion, and the most ardent champion of freedom from superstition, that we have ever had in this country. . . . All hail to thee, great liberator of the human mind . . . thou didst live for posterity. Posterity will remember thee."

Dietrich's words recall those of Edgar Lee Masters:

> *To the lovers of liberty everywhere,*
> *But chiefly to the youth of America*
> *Who did not know Robert G. Ingersoll,*
> *Remember that he helped to make you free!*

Acknowledgments
and
Bibliography

ACKNOWLEDGMENTS AND BIBLIOGRAPHY

The author is greatly indebted to Mrs. Eva Ingersoll Wakefield, granddaughter of Robert Ingersoll, and her husband, Sherman D. Wakefield, for freely putting at his disposal many letters from, to, and about Ingersoll, several albums of newspaper clippings, and much manuscript material, and also for many helpful suggestions and comments.

The author is also indebted to Mrs. Clinton P. Farrell, sister-in-law of Robert Ingersoll, now deceased, for access to letters and newspaper clippings and for glimpses of Ingersoll which only she, who for years with her husband and daughter was a member of his household, could provide. Thanks also go to Robert Ingersoll Brown, a grandson of Ingersoll, for a day in the summer of 1948, when he guided the author around "Walston," the estate and mansion at Dobbs Ferry-on-Hudson, New York, where Ingersoll spent his summers from 1890 to his death in July, 1899.

The author is likewise indebted to the following for ready access to Ingersoll materials: the Division of Manuscripts of the Library of Congress; the Peoria Public Library, Peoria, Illinois; the Illinois State Historical Society Library, Springfield, Illinois.

In the Division of Manuscripts of the Library of Congress, there were thirty-five volumes of newspaper clippings and four boxes—some 750 pieces—of letters and manuscripts; at the Peoria Public Library files of the *Peoria Daily Transcript,* 1858-1868, and the *Peoria Public Democratic Union;* and at the Illinois State Historical Society Library, letters from, to, and about Ingersoll.

For the speeches, lectures, and writings of Ingersoll, the main references were the twelve volumes of the Dresden authorized version; also, for speeches and lectures, the David McKay edition and verbatim newspaper accounts.

The following books and pamphlets, periodicals and journals, have also been consulted:

BOOKS AND PAMPHLETS

ABBOTT, LYMAN, *Reminiscences,* Houghton Mifflin Co., Boston, 1915.
BAKER, I. NEWTON, *An Intimate View of Robert G. Ingersoll,* C. P. Farrell,
New York, 1910.
BEALE, HARRIET S. BLAINE, *Letters of Mrs. James G. Blaine,* vols. 1 and 2,
Duffield and Co., New York, 1910.
BEARD, CHARLES A. and MARY R., *The Rise of American Civilization,* vols.
1 and 2. Revised. The Macmillan Co., 1940.
BEVERIDGE, ALBERT J., *The Art of Public Speaking,* Houghton Mifflin Co.,
Boston, 1924.
BLAINE, MRS. JAMES G., *Letters,* vols. 1 and 2, Duffield and Co., New York,
1908.
BOWERS, CLAUDE G., *The Tragic Era,* Houghton Mifflin Co., Boston, 1929.
BRANCH, E DOUGLAS, *The Sentimental Years,* D. Appleton-Century Com-
pany, New York, 1934.
BROUN, HEYWOOD and LEECH, MARGARET, *Anthony Comstock,* The Literary
Guild of America, New York, 1927.
BUCKLE, HENRY T., *History of Civilization in England,* vol. 1, Longmans
Green and Co., New York, 1901.
CARGILL, OSCAR, *Intellectual America,* The Macmillan Co., New York, 1941.
CARR, CLARK E., *The Illini,* A. C. McClurg and Co., Chicago, 1904.
CARR, CLARK E., *My Day and Generation,* A. C. McClurg and Co., Chicago,
1908.
CLARK, JOHN SPENCER, *The Life and Letters of John Fiske,* vols. 1 and 2,
Houghton Mifflin Co., Boston, 1917.
COHEN, CHAPMAN, *Bradlaugh and Ingersoll,* Secular Society Limited, Pioneer
Press, London, 1933.
COLE, ARTHUR C., *The Era of the Civil War,* 1848-1870, Illinois Centennial
Commission, Springfield, Illinois, 1919.
COLEMAN, MCALISTER, *Eugene V. Debs, A Man Unafraid,* Greenberg Pub-
lisher, Inc., New York, 1930.
COLLIS, CHARLES, *I Died,* The Irving Press, New York, 1926.
CRAMER, C. H., *Royal Bob,* The Bobbs-Merrill Company, Inc., Indianapolis,
1952.
CULLOM, SHELBY, M., *Fifty Years of Public Service,* A. C. McClurg and Co.,
Chicago, 1911.
DARROW, CLARENCE, *The Story of My Life,* Charles Scribner's Sons, New
York, 1932.
DEPEW, CHAUNCEY M., *My Memories of Eighty Years,* Charles Scribner's
Sons, New York, 1922.
DIETRICH, JOHN H., *The Humanist Pulpit,* The First Unitarian Society,
Minneapolis, 1931.
DRAPER, JOHN W., *History of the Intellectual Development of Europe,* re-
vised edition, vols. 1 and 2, Harper and Brothers, New York, 1876.
ELMO (pseudonym), Editor, *Ingersollia,* Bedford, Clarke, and Co., Chicago,
1882.

FISKE, JOHN, *The Letters,* edited by Ethel F. Fiske, The Macmillan Co., New York, 1940.
FURLONG, J. R., *Is Ingersoll in Hell?* 2nd ed., J. R. Furlong, Boulder, Colorado, 1910.
GARLAND, HAMLIN, *Roadside Meetings,* The Macmillan Co., New York, 1930.
GARRISON, WINFRED ERNEST, *The March of Faith,* Harper and Brothers, New York, 1933.
GLADDEN, WASHINGTON, *Recollections,* Houghton Mifflin Co., Boston, 1909.
GOLDTHWAITE, VERE, *The Philosophy of Ingersoll,* Paul Elder and Co., New York, 1906.
GORHAM, CHARLES T., *Robert G. Ingersoll,* Watts and Co., London, 1921.
GREELEY, HORACE, *The Autobiography,* E. B. Treat, New York, 1872.
GRIFFITH, WILL, Editor, *Idols of Egypt,* Egypt Book House, Carbondale, Illinois, 1947.
HALL, THOMAS C., *The Religious Background of American Culture,* Little, Brown, and Co., Boston, 1930.
HOAR, GEORGE F., *Autobiography of Seventy Years,* Charles Scribner's Sons, New York, 1903.
HUBBARD, ELBERT, *Little Journeys to the Homes of Great Americans,* The Roycrofters, East Aurora, New York, 1911.
HUBBARD, ELBERT, *Little Journeys to the Homes of Eminent Orators,* G. P. Putnam's Sons, New York, 1907.
HUSTED, H., *Robert G. Ingersoll's Religious Teachings,* H. Husted, White Plains, N. Y., 1925.
INGERSOLL, ROBERT, and Others, *The Limitations of Tolerance,* The Truth Seeker Company, New York, 1889.
INGERSOLL, COL. R. G., *Complete Lectures,* M. A. Donohue and Co., Chicago and New York, undated.
INGERSOLL, ROBERT, *The Gods,* Transcript Book and Job Print, Peoria, Illinois, 1872.
INGERSOLL, ROBERT, *The Gods and Other Lectures,* Copyrighted by Ingersoll, Peoria, Ill., 1874.
INGERSOLL, ROBERT, *Ingersoll to the Clergy,* The Truth Seeker Co., New York, 1897.
JULIAN, G. W., *Political Recollections,* Jansen, McClurg and Co., Chicago, 1884.
KITTREDGE, HERMAN A., *Ingersoll, A Biographical Appreciation,* Dresden Publishing Co., New York, 1911.
LA FOLLETTE, ROBERT, *Autobiography,* The Robert M. La Follette Co., Madison, Wis., 1913.
LAMBERT, L. A., *Notes on Ingersoll,* 6th ed., Buffalo Catholic Publishing Co., Buffalo, N. Y., 1884.
LUSK, DAVID W., *Politics and Politicians, Third Edition,* H. W. Rokker, Springfield, Ill., 1889.
MACDONALD, E. M., *Col. Robert G. Ingersoll as He Is,* The Truth Seeker Co., New York, 1910.
MASTERS, EDGAR LEE, *Whitman,* Charles Scribner's Sons, New York, 1937.
MCCABE, JOSEPH, *Robert G. Ingersoll: Benevolent Agnostic,* Little Blue Book No. 1215, Girard, Kansas.
MUZZEY, DAVID SAVILLE, *James G. Blaine,* Dodd, Mead and Co., New York, 1935.
PAINE, THOMAS, *The Age of Reason,* Patriots' Edition, William M. Van der

Weyde, ed., vol. VIII, Thomas Paine National Historical Association, New Rochelle, New York, 1925.

PARRINGTON, VERNON LOUIS, *Main Currents in American Thought,* Harcourt, Brace and Co., New York, 1927.

PERRY, BLISS, *Walt Whitman,* Houghton Mifflin Co., Boston and New York, 1934.

RHODES, JAMES FORD, *History of the United States,* Macmillan Co., New York, 1892-1919.

ROGERS, CAMERON, *Colonel Bob Ingersoll,* Doubleday, Page and Co., New York, 1927.

SMITH, E. G., *The Life and Reminiscences of Robert G. Ingersoll,* The National Weekly Publishing Co., New York, 1904.

STERN, PHILIP VAN DOREN, *The Life and Writings of Abraham Lincoln,* The Modern Library, New York, 1942.

TRAUBEL, HORACE, *With Walt Whitman in Camden,* vol. 1, (March 28-July 14, 1888), Small, Maynard and Company, Boston, 1906.

TRAUBEL, HORACE, *With Walt Whitman in Camden,* vol. 2, (July 16-October 31, 1888), Mitchell, Kennerley, New York, 1915.

TWAIN, MARK and WARNER, CHARLES DUDLEY, *The Gilded Age,* Harper and Brothers, New York, 1903.

VOLTAIRE, *A Philosophical Dictionary,* vols. 3 and 6, Done by the Craftsmen of the St. Hubert Guild, Copyrighted by E. R. Dumont, New York, 1901.

WAKEFIELD, EVA INGERSOLL, *The Letters of Robert G. Ingersoll,* Philosophical Library, New York, 1951.

WHITLOCK, BRAND, *Forty Years of It,* D. Appleton-Century Company, New York, 1914.

PERIODICALS AND JOURNALS

ABBOTT, LYMAN, "Flaws in Ingersollism," *North American Review,* 150, (April, 1890), 446-457, 654-55.

BEACH, STEWART, "Apostles of Liberty," *Independent,* 118, (June 18, 1927), 640.

BRANN, HENRY, "Robert G. Ingersoll," *Catholic World,* 69, (September, 1899), 787-790.

CHAPMAN, EDWARD, "Robert G. Ingersoll, Theologian," *Forum,* 48, (September, 1912), 339-353.

EDITORIAL, "Ingersoll after Twenty Years," *Current Opinion,* 71, (September, 1921), 336-338.

ABBOTT, LYMAN, Editorial, "Robert G. Ingersoll," *Outlook,* 62, (July 29, 1899), 696-698.

EDITORIAL, "Ingersoll Still Troubling the World," *Current Literature,* 51, (December, 1911), 649-651.

MANNING, HENRY EDWARD, (Cardinal Manning), "The Gladstone-Ingersoll Controversy," *North American Review,* 147 (September, 1888), 241-269.

FARRAR, FREDERIC, "A Few Words on Colonel Ingersoll," *North American Review,* 150, (May, 1890), 594-608.

FIELD, HENRY, "An Open Letter to Robert G. Ingersoll," *North American Review,* 145, (August, 1887), 128-145.

FIELD, HENRY, "A Last Word to Robert G. Ingersoll," *North American Review,* 145, (December, 1887), 616-628.

FIELD, HENRY, "The Influence of Robert G. Ingersoll," *North American Review,* 169, (September, 1899), 322-328.

FORCYTHE, S., "Col. Ingersoll and Christianity," *North American Review,* 146, (January, 1888), 103.

GILLIS, J. M., " 'Bob' Ingersoll," *Catholic World,* 121, (May, 1925), 216-226.

GLADSTONE, WILLIAM, "Colonel Ingersoll on Christianity," *North American Review,* 146, (May, 1888), 481-508.

HUGHES, JAMES, "World Leaders I Have Known," *Canadian Magazine,* 60, (April, 1923), 563-570.

INGERSOLL, ROBERT, "The Divided Household of Faith," *North American Review,* 147, (August, 1888), 150-164.

INGERSOLL, ROBERT, "Tolstoi and 'The Kreutzer Sonata'," *North American Review,* 151, (September, 1890), 289-299.

INGERSOLL, ROBERT, "Letter to Dr. Field," *North American Review,* 146, (January, 1888), 31-46.

INGERSOLL, ROBERT, "A Reply to the Rev. Henry M. Field, D.D." *North American Review,* 145, (November, 1887), 473-505.

KITTREDGE, HERMAN, "Ingersoll as an Idealist," *Arena,* 31, (March, 1904), 244-261.

KITTREDGE, HERMAN, "Ingersoll: His Genius, Philosophy, Humanity, and Influence," *Arena,* 31, (January, 1904), 50-69.

LA FOLLETTE, ROBERT, "Autobiography," *American Magazine,* 72, (October, 1911), 660-674.

MORE, P. E., "Ingersoll: a Biographical Appreciation," a review of Herman Kittredge's biography, *Nation,* 93, (October 5, 1911), 313-315.

MYALL, WILLIAM, "Mr. Ingersoll as a Reformer," *International Review,* 12, (March, 1882), 225-240.

PHELPS, ELIZABETH, AND OTHERS, "The Combat for the Faith: The Field-Ingersoll-Gladstone Controversy," *North American Review,* 147, (July, 1888), 1-36.

SUNDERLAND, J. T., "Robert Ingersoll after Nine Years," *Arena,* 41, (March, 1909), 295-301.

WARD, WILLIAM, "Colonel Ingersoll," *A Review of Reviews (N.Y.),* 20, (September, 1899), 317-321.

ZERBE, L. R., "Colonel Ingersoll on Christianity," *North American Review,* 146, (March, 1888), 344.

The articles below, all from issues of the *Journal of the Illinois State Historical Society,* were very helpful on the persons, places, and events of Ingersoll's Illinois years:

Volume 16:

1. TRUMBULL, LYMAN, *A Collection of Letters from Lyman Trumbull to John M. Palmer, 1854-1858,* edited by George Thomas Palmer, 20-41.

Volume 22:

1. LYLES, STELLA PENDLETON, *Shawneetown,* 164-191.

Volume 23:

1. KIMBALL, E. L., *Richard Yates,* 1-83.

Volume 24:

1. HOFER, J. M., *Development of the Peace Movement in Illinois During the Civil War,* 110-128.

2. PRATT, HARRY E., *The Repudiation of Lincoln's War Policy in 1862—Stuart-Swett Congressional Campaign,* 129-140.

Volume 26:
   1. YOUNG, JOHN EDWARD, *Journal* (extracts entitled "An Illinois Farmer During the Civil War"), pp. 70-135.
Volume 27:
   1. RENNICK, PERCIVAL GRAHAM, *The Peoria and Galena Trail and Coach Road and the Peoria Neighborhood*, pp. 351-431.
Volume 33:
   1. ANGLE, PAUL M., *The Story of an Ordinary Man*, 212-232.
Volume 34:
   1. DAYTON, ARETAS A., *The Raising of Union Forces in Illinois During the Civil War*, 401-438.
Volume 35:
   1. Galesburg: *Hot-bed of Abolitionism*, HERMAN R. MUELDER, 216-235.
Volume 36:
   1. *The Political Metamorphosis of Robert Green Ingersoll*, C. H. CRAMER, pp. 271-283.
   2. *Owen Lovejoy in Princeton, Illinois*, RUTH EWERS HABERKORN, 284-315.
Volume 37:
   Letter on "Campaign of 1860 in Peoria," p. 362.

Notes

NOTES

The Devil Moves in Mysterious Ways

1. Quoted in *Ingersoll, A Biographical Appreciation* by Herman A. Kittredge, p. 23.
2. Ingersoll in a letter, October 31, 1877, to Mrs. Ada W. Pick.

The Boy Learns of God

1. Ingersoll in his lecture, *The Liberty of Man, Woman and Child,* in Dresden edition, vol. 1, p. 377.
2. *Ibid,* p. 379.
3. Ingersoll in an interview, *Chicago Times,* Nov. 14, 1879.

The Boy Learns Other Things Too

1. John P. Robert's reminiscences in Cleveland *Plain Dealer,* Dec. 20, 1896.
2. Quoted in *Op. Cit.,* Kittredge, p. 29.
3. *Op. Cit.*
4. Quoted in *Op. Cit.,* Kittredge, p. 26.
5. Letter from Cincinnati, Ohio, Jan. 9, 1851.
6. *Ibid.*
7. Carson, Will C., editor, *Historical Souvenir of Greenville, Illinois,* 1905.
8. Reminiscences in *Milwaukee Sentinel,* March 10, 1897.
9. *Ibid.*
10. *Ibid.*
11. Ingersoll in a speech at Lotos Club dinner in honor of Anton Seidel, New York, Feb. 2, 1895, in Dresden edition, vol. 12, p. 172.
12. *Ibid,* p. 173.
13. Ingersoll in his lecture, *Why I Am An Agnostic,* Dresden edition, vol. 4—for this and the other references to theological writings.

What To Do

1. Ingersoll in a letter to his brother, John, and sister, Mary, Sept. 16, 1852.
2. *Ibid.*
3. *Ibid.*
4. Ingersoll in a letter to John, Jan. 14, 1853.
5. Mrs. F. W. Ingersoll, stepmother, in a letter to John, April 20, 1853.
6. *Ibid.*
7. Letter from Greenville, Illinois, to John, July, 1851.
8. Lute H. Johnson in a letter to Herman E. Kittredge, April 26, 1911.
9. Letter to John and wife, Dec. 29, 1853.
10. *Ibid.*
11. Clark Ingersoll in a letter to John, Nov. 5, 1854.
12. Herman Kittredge, *Op. Cit.,* p. 38.
13. Stella Pendleton Lyles, "Shawneetown," *Journal of the Illinois State Historical Society,* vol. 22, pp. 164-191—for this and other details on Shawneetown.
14. Letter to John, June 25, 1857.

"I Think We Are Going to Make Lots of Money."

1. Letter to John, February 26, 1858.
2. Letter to John, March 23, 1858.
3. Letter to John, May 6, 1858.
4. *Ibid.*
5. Letter to John, March 23, 1858.
6. Letter to John, June 25, 1857.
7. Letter to John, May 6, 1858.

Robert Enters Politics

1. Letter to John, March 23, 1858.
2. Peoria *Journal*, Aug. 4, 1899, a letter from J. W. Kimsey, Sheriff, Peoria County, to Alexander S. Bacon, a New York City lawyer. Quoted in the letter are the comments of Barrett White, Henry Baldwin, and John Warner.
3. Clark Carr, *My Day and Generation*, p. 335.
4. *Ibid*, p. 337.

Colonel Ingersoll

1. Letter to John, March 9, 1862.

The Eleventh Illinois Goes into Action

1. *Ibid.*
2. Letter to John, March 20, 1862.
3. James Ford Rhodes, History of the United States, vol. 111, p. 622—this quoted in Rhodes as taken from *Official Records of the War of the Rebellion.*
4. Letter to Clark, April 11, 1862, quoted in *Colonel Bob Ingersoll* by Cameron Rogers, p. 137.
5. *Ibid.*
6. *Ibid*, p. 138.
7. Letter to Clark, May 9, 1862, quoted in *Colonel Robert Ingersoll,* p. 141.
8. Letter to Clark, May 6, 1862.
9. Letter to John, May 22, 1862.
10. Letter to Clark, June 9, 1862, in *Colonel Robert Ingersoll,* pp. 142-143.
11. Letter to John, July 8, 1862.
12. Letter to Clark, Aug. 3, 1862, in *Colonel Robert Ingersoll,* p. 143.
13. Letter to John, Sept. 10, 1862.
14. *Ibid.*
15. Major L. H. Kerr of the 11th Cavalry in a letter to the Peoria *Transcript,* Aug. 12, 1862.
16. In the running account of the soldier named John, *op. cit.*
17. Report was printed in the Peoria *Transcript,* Oct. 14, 1862.
18. Major Kerr, *Op. Cit.*
19. Letter to Clark, Sept. 26, 1862, in *Colonel Robert Ingersoll,* p. 155.
20. Frank E. Nevins in a letter to his father, Oct. 5, 1862, in **Peoria** *Transcript,* Oct. 10, 1862.
21. *Ibid.*

"I hardly know what to think"

1. Letter to Clark, Oct. 7, 1862.
2. Letter to Clark, Sept. 22, 1862, quoted in *The Letters of Robert G. Ingersoll,* p. 125.
3. Letter to Clark, Sept. 29, 1862, quoted in *The Letters* . . ., pp. 127-128.
4. Letter to Clark, Oct. 7, 1862.
5. *Ibid.*
6. Letter to Clark, Nov. 1, 1862, quoted in *The Letters* . . ., pp. 130-131.
7. David W. Lusk, *Politics and Politicians,* p. 145.
8. Letter to Clark, March 16, 1863.
9. *Ibid.*
10. *Ibid.*
11. *Ibid.*
12. Letter to Lieut. Col. Henry Benmore, 16th Army Corps, Memphis, Tenn., June 18, 1863.
13. Letter to John, June 2, 1863.

"Colonel Ingersoll Flaying Copperheadism!"

1. Letter to John, June 2, 1863.
2. Letter to John, July 23, 1863.
3. *The Transcript,* Peoria, Sept. 1, 1863.
4. *Ibid.,* Nov. 2, 1863.
5. *Ibid.,* Oct. 21, 1863.
6. *Ibid.,* March 15, 1864.
7. Lusk, *Op. Cit.,* pp. 162-165.
8. *Ibid.,* p. 440.

The Deist Emerges

1. *Peoria Daily Transcript,* April 20, 1865.
2. *Ibid.,* Aug. 30, 1865.
3. Letter to John, Aug. 30, 1865.
4. Dresden edition, vol. 4, pp. 423-476. Ingersoll delivered a lecture entitled *Progress* in 1860 and again in 1864. While we cannot be sure that these versions were unexceptionable to the orthodox, we think so, for the following reasons:
   1. Ingersoll ran for congressman-at-large in 1860. It was a bitter time and a bitter campaign. It was not a time for sorties against God and church.
   2. In 1864, he was busy with "war speeches" against Copperheadism. Neither he nor the people were in the mood for iconoclasm. Also in 1864, he was active in his brother's campaign for congressman.
   3. In *1865,* his speeches bespoke acceptance of God and church.
   4. On May 5, 1866, he wrote Clark: "Week after next I am going to deliver a lecture in Rouse's Hall on 'Progress.' I wish that you were here, I would like your advice about it." Again, on May 12, he wrote: "I have it all written." That he sought Clark's advice on the lecture, that he never referred to a previous version, and that he said, "I have it all written,"— these are indications of a new lecture.
5. *Peoria National Democrat,* May 5, 1866.
6. *Peoria Daily Transcript,* May 5, 1866.

"Stand by principles, old boy"

1. Letter to John, March 17, 1865.
2. Letter to Clark, March 13, 1865.
3. Letter to Clark, March 1, 1866.
4. *Ibid.*
5. Letter to Clark, April 3, 1866.
6. As told by Shelby Cullom in *Fifty Years of Public Service.*
7. Letter to Clark, May 12, 1866.
8. Letter to Clark, June 27, 1866.
9. Letter to Clark, June 28, 1866.
10. Letter to Clark, June 27, 1866.
11. Letter to Clark, July 6, 1866.

". . . the bread and butter brigade . . ."

1. Letter to Clark, July 14, 1866.
2. Letter to Clark, Dec. 6, 1866.
3. Letter to Clark, Jan. 23, 1867.
4. Letter to Clark, May 22, 1867.
5. Letter to Clark, June 6, 1867.
6. Letter to Clark, April 1, 1867.

He Would Like to be Governor

1. Letter to Clark, Jan. 27, 1868.
2. Letter to Clark, March 2, 1868.
3. Letter to Clark, March 13, 1868.
4. Letter to Clark, April 29, 1868.
5. Letter to Clark, April 9, 1868.
6. Letter to Clark, Feb. 27, 1868.
7. Letter to Clark, March 26, 1868.
8. Letter to Clark, April 29, 1868.
9. *Ibid.*
10. *Transcript,* May 7, 1868.
11. Palmer's letter to *Transcript,* May 11, 1868.
12. Quoted in *Peoria National Democrat,* May 9, 1868.
13. *Peoria National Democrat,* May 10, 1868.
14. Letter to Clark, May 14, 1868.
15. Letter to Clark, June 7, 1868.
16. *Ibid.*
17. *Ibid.*
18. Letter to Clark, Sept. 7, 1868, in *"The Letters . . .,"* p. 155.
19. *Ibid.*
20. *Ibid.*
21. Dresden Edition, vol. 9, pp. 51-52.
22. Lusk, *Op. Cit.,* pp. 162-165.
23. Letter to Clark, Jan. 15, 1869.
24. Letter to Clark, April 18, 1869.

The Infidel Unfolds

1. All the quotations of the paragraph taken from the *Peoria National Democrat.*

2. In *The Complete Lectures of Robert G. Ingersoll* (For the trade) p. 3 of "Humboldt."
3. John Fiske, *The Letters,* p. 477.

The Only Deity I Worship

1. The *Transcript,* April 30, 1870.
2. Lusk, *Op. Cit.,* p. 204.
3. In the *Transcript,* March 30, 1872.
4. *"The Liberty of Man, Woman and Child,"* Dresden edition, vol. 1, p. 385.

"Impious Pope Bob"

1. "Thomas Paine," Dresden edition, vol. 1, pp. 121-165.
2. "The Gods," *Ibid.,* pp. 7-90.
3. *Ibid.,* p. 42.
4. *Ibid.,* p. 44.
5. The *Democrat,* April 26, 1872.
6. *Ibid.,* Feb. 20, 1873.
7. "Voltaire," Dresden edition, vol. 3, pp. 177-248.
8. The *Democrat,* Sept. 7, 1873.
9. *Chicago Times,* as quoted in the *Democrat,* Dec. 25, 1873.
10. "Heretics and Heresy," Dresden edition, vol. 1, p. 247.
11. Letter to Clark, March 7, 1874.
12. *Ibid.*
13. *Ibid.*
14. Interview in *The Globe-Democrat,* St. Louis, 1893, in Dresden edition, vol. 8, p. 521.

The Plumed Knight Speech

1. Letter April 6, 1872, to Jesse W. Fell, a lawyer of Boomington, Illinois.
2. *Chicago Times,* June 16, 1876, in Dresden edition, vol. 9, p. 55.
3. Dresden edition, vol. 9, pp. 56-60.
4. *Op. Cit.*
5. Chicago *Evening Journal,* Oct. 23, 1876.
6. Letter to Clinton and Sue Farrell, Sept. 8, 1876.
7. "Bangor Speech," Dresden edition, vol. 9, pp. 97-122—for all the quotations of the paragraph.
8. In the Dresden edition, vol. 9, p. 97.
9. *New York Tribune,* Sept. 11, 1876, in the Dresden edition, vol. 9, p. 125.
10. *Ibid.*
11. Chauncey M. Depew, *My Memories of Eighty Years,* p. 320.
12. "New York Speech," *Op. Cit.,* p. 132.
13. "Indianapolis Speech," *Ibid.,* pp. 167-170.
14. *Chicago Tribune,* Oct. 21, 1876, *Ibid.,* p. 191.
15. Harriet G. Blaine, *Letters.*

"Hayes Is a Coward. . . ."

1. Letter to Sue Farrell, Feb. 20, 1877.
2. *Ibid.*

3. Letter to the Farrells, Feb. 22, 1877.
4. Letter to Clinton Farrell, March 3, 1877.
5. Letter to Clinton Farrell, March 8, 1877.
6. Letter to Clinton Farrell, March 9, 1877.
7. *Ibid.*
8. Letter to Sue Farrell, March 12, 1877.
9. Letter of March 27, 1877.
10. Telegram from Clark Ingersoll to Robert.
11. Letter to the Farrells, Nov. 25, 1877.
12. Letter to the Farrells, Nov. 29, 1877.

"My Reviewers Reviewed"

1. June 28, 1877.
2. May 26, 1877.
3. June 5, 1877.
4. May 10, 1877.
5. July 2, 1877.
6. May 15, 1877.
7. *Op. Cit.*
8. San Francisco *Daily Examiner,* May 26, 1877.
9. *Op. Cit.*
10. May 13, 1877.
11. April 22, 1877.
12. April 30, 1877.
13. October 5, 1877.
14. May 15, 1877.
15. April 27, 1877.
16. April 30, 1877.
17. June 5, 1879.
18. May 10, 1877.
19. *Ibid.*
20. March 27, 1877.
21. Letter to the Farrells, May 28, 1877.
22. Letter to the Farrells, June 28, 1877.
23. For this and other details see "Vindication of Thomas Paine," Dresden edition, vol. 5, pp. 447-524.

Washington

1. Letter to Clinton Farrell, Feb. 13, 1878.
2. Letter to the Farrells, Aug. 16, 1878.
3. Nov. 23, 1878.
4. Letter to the Farrells, Feb. 4, 1878.
5. Ingersoll in a letter to the *Chicago Times,* May 7, 1879, in Dresden edition, vol. 7, p. 113.
6. *Ibid.* p. 121.
7. *Ibid.* p. 117.
8. "Some Mistakes of Moses," Dresden edition, vol. 2, pp. 214-215.

"The world looks dark to me."

1. March 23, 1858.

2. Dresden edition, vol. 12, pp. 389-391.
3. Letter to Clinton and Sue Farrell, June 3, 1879.

Obscenity

1. Interview in *The Dispatch,* Pittsburgh, Oct. 27, 1879.
2. Heywood Broun and Margaret Leech, *Anthony Comstock,* p. 180.
3. Letter from Bennett to President Hayes, printed in the *Truth Seeker,* July 5, 1879.
4. June 17, 1879.
5. June 22, 1879.
6. *Ibid.*
7. Letter to President Hayes, July 16, 1879.
8. July 22, 1879.
9. July 18, 1879.
10. Nov. 4, 1879.
11. Sept. 25, 1879.
12. Nov. 14, 1879.
13. Oct. 27, 1879.
14. Letter to T. B. Wakeman, Aug. 15, 1879.
15. *Ibid.*
16. "The Third Annual Congress of the Liberal League," *Truth Seeker,* vol. 6, Sept. 27, 1879, pp. 614-620.
17. Nov. 6, 1879.
18. "National Liberal League Congress," *Truth Seeker,* vol. 7, pp. 635-637, 640.
19. "The National Liberal League," *Truth Seeker,* vol. 9, pp. 646-647.

The Hewer of Wood and the Drawer of Water

1. Letter to brother, John, July 6, 1880.
2. *Ibid.*
3. July 9, 1880.
4. *New York Herald,* Oct. 31, 1880, in the Dresden edition, vol. 9, pp. 347-348.
5. *Ibid.*
6. *New York Herald,* Nov. 7, 1880, in the Dresden edition, vol. 8, pp. 40-42.
7. Letter, July 10, 1880.
8. Telegram, Oct. 13, 1880.
9. Letter, Oct. 16, 1880.
10. Oct. 31, 1880.
11. Nov. 10, 1880.

Blasphemy!

1. Interview with Ingersoll, *Chicago Times,* Feb. 14, 1881, in Dresden edition, vol. 7, p. 483.
2. *Ibid.* p. 482.
3. *Ibid.* p. 490.
4. April 24, 1881, in the Dresden edition, vol. 8, p. 80.
5. *Ibid.,* p. 82.

Ingersollism and Assassination

1. This and other details of the paragraph, are in an interview with Ingersoll, *Sunday Gazette,* Washington, July 24, 1881, in Dresden edition, vol. 8, pp. 100-101.
2. Letter to John, July 5, 1881.
3. *Ibid.*
4. *Ibid.*
5. *Ibid.*
6. *Op. Cit.,* p. 102.

Theological Polemics

1. For this and other details of the reply, Dresden edition, vol. 6, pp. 29-59.
2. *Ibid.,* pp. 60-117.
3. May 31, 1882.

The Star-Route Trials

1. Sept. 6, 1882.
2. Sept. 16, 1882, in the Dresden edition, vol. 10, p. 39.
3. *Nation,* Sept. 14, 1882, for the substance of this paragraph.
4. *Ibid.*
5. Sept. 23, 1882.
6. *Op. Cit.*
7. Letter to Clinton Farrell.
8. Letter to John, May 29, 1883.
9. June 15, 1883, in the Dresden edition, vol. 10, p. 531—for this and ensuing details.
10. Letter to John, June 17, 1883.

"The Real Temple Is Home"

1. *The Letters* . . . , p. 501.
2. Letter to Ingersoll, Dec. 9, 1882.
3. Nov. 30, 1881.
4. The New York *World,* April 28, 1889.
5. *Ibid.*
6. April 26, 1883.

"Royal Bob"

1. Feb. 27, 1882.
2. March 31, 1881.

"A Positive Genius for Losing Money"

1. Letter from John Ingersoll to son, John, Dec. 2, 1881.
2. Letter from Burton to his brother, John, Dec. 12, 1881.
3. April 17, 1889.
4. Chicago *Times,* Feb. 21, 1884, for this and other financial details on ranch and Palo Blanco Cattle Company.
5. Oct. 16, 1884.
6. Letter to John, August 1, 1891.

Notes

301

"I Was Afraid of Frightening the Preachers Away"

1. *Evening Post,* San Francisco, Sept. 16, 1884, in Dresden edition, vol. 8, p. 206.
2. Letter to Clinton Farrell, Aug. 13, 1884.
3. *The Plain Dealer,* Cleveland, Dec. 11, 1884, in *op. cit.,* p. 221.
4. *Ibid.*
5. Letter to Clinton Farrell.
6. *Ibid.*
7. *Ibid.*

Lectures, Home and Abroad

1. *The Herald,* Cleveland, June 28, 1884.
2. Brooklyn *Daily Eagle,* Feb. 2, 1885.
3. *Rockford Daily Gazette,* May 24, 1885.
4. Oct. 3, 1884.
5. For the substance of this paragraph—"The Brooklyn Divines," Dresden edition, vol. 7, pp. 169-215.
6. *New York Herald,* Feb. 23, 1885.
7. Dec. 29, 1884.
8. *Tribune,* Feb. 25, 1885.
9. Dec. 29, 1884.
10. *Philadelphia Press,* May 24, 1884, in Dresden edition, vol. 8, p. 202.
11. *Ibid.,* p. 204.
12. For this and other details of paragraph, *Evening Post,* San Francisco, Sept. 16, 1884, Dresden edition, vol. 8, p. 204.
13. For the interview, Dresden edition, vol. 8, pp. 179-188.
14. Nov. 21, 1883.

"A Splendid Bargain"

1. Letter to Clinton Farrell, Oct. 27, 1885.
2. *The Truth Seeker,* Jan. 14, 1888, in Dresden edition, vol. 8, p. 298.

"The Law and the Profits"

1. Letter to John, Nov. 13, 1885.
2. *An Intimate View of Robert G. Ingersoll,* pp. 21-22.
3. To Sue Farrell.
4. This and other details of the case, *The New York Times,* May 20, 1887, in the Dresden edition, vol. 11, 55-56.
5. *Ibid.*
6. *Ibid.*
7. *Ibid.*
8. June 21, 1881.

The Haymarket Affair

1. Dresden edition, vol. 4, p. 223.
2. *Ibid.,* p. 226.
3. *Ibid.,* vol. 8, p. 278.
4. *Forty Years of It,* p. 73.

5. In a letter by George Schilling to Mrs. Eva Ingersoll Wakefield, in *Letters,* p. 628.
6. Interview, New York *Mail and Express,* Nov. 3, 1887, in Dresden edition, vol. 8, p. 293.
7. *Ibid.*
8. *Ibid.,* p. 291.
9. Schilling, *Op. Cit.*
10. Interview, *Op. Cit.,* p. 292.
11. Letter to Schilling, Nov. 3, 1887, in *Letters,* p. 629.

"Think of It. 55."

1. Letter to Ingersoll from Holyoake, June 16, 1888.
2. *With Walt Whitman in Camden* (March 28-July 14, 1888), p. 69.
3. *Ibid.,* pp. 81-82.
4. *Ibid.,* p. 273.
5. April 29, 1888.
6. June 13, 1889.

Walston and 400 Fifth Avenue

1. May 6, 1886.
2. May 6, 1891.
3. Interview in *New York Star,* Dec. 23, 1888, in Dresden edition, vol. 8, pp. 430-437.
4. Jan. 22, 1888, in "The Letters . . .," p. 432.
5. Feb. 26, 1889, *Ibid.*
6. *Peoria Transcript,* Dec. 29, 1890.
7. *The Letters . . . ,* p. 433.
8. Letter to Mr. Fiske, April 3, 1897.
9. Dresden edition, vol. 12, p. 96.
10. Jan. 27, 1889.
11. Letter from Barrett to Ingersoll, March 27, 1889.—"We are all anxious to have you in this club—Booth and myself especially."
12. Letter from Barrett, Dec. 12, 1889.

Mark Twain and Walt Whitman

1. *The Letters . . .,* p. 87.
2. Letter, Mark Twain to Ingersoll, Dec. 14, 1879.
3. *With Walt Whitman in Camden* (March 28-July 14, 1888), p. 37.
4. *Ibid.,* p. 114.
5. Quoted in *The Letters . . .,* p. 386.
6. *Op. Cit.,* p. 114.
7. Ingersoll to Traubel, June 29, 1896, in *The Letters . . .,* p. 401.
8. *Op. Cit.,* p. 386.
9. *Ibid.,* p. 293.
10. From Ingersoll to Whitman, June 5, 1890, in *The Letters . . .,* p. 390.
11. *Ibid.*
12. *The Letters . . .,* p. 392.
13. *Dresden edition,* vol. 3, p. 258.
14. *New York Herald,* March 31, 1892, Dresden edition, vol. 12, p. 473— for this and other details of the occasion.
15. Dresden edition, vol. 12, pp. 473-477.

". . . I Shall Be 58"

1. To Clinton and Sue Farrell, Aug. 11, 1891.
2. To John, Aug. 1, 1891, in *Op. Cit.,* p. 203.
3. To Sue Farrell, Aug. 25, 1891.
4. Dresden edition, vol. 10, pp. 535-536.
5. *Anaconda Standard,* Sept. 5, 1891, in *Ibid.,* p. 535.
6. Sept. 4, 1889.
7. *Telegram,* Jan. 2, 1892.
8. *Ibid.*
9. *Ibid.*
10. *Telegram,* Jan. 12, 1892.
11. Dresden edition, vol. 7, pp. 327-328.

Lecturing—"A Bad Business."

1. Letter to "Dear Girls," March 15, 1894, in *Letters* . . . , p. 572.
2. *Ibid.*
3. Jan. 29, 1894.
4. For this and other details of the affair, *New York Daily News,* Feb. 24, 1895; *Boston Herald,* Feb. 25; Pittsburgh *Dispatch,* Feb. 25; New York *Sun,* Feb. 25; Buffalo *News,* Feb. 25; Paterson *Press,* Feb. 25.

Ingersoll Converted!

1. Oct. 30, 1896.
2. March 28, 1897.
3. New York *Journal,* April 12, 1897.
4. Philadelphia *Record,* Nov. 29, 1895.
5. Jan. 23, 1896.

The Campaign of '96

1. Letter to Clinton and Sue Farrell, Aug. 19, 1892.
2. Letter to John, June 30, 1896, in *The Letters* . . . , p. 215.
3. *Ibid.*
4. In *The Letters* . . . , p. 210.
5. Interview, New York *Journal,* Dec. 24, 1895, in Dresden edition, vol. 8, p. 585.
6. *Ibid.*
7. Letter to John, Sept. 19, 1896.
8. For this and other points of the speech, Dresden edition, vol. 9, pp. 535-582.
9. For this and other details of the occasion, Peoria *Transcript,* Oct. 17, 1896, in *The Letters* . . . , p. 212.
10. Letter to Putnam, Nov. 6, 1896.
11. *Ibid.*
12. Letter to John, Nov. 4, 1896.

A Hard Way of Taking It Easy

1. Letter to John, March 24, 1898.
2. Oct. 23, 1897.
3. April 14, 1899.
4. Chicago *Times,* March 8, 1897.

5. Kansas City *Journal,* April 13, 1897.
6. Louisville *Commercial,* April 19, 1897.
7. Hartford *Telegram,* March 22, 1897.
8. Kansas City *Times,* April 14, 1897.
9. Feb. 1, 1898.
10. Letter to "Dear Girls," April 14, 1898, in *The Letters* . . . , p. 591.
11. *Ibid.*
12. Letter to "Dear Girls," Feb. 11, 1898, in *The Letters* . . . , p. 591.
13. Jan. 26, 1899.
14. Dresden edition, vol. 4, p. 313.
15. *Ibid.,* p. 354.
16. *Ibid.,* pp. 406-408.
17. *Ibid.,* pp. 479-508—for these and following points of the speech.

The Posthumous Man

1. *The Letters* . . . , p. 63.
2. *Ibid.*
3. *Ibid.,* p. 64.
4. *Ibid.*
5. July 26, 1899.
6. July 31, 1899.
7. Quoted in *The Letters* . . . , p. 502.
8. *American Magazine,* Oct., 1911.
9. Nov. 15, 1916.
10. *Darrow, Story of My Life,* p. 381.
11. Chicago *Inter-Ocean,* Aug. 27, 1900.
12. "Senator at Large—William E. Borah" by Will Griffith in *Idols of Egypt,* p. 64.
13. Beveridge, *The Art of Public Speaking,* pp. 12-13, for this and following statements.
14. Garland, *Roadside Meetings,* pp. 44-47, for this and other comments of paragraph.
15. Depew, *My Memories of Eighty Years,* pp. 319-321.
16. Letter to Charles H. Betts, July 13.
17. Letter to Mrs. Walston Hill Brown, March 2, 1921.
18. Masters, "Robert G. Ingersoll" in his *The Great Valley.*

Index

INDEX

307

DATE DUE

NOV 2 9 1962			
MR 26 '63			
MAY 3 1963			
MY 34 '63			
GAYLORD			PRINTED IN U.S.A